FOXHUNTING IN WESTERN PENNSYLVANIA

S. Todd
'97

THE DERRYDALE PRESS

FOXHUNTERS' LIBRARY

FOXHUNTING IN WESTERN PENNSYLVANIA

A Memoir and a History

SUSIE TODD

THE DERRYDALE PRESS
Lanham and New York

THE DERRYDALE PRESS

Published in the United States of America
by The Derrydale Press
A Member of the Rowman & Littlefield Publishing Group, Inc.
4501 Forbes Boulevard, Suite 200, Lanham, Maryland 20706

Distributed by NATIONAL BOOK NETWORK, INC.

First Derrydale Printing 2003

Library of Congress Cataloging-in-Publication Data

Todd, Susie, 1925–
Foxhunting in western Pennsylvania : a memoir and a history / Susie Todd.
p. cm.—(The Derrydale Press foxhunters' library)
ISBN 1-58667-103-0 (cloth : alk. paper)—ISBN 1-56416-206-0 (clamshell)
1. Fox hunting—Pennsylvania—History. 2. Hunting and fishing clubs—Pennsylvania—History. 3. Todd, Susie, 1925– I. Title. II. Series.
SK287.U62P48 2003
799.2'59775'09748—dc21

2003003910

∞™ The paper used in this publication meets the minimum requirements of American National Standard for Information Sciences—Permanence of Paper for Printed Library Materials, ANSI/NISO Z39.48–1992.
Manufactured in the United States of America.

Dedication

To my loving family and my animal friends

Acknowledgments

This book would have never been completed without the invaluable help of Jed Lyons, Bob Gangewere, and Steve Glasstetter.

Contents

Part I

Memoirs

Introduction

My father loved horses, and he started his children riding at a very early age—we all adapted enthusiastically. The thrills and spills that ensued over the years did not deter us, but my non-horsey mother found it devastating. Despite this she was a good sport, nervously watching us as we competed in horse shows and even riding in point-to-points. We found it fulfilling to enjoy a group sport with our horses and foxhunting has provided me with many great experiences in the company of lots of nice people.

I was born in 1925 and remember the twelve foxhunts that existed in western Pennsylvania. Now there are only two remaining active: Sewickley and Rolling Rock. Many of the early foxhunters were my parents' friends so my association with these people extended beyond horse activities. Seeing lists of those involved provided me with many pleasant visual and emotional recollections. With this in mind, I have included lists when available at the end of each hunt chapter. Much of the data was obtained in researching the files of Baily's, the Master of Foxhounds Association (MFHA), and *The Chronicle of the Horse*. While I have found some discrepancies, the fault seems due to the hunts not properly reporting changes. When in doubt, I have elected to record the memory of my friends.

I felt that the best way to approach this book was to entwine my personal experiences with the hunts of western Pennsylvania. I have known many masters and hunt members through the years, but my memory and that of my contemporaries is, unfortunately, fading. I'm sorry if I have omitted any people or important facts. The hunts will be included as I encountered them during my lifetime, rather than by the dates of their origin. The hunt chapters each vary with the records of that hunt, with the contributions from people involved, and with my memories as well as with anecdotes that bring more warmth to the description. The reader can skip about without any fear of losing the continuity. I have avoided providing lists of people involved when I could not obtain a complete list, but I have included some made by other contributors. I am sorry to say that some of my favorite hunting companions are not in the available lists.

I found rereading J. Blan Van Urk's *The Story of Rolling Rock*, published in 1950, to be an inspiration and a marvelous source of information. His beautifully written book is primarily about Rolling Rock, but does include many of the activities of the other hunts in the area. I knew Jack and his bubbly wife, Ginny, while they were staying in Ligonier during the writing of the book for General Richard K. Mellon. They were a marvelous couple and were enthusiastically accepted by the community. Jack was not only an avid foxhunter but he knew the sport well. He was a prestigious author, and among his numerous works is the notable *The Story of American Foxhunting*, two volumes: *1650–1861, 1865–1906.*

My illustrations of the hunt buttons are my freehand interpretations of the records of the Masters of Foxhound Association, *The Chronicle of the Horse*, and Baily's. Needless to say, the drawings are similar to the originals, but not identical. There is one exception—I could not find one for the Harkaway Hunt so I simply designed it. The other sketches are my own inspiration.

I decided to make the first half of this book an account of the wonderful life that I have had. Of course, this usually involved horses but does deviate into other pursuits.

Although my husband Burt and our family are the most important things in my life, this book is not about them. Hopefully, you will get to know them as they appear. Our eldest daughter Laurie married Eric P. Widing, and they have two girls, Kathryn and Elsie. Franny married Charles P. Stewart Jr. and they have two girls, Natalie and Julia, and a son named Chas. We are very proud of these grandchildren. Burt and I often reflect on how fortunate we are to have such a wonderful family.

Other than Jock, my farm collie, I have completely excluded my very best friends—my dogs—from this memoir. I have owned many different breeds and some of them have been very special. My daughter Franny once accused me of being nicer to my dogs than to my children. I hope that is not true. My defense has always been that since dogs cannot talk they need a lot of "tender loving care." To this day, my daughters' families, the Widings and the Stewarts, use Foxley Farm as their boarding kennel, knowing that I will take good care of their dogs. When I add a Golden Retriever and a Welsh Corgi to my two female Bernese Mountain Dogs, my Legacy Subaru is packed. My dogs are very polite about giving up their favorite space because they always love to put their heads out of the windows when the car is going slowly. We create quite a picture, since those big black heads make the car look as though it has sprouted elephant ears.

I have traveled a great deal, yet I still feel that there is no place like home in western Pennsylvania. I love the rolling countryside, the changes of seasons, the people, the variety of sporting and horse-related activities, and most of all—living in Ligonier Valley.

Calling in

My Family

I was born in 1925, the third child of John Crossan Hays and Frances Dalzell Hays. My family seemed to like nicknames—I have always been Susie, although my christened name is Frances. My sister Mary was always called Molly, and brother John was always Jack. Jack (John C. Hays, Jr., 1923–1954) was exactly, to the day, two years older than I was, and Molly (Mary D. Hays, 1919–1998) was six years older.

Of course as children we all fought, but our relationship grew into admiration as we matured. Molly and Jack resembled the Hays family in their height and grace. I, on the other hand, was built low to the ground but with ample coordination. Molly was my idol and I usually followed in her footsteps doing the things that she did. She was a good athlete, excelling in riding, skiing, and golf, and in later life became a fanatic about the game of bridge. She was always kind to people and was adored by her friends. Jack was a handsome fellow, well liked, and a good athlete. My husband Burt said Jack had "a superb command of swear words," but I never saw this side of him. I found him sweet.

We lived on Gladstone Road near the Pittsburgh Golf Club, but in 1929 during the summer my parents rented the clubhouse of the Pittsburgh Hunt on Hunt Road in the suburb of Fox Chapel. It was real country then, and the

Hays children would hang out of the car window on our weekend trips, shouting excitedly, "We're going to the country." It was such fun staying in the old, frame building and having all the activity of the horses and hounds right on the property. The house was always busy, and I remember once, as a child, when eavesdropping on a party from the top of the old stairway, losing my balance and rolling all the way down the steep stairway, gathering enough momentum to plummet into the middle of the party taking place in the glassed-in porch. Being a well-padded, tough child, the only harm I suffered was to my ego.

My father, Crossan, was the youngest of the four children in the family of William and Kate Crossan Hays. The eldest son was also named William (married Anita Woods), then there was Mary (married Francis Guthrie), and Caroline (married Grant Curry). The William Hays family lived in the East End of Pittsburgh at 5200 Westminster Place in Shadyside, in a wonderful big house with a stable in the backyard.

My father started early in life with a love for animals. One of his favorite possessions was a goat and cart, and he would not let his favorite cousin, Dorothy Dilworth (Witherow), ride in it for fear that her excessive baby-fat would crush the cart. He also had two fox terriers, Sport and Trixie, and a bay pony called Annie. The neighborhood boys formed a club and called themselves the Rough Riders. With careful planning, they acquired complete Western outfits and managed to stage a cowboy and Indian fight. Using an empty lot on Fifth Avenue near the Duquesne Gardens, the Rough Riders produced an exciting show with banging cap pistols and wild riding attacks on a shack. This performance somehow attracted the attention of the national periodical, *The American Boy*, published in Detroit, Michigan. In May 1903, my father appeared on the cover in his Western finery with an article about the "Pittsburg Rough Riders." Note the spelling of the city's name without the present "h" that the citizens of Pittsburgh later insisted on restoring.

My great, great, grandfather, William Hays married Lydie Semple. He was a Judge of Allegheny County in 1796, and founded the Iron City Tool Works in 1815. The company certainly did well by the family for many years;

it was finally sold in the late 1940s, after my father became too ill with arthritis to manage it. William Hays, Jr. was born in 1813 in the Hays' mansion, in the heart of Pittsburgh at the location of the future Jenkins Arcade. It is hard for me to picture downtown Pittsburgh as a desirable place to live, but one person has recorded seeing the inhabitants of that time sitting outside of their homes or promenading along the streets to the rivers.

Unfortunately I did not know my father's parents, but William Henry Hays, my grandfather, was born in 1847 and married Kate Crossan, a very beautiful woman. Her father, John McDonald Crossan, owned and operated the famous Monongahela House, a hotel at the corner of Smithfield and Water Streets. It was reputed to be the largest hotel between New York and Chicago, renowned for its excellent accommodations and service. The hotel was built in 1842, burned in the great Pittsburgh fire of 1845, and rebuilt in 1847.

My father, John Crossan Hays (1892–1968) was a tall, soft-spoken, handsome man with a great wit, adored by the ladies. After graduating from St. Paul's School in New Hampshire, he went on to Yale University. He was a good athlete, but he unfortunately lost an eye while playing hockey. Graduating from The Sheffield School of Engineering, he found employment at the Farmers Savings Bank and later joined The Iron City Tool Works, becoming President in 1926. He was successful running the company and shared the profits with his siblings. Crossan Hays had a reputation of being a hard bargainer and being "close" with his money. Like most fathers, his normal reply to a request for funds was a simple "NO," but we learned that he did not always mean it.

Crossan was a precise businessman, and his checkbook in 1933 reveals the costs of being a hunt club member in those years. Membership in the Pittsburgh Hunt for three months was $6.25, plus $.63 tax, or $6.88. The same fee was required for the Fox Chapel Hunt. Both he and my sister Molly were members. The Rolling Rock Club was also reasonable, with membership dues of $40.00 a year. Vanning a horse 50 miles from Pittsburgh to Rolling Rock, and return, cost my father $10.00. Shipping two horses, including return, 12 miles from Fox Chapel to the Sewickley Horse Show required him to pay $15.00. My friend Milt Selznick ran a riding stable, and his good blacksmith with two helpers would arrive in a truck and hot shoe his horses for $1.50 a head.

My mother, Frances Dalzell (1895–1968), was a small attractive lady who loved people, parties and the fashionable way of life. She was a good athlete in golf and tennis, but did not share the love of animals that the rest of the Hays family enjoyed. The story went that as a child she was knocked down the stairs by a St. Bernard, and an appreciation of horses was definitely out of the question. She was a compassionate mother, a marvelous homemaker, artistic with her sewing, and very clever in making adorable decorations. Fanny, as her friends called her, was loved by many. In hindsight, Mother must have found the move to the country traumatic, but she settled in nicely amongst the nifty people in the growing Fox Chapel community. She also must have found it frustrating to have three children who preferred informal blue jean activities rather than getting dolled up for dancing school or parties. Of course, she was right, and it was necessary for us to learn the niceties of the social life, despite our strong objections at the time.

Mother came from an illustrious background. Her grandfather was the Hon. John Dalzell, who in 1886 was elected to the Fifty-third Congress and was re-elected through the Sixty-second Congress. According to a Pittsburgh paper, during his tenure he was instrumental in "making the State of Pennsylvania the greatest industrial sovereignty in all history." He also held the important position of Chairman of the House Ways and Means Committee. He married Mary Louise Duff and they had two sons, William and Robert.

Mother's father, William Sage Dalzell (1868–1934) married Mary Ruth Hough and they had three children, Frances (married John Crossan Hays), Catherine (married F. D. Armstrong) and Marjorie (married Smith then Harold Schaff) and John Dalzell II (married Virginia Clifford).

William S. Dalzell distinguished himself as a lawyer and a civic leader in Pittsburgh. My grandmother died early and Grandpa married Elizabeth Gil-ford, a wonderful lady, who would take me to Pike Run Club for a delightful short stay.

The Pike Run Club has a beautiful location near Donegal and still has not lost its charm. I remember staying in the house near the main building–a soft, cool breeze fluttered the white curtains at my open window; the pool was very invigorating; the people and the food were special. The club is still popular with the long-standing members.

William S. Dalzell became President of the Allegheny and Pennsylvania Bar Association and was eulogized by his associates at the time of his death in 1934. Grandpa was a member of the board of the Pennsylvania Railroad and was its chief council. My family enjoyed this association, because occasionally we were invited to travel in his luxurious private railroad car. William Sage Dalzell was not only successful, but he was also known in the community as a very kind, compassionate man. The Hays family was often invited to Kentucky Avenue for Sunday lunch. I loved sitting in Grandpa's lap as he sat in his red high-backed chair in the corner of the living room. He had nice big blue eyes, and I felt very warm and content.

It would be remiss of me not to stress the importance to me and to my family of the Iron City Tool Works, the family company founded in 1815 by my great, great grandfather William Hays. The company carried on through the generations with William Hays Jr., William Henry Hays and my father John Crossan Hays. My brother John Crossan Hays, Jr. would have been the fifth generation to run the company. After learning about business at Babson Institute, Jack found it too frustrating to work with my father, who could not see any advantage to modern change.

This was a company with a lot of tradition. The logo of the six-pointed star, with "Iron City" stamped in the center, was a sign of business roots that went back to the era of iron manufacturing, before the development of steel as an industrial product. In my time the works was still living up to my grandfather's advertising motto from the 1880s: "Any tools bearing this design may be accepted as solid-cast steel goods and of the most superior make." The Works made picks, mattocks, grub-hoes, sledgehammers, blacksmith vises, railroad and mining tools, and standard and specialized tools of every kind. An 1890 publication called *Industries and Wealth of Pittsburgh* touted the company's "honorable business methods and unflagging efforts at progress in every branch of the business."

But progress in the delivery system had not, by World War II, eliminated the honorable tradition of using a matched team to deliver the product. My father was one of the last businessmen in Pittsburgh to maintain a horse-drawn delivery wagon, and my memories of his matched pair of blue-roan Percherons go back to the 1930s. My father took pride in his horses, purchasing them from a horse dealer in the Bloomfield district. It was important to him that each new horse was a close match to the one it was joining.

I have vivid memories of my early visits to the Works. It had an indelible musty quality that would have been perfect for a period theatrical production. The three-storied red brick building, flanked by cobblestone streets, was on Smallman Street near the 32nd Street Bridge in the Strip District. My recollections of the building in the 1930s and 40s make me believe that there had been little change since its construction. I first climbed the five green wooden steps, guarded by black iron railings, to the inner recessed wooden doors with their etched glass panes. Upon entering, I was restricted to a benched area enclosed by a wooden railing. On the other side of the gate with its hidden latch, I could observe the four men sitting on high stools pulled up to the slanted shelf that held their voluminous stacks of papers. Each man sat under a hanging light with a metal shade, and each wore a green visor to protect his eyes from the glare. The old gas jets were still in evidence despite the "modernization" of the Works. The brown tongue-and-grooved walls absorbed any reflective light, and complemented the bare plank floor that softly creaked with my steps.

I remember how Frank Stutz rose from his stool, opened the gate and ushered me into my father's office on the right. It was a large corner room with three long shuttered windows, sparsely furnished with two large cluttered wall tables and a few visitors' chairs. My father sat here behind an immense roll top desk, piled high with aged yellow papers. Perhaps there was a dearth of filing space, or maybe he just liked it that way.

My father took me on a tour, past the friendly office workers and through the sliding wooden doors into the warehouse, and after opening more doors we entered the factory with its huge forging machines and blazing fires. It was an impressive, noisy sight, as the men worked diligently in their hazardous setting. The noise was accented by the sounds of sizzling, red-hot steel products being dipped into vats of cooling water. One of the most popular items made by the company was a beautifully balanced lightweight pick, ideal for gardening. I still have some and treasure them.

The tour ended with a visit to the stable on the other side of the U-shaped courtyard. Gas jets on the wall illuminated the quarters of the two roan Percheron draft horses, standing in their stalls, happily munching hay.

I was enlisted to drive this team during the Second World War, because teamster Jack Havens was ill and a war shipment of picks had to go out for the Army. My mother was aghast at the idea of my driving the team, but my father was insistent. When I arrived, a man named Tony had the wagon backed up to the loading dock and the horses were harnessed and waiting in their stalls. We loaded the wagon, and lifted only eight pounds at a time, probably for my benefit. That day in 1944 we hauled three wagonloads of picks, unloading them into a freight car, which transported them to the Army.

After hitching up the horses we were on our way, and I was driving. As we proceeded down Penn Avenue to the freight yards in the Iron City Tool wagon, we created a sensation as people noticed who was driving the team. People began to line the streets, cheering us on, and office workers hung out of the windows shouting “Hi Ho Silver.” For each of our three trips to the freight yard we had an appreciative audience. Thank heaven for small blessings—it all went well, and certainly not due to my own skill. I don’t know if we loaded and unloaded 3,000 pounds or 30,000 pounds, but my back felt like the latter. The horses were positive angels. For me it was a memorable and exhausting war effort.

Due to my father's ill health the Iron City Tool Works was sold in the 1950s, and so the Hays family tradition at the Works, and the use of draft horses, came to an end.

Years later I had occasion to go to an address on Smallman Street, and I looked for the old Iron City Tool Works. The building was being used by a swimming pool company, and had a new façade and renovations. But it was exciting to be there again.

My earliest years of childhood were spent living on Gladstone Road near the Pittsburgh Golf Club, which had been very pleasant for us. I distinctly remember looking down from the hill to Forbes Avenue where horses were kept by the Joseph L. Roberts family. Their son Joe is still hunting with the Sewickley Hunt but he told me his father had moved the horses away from Forbes Avenue to Fox Chapel in the 1930s, after his brother had been hit by a streetcar while riding his horse across Forbes Avenue.

Pittsburgh became more crowded as it developed into a thriving industrial city. I can vividly remember when the family would drive to a point in Schenley Park to observe the spectacular view of the belching steel mills illuminating the dark night sky along the Monongehela River. This impressive sight did create a dirty atmosphere and whenever possible families moved to cleaner suburban areas. Needless to say, it was thrilling for the Hays children to move permanently to Fox Chapel, instead of just renting the Pittsburgh Hunt clubhouse for the summer months.

Ranging

Fox Chapel

Although we had several delightful summers renting the Pittsburgh Hunt clubhouse, by 1930 my father and his brother-in-law, Grant Curry, purchased the 115 acres owned by H.G. Lytle in Fox Chapel. This was to be our home, and the popular architect Brandon Smith built us a marvelous L-shaped house that incorporated the old frame clubhouse building. We each had our own bedroom, but our favorite sleeping place was the sleeping porch with three metal beds. There were windows on all three sides and I loved my bed, which was next to the windows on the right and I kept them open during the night. In the winter it was hard to warm up my bed, but I snuggled under the covers and paid no attention to the blowing snow that encrusted the covers and froze any wisps of exposed locks. It set for me a lifetime habit of insisting on an open window for a good night's sleep.

Our driveway entrance (now called Edgewood Drive) off Hunt Road had two stone pillars and it wound up the hill, passing between Lettie Lytle's house and the large Pittsburgh Hunt stable (torn down in the late 1950s). The house had a lovely stone terrace overlooking our large pasture and Hunt Road. The stable was an intriguing two-story bank barn with an L addition containing standing stalls for twenty more horses. The main downstairs had six box stalls, ten standing stalls, an aisle for grooming, and a large paneled room filled with lovely tack on wooden racks, marked with the owners' names. The upstairs had eight box stalls, a large haymow, and a tack room and a granary. In the fenced-in barnyard, there was a wooden mounting block and a huge open metal watering tank that had a pipe supplying an endless flow of fresh spring water. The tank contained numerous huge gold and white carp, which kept the water clean and provided endless entertainment. Below this area was a turn-out paddock with a circular schooling corral in the center. We found this a perfect place to ride our horses bareback with just their halters on.

There were four outbuildings—a cheery small cow barn with a space for the blacksmith to work, a springhouse with open concrete holding tanks, a kennel divided for dogs and bitches with their own runs, and another outbuilding. Bert Cence, who later became the huntsman for Chestnut Ridge, was the huntsman and ran the whole operation. The entire set-up provided endless opportunities for children to entertain themselves.

Below these buildings, there was a rather wet, swampy area, which drained into a rockier streambed and fell over a delightful waterfall. This led to a heavenly secluded, fern-covered area, perhaps fourteen feet down. We had a marvelous time paddling around in the water, lifting rocks in our search for the numerous hiding crayfish. We would catch them, despite their threatening claws, but would return them unharmed to the water. It was great fun but it must have been traumatic for them. We could follow the stream for a long distance, until eventually it came to Guyasuta's Falls and the Boy Scout camp.

My father's Percherons at the Iron City Tool Works had another use besides pulling the company delivery wagon. During haying season my father had the teamster, Jack Havens, bring them out to our farm in Fox Chapel, where they would be used to cut the hay and store it in the barn.

Jack Havens drove the horses and took excellent care of his equine friends. Jack was a man of small but powerful stature, with twinkling blue eyes and a wonderful happy disposition. Each summer the half-hour automobile trip from the city became a much longer horse-and-wagon journey because Jack had to rest the slow moving team, especially as they climbed the long hill rising up from the Allegheny River. For the last stretch, up the Kittanning Pike from Pleasant Valley, I remember that George Yaukovitz, our outside man, would meet the team at the bottom of the hill with the car. Jack would unhitch the team and lead them up to Mauer's Lane while George would pull the wagon with a car. The paved hill was too steep and slippery for the horses to keep their feet while pulling the heavy wagon.

It was always exciting to watch Jack mow the mature hayfield with the softly chattering mower. The next day he would release the rake as he made neat windrows. Then we were permitted to help Jack and George with the last stage, putting the sweet-smelling hay onto the old wooden hay wagon. After Jack tied down the load we would ride to the barn to unload the hay into the upstairs mow. John Crossan Hays was as proud of his Iron City Tool Works team in the field as he was of them in the city.

One summer day at the farm when I was about fourteen, my father asked me to water the Percherons. They were stabled in the upper level of the old Pittsburgh Hunt Club Barn, which, like most Pennsylvania bank barns, had a second story entrance on the hill. My job in watering them was to lead them one by one down the hill and around the barn to the long, green rectangular iron tank to drink.

These Percherons, like all heavy draft horses, were placid, kind and quiet, with a lot of sense, so a young girl like myself approached them without fear. I led the first horse out and down, let him drink, and took him back. The second horse came out, had his drink, but was suddenly spooked by something as I led him back up the hill. Immediately I found myself being pulled by the lead rope as he broke into a trot, and then I was on the ground, being dragged on my stomach along the cinders, as the 1,800-pound horse headed back towards his stall. My pride told me to hold on, but common sense told me to let go. And so I did. I lay in the cinders as the horse headed back up the hill, praying that he would return to the safety of his stall. Luckily he did just that and all I needed was a bath and a bit of Mercurochrome.

The Harts Run Junior Horse Show

This annual event holds wonderful memories for me and for many other Pittsburghers. Besides being an exciting day for young equestrians, it was a social event for which the ladies carefully chose their appropriate attire. Each year, *The Bulletin Index*, a Pittsburgh magazine, meticulously reported the day. For several years the show was held in June at the gorgeous estate of Mr. and Mrs. John W. Lawrence, called Hartwood Acres, which is now an Allegheny County Park.

The special quality of the day was enhanced as you passed the gated entrance and wound up the long, climbing, and beautifully landscaped driveway. The wooded area opened out into the meadow below the stately stone mansion. It was and still is a place of well-kept natural beauty and elegance.

The show ring was surrounded by numbered parking spaces and there were enclosures in the woods where you could tie your horse. Grooms held the other animals scattered around the area. Although it was an important event, it was pleasant for juniors, and it lacked the competitive atmosphere of modern-day showing.

One year I was fortunate in being able to ride the fabulous *Chestnut Prince*, who belonged to Johnny Beach. *Chestnut Prince* was so kind and capable that all you had to do was let him know where you wanted to go and he took care of the rest. It was a special treat to be chosen to ride *Chestnut Prince*. He was loved by many young riders and will be long remembered.

As my riding skills improved I was in great demand as a "catch-rider." Dealers and people with problem horses or ponies would ask me to ride for them. Riding in some of these classes was like being a whirling dervish, and so exciting. As soon as I came out of the ring I would be thrown up on another animal. There was little time for instruction and some of them were not well schooled. But I had plenty of determination—enough for both of us—it was great fun. In a single jumping class I may have ridden as many as five different animals.

The Fox Chapel District developed quickly. Far-sighted Pittsburghers knew that Fox Chapel would become a sought-after residential area. I found it interesting in my research to learn that The Pittsburgh Field Club was built in 1915, Shady Side Academy (the senior school for boys) was built in 1922, and the Fox Chapel Golf Club (the outgrowth of the Pittsburgh Golf Club) was built in 1923. With the advent of the automobile, many Pittsburghers had the urge to become suburbanites. By the early 1930s, quite a few of my parents' friends lived in Fox Chapel and the families would get together for group activities.

Dr. and Mrs. Ralph Lynch were our close neighbors and dear friends on Hunt Road and were a great family. They had four boys, Hugh, Ralph, Mac, and David. Their father could not understand why they were not interested in horses, especially when he advised them, "All the cute girls like to ride." Dr. Lynch was a delightful, small man with twinkling blue eyes and a marvelous wit. He was a good horseman, tennis player and skier. Mrs. "Tommy" Lynch, a Baltimorean by birth, kept up with her athletic family, and she was such a sweet, lovely person. She was also very talented and every Christmas, Mother and Tommy would exchange the most divine presents, cleverly created by fine stitchery or paint as needed to convey their inspiration. Everyone anxiously anticipated the opening of these special gifts. Mrs. Lynch's house and gardens were charming, and her dollhouse collection kept in a corner cupboard was absolutely superb. Dr. Lynch participated in most of the horse events, racing, showing, and became a Joint Master of the Westmoreland Hunt in 1951 with Torrence Miller. We did a lot of things together and I cherish the friendship that we had.

Dr. Lynch was particularly thrilled when I invited the famous Captain Vladimir S. Littauer to conduct a clinic in our ring in Fox Chapel in the early 1950s. Anne Sortwell Clement (her husband George was Master of the Rolling Rock Hunt) had known the Captain from clinics that she had attended in the Boston area. Anne and I went to one of his clinics held at Sweet Briar College in Virginia. As you can surmise, I knew how to ride but had never been exposed to a learned teacher. I hardly knew what he was talking about, and I was a bit crushed by his severe criticism, but I realized that I could learn a great deal from him.

Captain Littauer, a White Russian, had fled to New York after the Revolution, along with his compatriots Kadir Guirey and Sergei Kournakoff. They started the highly successful Boots and Saddle Riding School on East 88th Street in the city. The Captain, with his marvelous wit, recounted so many humorous tales about horses and riding that both he and his attentive audience would be reduced to tears of mirth. I was so enthralled with this man and his knowledge that I later invited him to have clinics at the Harts Run and Rolling Rock Hunts. I even spent several months in Syosset, at his request, teaching a class of beginners.

His lovely wife, Mary, was a Marshall from Pittsburgh and her family lived in the white house that is now The Pittsburgh Center For The Arts on Fifth and Shady Avenues. I loved visiting the Littauers at their fantastic home on Long Island. The house was so charming, filled with beautiful antiques. It was located on a large, secluded property with lovely gardens, fields and a perfectly proportioned small stable. They were both scholars, publishing books in their own fields of expertise, and it was a challenge for me to keep up with their erudite conversation. Although the Captain is gone, I still exchange Christmas cards with Mary.

Our friends in Fox Chapel included Dr. and Mrs. Edward J. McCague with their children, Peggy, Miney, Eddie, Willis and Johnny. They lived off of Pasadena Drive in an amazing Norman house with an enclosed courtyard and extensive gardens. It was always an exciting occasion to be invited to join the McCague family for a boat trip on the Allegheny River. Sometimes we would stop and picnic on one of the vacant islands. The Bud Snowdens with their children Bill and Betty were the McCague's closest neighbors. Mr. Snowden had been a classmate of Dad's at St. Paul's and Yale. Bill and Betty were close to Molly's age so the families often got together.

Dr. McCague and Miney were interested in horses. The Doctor had two wonderful chestnut mares, *Duhallow Lass* and *Princess Pat*. Miney, eventually, learned how to ride Lass and won many ribbons on her with their brilliant performances. After her marriage to Chizzy Anderson, Miney took the mare East and happily hacked her until the mare was thirty years old.

The McCague's stable was called Handley Court and the doctor employed Johnny Beach to run it. He permitted Johnny to keep horses of his own, and Johnny soon built up a large clientele of riders and prospective buyers. The Hays children spent a great deal of time there, enjoying the busy activity with all the other young riders.

Johnny Beach was a delightful Virginian who made his mark in western Pennsylvania. He was a small cheerful man with a big rather toothy smile. He was a gentleman to a degree, but he did seem to stretch the truth. Daddy would often remark with a chuckle, "I knew he was lying but I had to believe him." He was perpetually pressed for cash to support his nice wife Edith and three boys, Alan, Richard and Raymond. Johnny was constantly wheeling and dealing with horses. He charmed the horses as well as the people and somehow made a successful living. He was a great horseman, but he must have had nerves of steel to put novice riders on green horses. Yet everyone survived with only a few mishaps. He had a great deal of charisma and led a charmed life. Johnny later became well-known as the huntsman for the Harts Run Hunt.

Milt Selznick, a contemporary horseman of the 1930s, remembers Johnny very well and admired him, despite their different approaches to training horses. Milt was interested in the classical approach of dressage training, whereas Johnny only wanted a horse to go on and jump well. Milt once described Johnny: "He had big hands and arms just like the cartoon character, 'Popeye'."

Milt also recalls the "Thistledown horse deal," involving Johnny. It was in the depression years and Milt needed another horse for his riding business. He saw one that he liked at the Thistledown Race Track near Cleveland. The lady in charge wanted $100 for the weedy-looking three-year old, and Milt said, "I'll take him for $30 if you deliver him to Pittsburgh." End of conversation—the lady went off in a huff. But that night her husband called to renegotiate: "I'll deliver three horses to you for $100." Milt agreed, although he had never seen the other two horses. In a couple of days the van arrived with Johnny Beach in the lead. "Mildon [as he always called Milt], this man couldn't find your place so I was glad to show him." The van was opened, and in it was just the unimpressive little chestnut, so Milt paid his $30. Everyone knew what had happened, but nobody said a word. Milt admitted that his horse had bad conformation, but it turned out to be one of his most valuable assets. Johnny, on the other hand, had two good horses.

Handley Court, where Johnny was in charge, was for the Hays children our home away from home. We happily rode anything that Johnny would put us on and some of the horses were plenty green. I don't think we got any instruction other than, "Go jump that fence," or an occasional, "Leave his head alone." There were lots of spills with this haphazard method, but those who survived did learn how to ride.

When I was a little older, I was schooling a wild-eyed brown horse named *Oscar*. He was a very good jumper and we happily sailed over the fences in the ring, so Johnny told me to jump out over the ring fence. But as we came back up the hill, in mid-air the saddle slipped back on *Oscar*'s loins, and he landed bucking. I stayed with him until he turned. Off I went, breaking my collarbone. This did not dampen my spirit, but I did learn to check a horse's girth before schooling.

Mr. and Mrs. William Forman Bickel with their children, Bill, Harry and Polly lived off Squaw Run Road (East), on the hill that overlooks the third hole of the Fox Chapel Golf Course. They had started off in a little farmhouse in 1927, halfway up the hill on the right, but soon built a large elegant stone house with an enclosed courtyard.

Bill became an enthusiastic rider on his large mare, *Toxaway*, and remembers hunting with the Pittsburgh Hunt. Bill also remembers the Shadyside Academy, an upper school for boys in Fox Chapel, and playing polo for a few years on the school's own field. Like most boys, Bill's interest in horses took second place when he became involved in football. Polly was my good friend and we went to school together for a long time. I still shudder when I remember how I followed Polly one afternoon as we crawled over the high roofs of her house. I swallowed my acrophobia, but I was very unhappy during this adventure. She probably felt a few qualms, herself, when we rode together. Polly later married Robert W. Off, a brother of my brother-in-law Sam.

It was just a short ride cross-country to the home of Mr. and Mrs. Thomas Robinson with their daughter, Jane, and son, Hillary. They had a beautiful, white painted brick house on Fairview Road. They had two adorable black and white ponies, *Susie* and *Star*. I particularly liked *Susie*, who was a bit naughty, but I was not intimidated by her and we had a great time together. Jane had a neat two-room playhouse with a porch and we played "settlers," with the ponies often tied to the porch between our riding ventures. My closest Fox Chapel playmates were Jane, Polly Bickel, Elsie Hilliard, and Maddie and Betty Blackburn. We all went to Ellis School in the East End and became lifelong friends.

Speaking of Ellis, the "riders" dominated the recess periods of the school by having everyone play horse show. It became the "in thing to do" and the girls performed walk, trot, and canter, even with classes for jumping over fences. You would be judged on your way of going and your jumping performance. I would not say that everyone loved it, but we all do have a good laugh when we remember those days.

Playing horse show as an entertainment fell apart when an interest in boys began to cloud the minds of most of the young ladies. The weekends became filled with boys and girls gathering at the Henderson's, the Robinson's or other places to ice skate, play softball, football, or some other kind of group activity. Bill and John Henderson lived off Squaw Run Road. Bill Henderson enjoyed riding and loved the thrill of "steeplechasing." The Blackburns had moved from the Rowe house on Fox Chapel Road to the Henderson property. Their house was convenient to a lovely big white barn with comfortable box stalls for the horses.

On weekends during the school year and during the summer months, I would meet my friends, Maddie (Lewis) and Betty Blackburn (Taylor) at some appointed spot for a day with our horses and dogs. The Blackburn home on the Hendersons' place was adjacent to Earl B. Gould's, now the site of the Fox Chapel Episcopal Church.

Our dogs consisted of my Jock, Maddie's collie, Lad, and Betty's Welsh terrier, Tippy. They worked out a very effective strategy for catching rabbits. The two larger dogs would work a hillside to flush out the poor bunny and the terrier would nail the fleeing prey. We would rescue the body and perform a funeral service with a hymn of "Onward Christian Rabbits, marching on to heaven. . . ." The dogs were disappointed but would patiently sit during the whole procedure. Maddie would hold the horses while Betty and I would take care of the burial site.

The Thomas J. Hilliard family with Mary, Tommy, Toby, Elsie, and Billy had lived at Ramblewood, a wonderful sprawling frame house off Harts Run Road. When they suffered a disastrous fire in the late 1930s they moved to Old Mill Road. Mary was Molly's friend, Toby was Jack's, and Elsie was my age and lifelong friend. Elsie and I played together a lot but she drew the line when it came to riding. This definitely was not her cup of tea, but she did play horse during recess. Other than riding, Elsie was game for anything. Without her parents consent, we would take one of the cars and drive it around the property. We stalled and got stuck a great deal and had to be rescued by their wonderful houseman, Chris.

Tommy Hilliard was given a beautiful gray pony by his Aunt Lila and he was later made Master of the Harts Run Junior Hunt under the auspices of John W. Lawrence. I was not the right age to know Tommy at that point in life, but he later married my good friend, Audrey Hillman, and we are very close to them and their nice family. Toby Hilliard had a little bay thoroughbred, *Bashful Boy*, which he gave to me when he went away to St. Paul's School with my brother, Jack.

Bashful Boy was a sweet, lop-eared thoroughbred who would get a little frantic when things got too much for him. My first foxhunting experience in 1938 was with *Bashful Boy*, when my father took us into the Hartwood woods on a Fox Chapel Hunt. I was trying to stay behind my father but I had little or no control. We careened through the woods of Hartwood Acres and flew wildly over fences. There was no point in fighting the horse so I just had to try to quietly ease the situation. We were both exhausted by the end of the day. I also lost a good bit of faith in *Bashful Boy* when he simply fell down with me, two Saturdays in a row while we were showing. It was quite a shock because our approach was fine, but he just seemed to misjudge the height of the fence.

Another *Bashful Boy* episode occurred during the war when Molly drove the horse in a breaking cart to pick up her husband, Sam, who had taken the train to Aspinwall. Thinking that she had been delayed, Sam began walking up the road to meet her. He became suspicious however when he kept finding bits of harness along the way. Eventually he found Molly and the capsized cart on the curve of Hunt Road hill. Molly later said everything had been going along fine until they started down the hill and the horse started shaking his head. Before she could stop him, the bridle fell off and *Bashful Boy* took off at a mad gallop. Thank heavens Molly was not seriously hurt, and the horse somehow returned to our stable unscathed. In hindsight, it is amazing that we young people survived all our mishaps with horses—including many which could have been avoided with more precaution.

My parents were great to let their children ride freely through the undeveloped country of Fox Chapel. Despite the possibility of a riding accident, we were perfectly safe in those days. All the roads in Fox Chapel were cindered, with hardly any traffic. Due to the previous existence of the Pittsburgh and Fox Chapel hunts, the countryside was honeycombed with many trails as well as a few remaining hunt fences to add to our enjoyment. My father and several other horsemen organized the Fox Chapel Trail Association, which did a great job in maintaining the riding trails.

We covered a lot of territory on our horses, unwittingly keeping them mentally and physically fit. One of our favorite outings was a trip to the cavalry reserve field. Colonel George Cherrington of the 108th Cavalry Reserve unit had given us permission to use their field on Fox Chapel Road. (This field is presently part of Fox Chapel Mews.) The nicely cleared field had several fences and a wonderful log cavaletti set-up that our horses happily jumped. It was fun, and a good schooling for the horses.

Although I have had other dogs in my life, my collie Jock was such a special friend. When the Blackburns first moved to Fox Chapel, their house was near the Teats farm where there was a litter of puppies. Despite the fact that Daddy did not like collies, naughty Susie chose a sweet sable and white fellow. To buy him, I had boldly lied, "I need fifty cents because we are going to the drugstore." I cannot remember the repercussions when I returned home with my soft bundle of joy. But I was allowed to keep him. We developed a fantastic bond that I shall never forget.

We often had special projects to occupy our energies. My friend Betty Blackburn Taylor (who now lives in Denver) recently asked me, "Don't you remember our secret 'YSP' camp?" While we were building a corral for the horses in the woods, there was a yellow Piper Cub circling overhead, so we named our place the "Yellow Spy Plane." This was in the expansive, undeveloped Ross-Delafield property adjacent to the Heinz property. While we were building this camp, Polly Bickel almost cut my finger off with loping shears. This incident was just one more accident that Mother had to cope with.

Every spring we would take our horses to Dr. Lynch's ring to practice for the hunt team class at the Hart's Run Junior Horse Show. Dr. Lynch welcomed us and gave us encouraging advice. I was on *Tish*, Betty on her good little mare, *Charcoal*, and Maddie on her mare, *Meadowlark*. Our practice efforts went fairly well, but, somehow, Maddie and *Meadowlark* would mess up on the day of the horse show. It was not that important to us because the real fun was the preparation and the anticipation.

Maddie was not naturally athletic. When we first started playing golf, she proudly stated that she had a 43, but, unfortunately, that was just for the first hole! We all improved when we started taking lessons. Fortunately, I was athletically inclined, but I did not have the mental ability or desire to excel at any one sport, and riding was my favorite occupation. What a wonderful carefree youth we had. Betty and I agree that our early years playing in the woods and fields of Fox Chapel were a special time in our lives.

Ware hole

Education and Adventure

In 1940 Polly Bickel (Off), Audrey Hillman (Hilliard), Elsie Hilliard (Hillman) Janet Ketchum (Grayson, Whitehouse) and I left Ellis School to attend Chatham Hall, a boarding school in Chatham, Virginia. For many years it was a popular school for Pittsburghers, and my sister Molly had gone there. I enjoyed my three years there and managed to maintain good grades through my wits rather than a quest for knowledge. I made lots of good friends and seemed to concentrate on the fun things that the school offered. I became the President of the Riding Club, served on the Student Council, sang in the choir, and played all the sports.

My English teacher at Chatham Hall, Miss Denniston, would be amazed to hear that I have written a book. I was not one of her star students, but I did thoroughly enjoy listening to her read the classic book *Ethan Frome*. The only other accomplishment that I remember from her class was the following limerick that I had to write after I was absent from school due to an appendectomy operation.

I once had a pair of rabbits.
I did not know their habits.
In a short time

I soon had nine.
Now I know the habits of rabbits.

I cannot remember the grade that I received, but at least I did not fail the course.

I became very good friends with Retta Ferguson (McDowell), my roommate for two of our three years at Chatham. Her family, the Robert W. Fergusons, lived at Greyfield on Cumberland Island off the coast of Georgia. The family welcomed me into their fold of two boys, Bobby and Ricky, and two girls, Retta and Cindy. Bob Ferguson was a handsome capable man and his wife Lucy, who was hard of hearing, resembled an attractive Indian woman who was thoroughly at home in the wilds of the island. The wonderful big house Greyfield is now an Inn run by Retta's relatives. The Inn hit the tabloids in 1996 when John Kennedy chose Greyfield for his secluded wedding party.

Retta had invited me to stay with her neat family on numerous vacations. We had a fantastic time riding the small native horses, hunting, exploring, watching sea turtles lay their eggs, swimming, digging for clams and even shooting rats in the pigeon house. Thomas Morrison Carnegie, the younger brother of Andrew, knew what he was doing when he purchased the marvelous island. Thomas and his wife Lucie Coleman were captured by the charm of the island in 1880 and subsequently bought it.

During WW II, Retta and I would spot planes from the roof of Carnegie's fabulous house, Dungeness. It had not been kept up but it was easy to imagine the elaborate lifestyle of its heyday—gold fixtures in the numerous bathrooms, an indoor swimming pool, and squash courts. It was spacious to accommodate his frequent large house parties. How fortunate I was to be included into the Ferguson clan—to know them and to experience the wonders of life on Cumberland Island.

During our Chatham years, we all did mature a bit and made the most marvelous friends. The proof of this is that fifty years later, we celebrated a reunion with our spouses for a three day stay at Yeaman Hall in North Carolina playing golf and renewing old times. We were all grateful to Gussie (Wolcott) and Kenny Howes for organizing this perfect outing. It was amazing that the ten Chathamites (there were others invited who could not make it) retained their friendship and were married to such nice men that we all had a splendid time together. It is true that a good friend is a friend forever.

Despite my pleasant time at school, it was nice to graduate from Chatham Hall and feel free to stretch my wings. I was so relieved that I had not taken the offer from the school to return as their riding instructor. I did not have a plan or a pursuit, so my life became full of endeavors in many directions. In time I was to learn that the lack of a college education did limit my access to many positions. I am not convinced that a college degree was anything more than a screening standard, except in the case of a technical environment that would require a specific education. If I had gone to college, I probably would have gone to a Veterinary School. I have a close affinity with animals and find medicine interesting. With this lesson about education learned, we did encourage our daughters to go to college. Laurie went to Oxford University in England and Franny went to Williams College in Massachusetts. Their education broadened their horizon and they made many good friends.

You may think that the following years were a deviation from my interest in horses, but that is not the case. I have always owned one or more horses since I was nine years old. When I graduated from Chatham, my family gave me a beautiful gray mare, and she eventually had a foal, *Mystic Marron*. My trips or excursions never lasted too long, and my father and George Yaukovitz took good care of my horses, who enjoyed their vacations. They remembered their manners and easily went back to work for me on my return.

In the summer of 1943, after graduation, I went with a classmate, Anne (Andy) Campbell to work at the E Quarter Circle ranch in Maher, Colorado. Her Uncle Bill had spent several summers as a paying guest at the Donald Meek ranch, and he arranged to have us work there during his visit. I had gone to Eaton's Ranch in Sheridan, Wyoming in 1936 with my family and I loved the open spaces of the West and the life that it offered.

Our two months spent in Colorado were delightful, filled with work and adventure. We learned how to bring in the cows and milk them, wrangle horses, work in the garden, help with the harvesting and storing of the essential hay crop, and wash lots and lots of dishes. The Meek family was extremely nice to us and consisted of Mr. and Mrs. Donald Meek and their son Carton and his wife Ruth. They also employed two nice local boys, Cecil and Oscar, who were very patient in teaching us how to do things. I had never worked with cows and it took awhile to anticipate the idiosyncrasies of the bovine mind.

With the help of Don Meek, I did break and train two colts that he had raised. They had not been handled, so I did need Don's help with his rope in the beginning. *Drummer* and *Pilot* were both nice colts and it did not take very long before I could work with them by myself. Don was very pleased with my training because he later sold them at a very good price.

I have to admit that we were a bit of a disappointment to Mrs. Meek because we were not thrilled with the garden work or washing the mounds of dishes. It was a lot more fun doing the other "chores" and playing tennis on the concrete court with the guests and the men on the ranch. After dinner and the dishes, we spent the evenings playing checkers and learning the game of chess.

After this very pleasant summer, I was later thrilled to accept Peggy Frew Conderman's invitation to work on her ranch, The Bar BC, in Jackson's Hole, Wyoming. Peggy ran the ranch as a limited guest ranch to help defray the cost of supporting her inheritance. I had a wonderful time working as the wrangler and jack-of-all-trades. Jackson's Hole is a fantastically beautiful area with imposing mountains protecting an open valley. The river offered excellent trout fishing, there was an abundance of wildlife, and a part of Yellowstone Park was close by. Peggy had a wonderful sense of humor and we really had a good time together.

One of the most worthwhile things I did in 1943 and 1944 was to serve as a courier, three different times, at The Frontier Nursing Service (FNS) in Wendover, Kentucky.

The Frontier Nursing Service was started by Mary Breckinridge in 1925 to serve the needs of the Kentucky people and also to educate midwives to perform in other isolated places in the world. Mrs. Breckinridge was a strong woman with a magnetism for her co-workers and the ability to attract many donors to her worthwhile cause. As you can imagine, all the people involved in the FNS were exceptional people—intelligent, warm, and purposeful. The FNS is still in existence, carrying on its excellent mission. I am glad that I was there before jeeps replaced the use of horses.

My first stint was with Mary Gellatly (Walker), an Ellis schoolmate and childhood friend. Molly, my sister, had also been a courier in previous years—I did seem to follow her leads in life. The volunteer couriers' job was to take care of the Service's horses and be prepared to ride between the outposts on various missions. It was an interesting eye-opener; life in the Kentucky Mountains was not easy. The people were poor and had to scrounge out a living by tilling their precipitous fields. The majority of the people were of English stock, retaining many of their old customs and rarely leaving the area. They were fine people, but fists and guns were often the way they settled a dispute.

The FNS was highly respected by the local people and all its workers were perfectly safe, but once I put myself in a ticklish situation. While traveling to an outpost, I stopped my horse to take a photograph of a particularly charming farmhouse. A child spotted me and scurried off to find Daddy, who came out brandishing a large gun. Unknowingly, I had chosen a farm that ran a still! Luckily, he held his fire and I made fast tracks away.

Another trip that I remember well involved taking a nurse's horse back from an outpost to Wendover, a three-hour ride over unfamiliar territory. My vague directions went something like this: "Turn left outside the post, at the bottom of the hill cross the stream and at the second fork bear to the right until you come to the fourth cabin, where you find a small trail angling off to your left. . . ." This is just a smattering of my written instructions, and I really began to wonder if I were going the right way as the day passed. I did stop and ask a man sitting on his porch, but he was hardly communicative. Needless to say, I was relieved when I began to recognize familiar landmarks.

During another stay at the Service, I was kicked a glancing blow by a horse that I was doctoring, but as I fell I hit a rock and had a concussion. I briefly awoke as some men were carrying me by stretcher over the flooded river so I could be transported by car to the fully equipped hospital in the town of Hyden. I thought I was dreaming when I woke up and saw a handsome, redheaded doctor putting in the finishing stitches in my lower lip. Poor Mother and Daddy (Daddy had to seek relief in warmer winter climates due to his advancing arthritis) were sitting by the pool at the Tucson Inn in Arizona when they received a telegram: "Susie kicked in the face by a horse, but doing fine." They immediately envisioned a big hoof print on the face of their darling daughter, but a phone call cleared up that horrible thought.

When I returned to Pittsburgh, I tried to contribute to the war effort by taking a job at Spang Chalfont in Etna, where they made the casings for incendiary bombs—very tedious work. At one point I was running a machine that cut lengths of pipe, and I was told by my boss in no uncertain terms to "take a break." I turned off the machine, instead of continuing to run it and waste all the lubricating oil. The tough woman exclaimed, "Who the hell are you working for—the company?" There was obviously no point in discussing it. One nice girl did help me pass the dull hours on the assembly line, but the job was far from self-fulfilling and there were many applicants, so after several months I took my leave. My next military effort did not last long either: driving military personnel around Pittsburgh. I wore a uniform, and managed not to wreck any of the cars.

One of my first jobs in Pittsburgh was as a page in the Union Trust Company. I accomplished this efficiently and after several months my pleasant boss announced he wanted to promote me to the bookkeeping department. Unfortunately, my third grade teacher had told me that I was hopeless at math and I completely closed my mind to the subject–a scar that has lasted a lifetime. Knowing my stupidity with numbers, I told him frankly that he would be there until midnight trying to rectify my mistakes, and I had to say, "Thanks, but no thanks."

Then I attended the Art Institute of Pittsburgh, which was run by Dr. Vincent Nesbitt. But I was not thrilled with commercial art, and left after I was told that I had a great talent for lettering—ugh! Years later, in the 1970s, Burt and I built an addition to Foxley Farm. Burt went to the Mountain View Inn near Greensburg to a sale of books collected by Mr. Nesbitt. He purchased about 5000 nicely bound books for a very nominal fee to fill our extensive bookshelves. It is odd the way the paths of your life often entwine themselves. I am sure that Mr. Nesbitt would be very pleased that his carefully selected collection has a happy home. We did give the Russian books to a deserving group who could fully appreciate them.

During the next few years, between various jobs, I had a wonderful time going to great ski resorts with Pittsburghers and ex-Chathamites. I first went to Aspen with Caroline Hartwell (married C.P. Stewart, and future mother-in-law of Franny Todd Stewart), and Taitsie Walton (married Walter J.P. Curley, eventually Ambassador to France). We had a marvelous time and I was considered a rising skiing star—but this was only due to boldness and lack of control.

One day they mistakenly promoted me to a class that reveled in skiing deep powder. I did not have a clue about the technique, and fell repeatedly, often under a tree that dumped more snow on top of me. It was exhausting trying to get up again from the deep, soft snowdrift. Towards the end of the powder slope I surveyed the class waiting patiently for me and decided to schuss the ravine. Through sheer determination I flew towards the class, becoming airborne over the last rise—luckily stopping before the trees. We proceeded down the mountain on a packed trail, and I had to be thawed out of my frozen jacket.

In the winters that followed I had many great ski trips and eventually learned the art of skiing. Mimi Cameron and I had a ball working at a ski lodge in Stowe, Vermont. Unfortunately, I wrecked my leg while taking a lesson, but my family let me join them in Ocho Rios, Jamaica, to recuperate. I cannot recall the sequence, but I skied at Mont Tremblant, Sun Valley, Alta, and Switzerland. I became accomplished enough to spend a wonderful winter teaching skiing at Laurel Mountain in Ligonier. The Mellons owned the mountain at that time and Doc Des Roche and his wife, Toby, ran the ski school. It was a great life, and I found that the thrill of skiing in good conditions is comparable to riding a lovely moving horse.

While in Pittsburgh, I spent one winter exploring photography and taking various art courses. Farley Walton (Whetzel), Taitsie"s sister, was my buddy and we enjoyed photography and figure skating at the Duquesne Gardens. I also took lessons in oil painting from a capable artist. She became thoroughly frustrated with her stupid student who could not fathom the theory of color. In utter frustration, she gave me some plasticene, a non-drying type of clay, and told me to go home and sculpt something. Effortlessly, I made a very nice horse's ear and she was thrilled. When she enthusiastically proclaimed that I was a sculptor, I replied "but I do not want to be a sculptor." Years later, after I was married, I did take up sculpture and with the success that I reached I remembered her words. I still enjoy taking painting lessons, although I am not very good, I have improved somewhat.

I spent a year at the School of Horticulture and Agriculture (now part of Temple University) in Ambler, Pennsylvania. I went with my friend Jane Baker (Beach) from Pittsburgh and we had a good time. We both took a course in agriculture that we did not take very seriously. This little bit of knowledge later helped when Burt and I bought Foxley Farm and I could converse with the farmers who worked our land on a sharecropping basis.

Having worked in the 1940s in a gift shop, bookstore, and helping Mrs. Thomas J. Hilliard (my friend Elsie's mother) with her production of fireplace fans, I decided I should take a short stenographic course with an emphasis on speed writing. Trishie Disston, a Chatham friend from Philadelphia, and I then delivered a car to Tucson, Arizona on our way to San Francisco.

We must have had a "Guardian Angel" protecting us on our eventful trip from New Orleans to Houston. There had been a rare freeze during the night and we were happily cruising along, admiring the frozen trees, when we crept up on a car cautiously traversing an icy bridge. I could not slow down and rather than ramming the car, I tried to go around and this put the old LaSalle into a wild spin. For some unknown reason, no one was hurt and we carefully proceeded on our way.

We were both good drivers and not really speeding. It was Trishie's turn at the wheel and as she was passing a slow moving car, it suddenly made a left turn. Trishie, who had ferried planes for the WAAC's during World War II, reacted magnificently but it was definitely wild as we made several spins along the road and the car came to rest with the rear tires in the mud bordering a canal. After giving our "thanks for survival," I tried to push the car out of the mud to no avail. I saw a man "frozen" in front of his gas station and called to him for assistance. He ambled across to us muttering softly, "I thought you were goners."

It is hard to believe that we had one more hair-raising episode as we entered Houston. It was dark and raining and we were in a line of traffic when a railroad gate came down in front of us, capturing us in the path of an approaching train. It definitely was a ticklish situation, but thankfully an alert attendant lifted the gate for us to escape unscathed. Needless to say we were happy to reach the Houston home of Anne Loomis, a classmate from Chatham Hall. I do not think that we ever told our families about our action packed day—it was too horrendous.

When we finally arrived at our final destination, San Francisco, I exaggerated my stenographic accomplishments and got a job at an insurance company. My position entailed typing accident reports. I was told to make corrections on the duplicate forms by using a straight edge razor. The first day, nervously, I dropped the razor into the bowels of the typewriter. Afraid to type, I tried to shake the razor out. The horrified manager asked me what I was doing. I explained, and she responded, "Does it still work? Forget it and keep working." I did get the hang of it, and when I finally left, they offered me a job if I wanted to return. I considered the offer a great compliment.

A few years later, in 1952, I ventured to New York seeking a new way of life in the action-packed city. I stayed at the Barbizon Hotel in a tiny cell-like room that was not expensive, and where I was safe. With my exaggerated "secretarial skills" and my knowledge of horses, I applied for a job at The Jockey Club, and was immediately accepted. The first day I was so nervous it took me an hour to type a letter for my boss, Mr. Cooper. I was obviously not going to succeed as a secretary. They were forgiving, and gave me another job—bringing up to date the files on the jockeys' infringement of the racing rules.

Jockeys were fined and suspended for many things—from crossing over, pulling horses, rough riding and numerous other infringements—and during this period I learned the lesson that "The best horse doesn't always win." The job was never-ending, and I worked diligently at it. In the spring The Jockey Club wanted me to go out to the Belmont Track—but instead I decided to accept an offer from Captain Littauer to teach riding in Syosset, Long Island. Unfortunately, I never knew what I was going to do at Belmont. It could have been interesting, and probably would have changed the course of my life.

With my checkered existence during this time I had a few very nice beaus, but the re-appearing Burt Todd kept coming back into my life. Burt and I had gone to dancing school together at the Twentieth Century Club in Pittsburgh, and later I had visited his nice family in Nassau and the Iron City Fishing Club in Georgian Bay, Canada. I really liked the Kirkland W. Todds. Mrs. Todd was a vivacious intelligent woman and Mr. Todd was very sweet to me. He had been a very successful businessman. In fact, the whole family was very much business orientated and I certainly took a back seat during these discussions. Burt also had a nice older brother, Kirk, who was a successful plastic surgeon and married to an intelligent, attractive girl, Adrienne Hill.

In 1953 Burt blew into town and we met at a party given by George Klinglehofer, where he told me he was going to South America with his friend Edward St. George. Although he considered me "his girl," I was fed up with his disappearing act, and told him to go to South America, and that I never wanted to see him again—and I meant it.

This shook him to the core, and the next night we went out and he told me we were getting married. This was not exactly a romantic approach, however intriguing. Later, at my insistence, he did present me with a ring, and we went through what I thought was the necessary and proper procedure.

Honeymoon in Bhutan

Burt Kerr Todd and I were married in June of 1954 and had a fabulous six-month honeymoon trip around the world. The only thing that marred this exotic year was that my brother, Jack, was killed in a car accident two weeks before our marriage. I don't know how my parents were strong enough to go through with the plans, but perhaps it salved their grief to have their thoughts occupied with something else. I am sure that they derived some vicarious pleasure because I wrote a constant stream of letters to keep everyone current with our adventures.

Air travel in those days was more gracious, and we made fast friends with Arthur and Linda Seeligson from San Antonio while we sipped refreshments in the cocktail lounge on our flight to Hawaii. We discovered that we shared the same wedding date and we would celebrate our anniversary together for many years to come. From Hawaii Burt and I continued our journey, making stops in Japan, Hong Kong, Singapore, Bangkok, and Calcutta. The main objective was a visit to Bhutan, a small country north of India and south of Tibet—I had to look it up on a map when Burt suggested going there.

While Burt was at Oxford, he had met Ashi Kesang Dorji, the daughter of Raja Sonam Tobgye Dorji, the Prime Minister of Bhutan. "Ashi" is an honorific title, similar to princess. Also "La" is often attached to a name as a matter of courteous recognition. After graduation from Oxford, Burt, Paul Bower and Edward St. George took a trip around the world. They visited the Dorji family at the Bhutan Government House in Kalimpong in northern India. They became very good friends with Ashi Kesang's brother, Jigme (Jigs) and his Tibetan wife, Tess-la. Burt was invited to return to Bhutan to attend the auspicious wedding of Kesang to Jigme Wangchuk, the King of Bhutan. He was the first American to visit Bhutan, just as I was to become the first American woman visitor.

The Dorji family and Bhutan had become an important part of Burt's life, and it was fabulous to be able to share this with him. We were guests of Jigme and Tess-la, and they warmly welcomed me. Jigs was a small man with a quick sprightly manner and a delicious sense of humor. Tess-la was stately, capable, yet warm and charming. Tess-la was the daughter of the notable Tsarong Shape of Tibet (he was executed by the invading Chinese). We stayed at Bhutan House in Kalimpong for a week before starting the trek into Bhutan.

Kalimpong, a sizeable town, located in northern India was known as the gateway to Tibet. It was a fascinating beehive of activity with a constant stream of belled, heavily ladened donkeys passing along the main road outside of the gates of Bhutan House. White prayer flags adorned the hillside of Bhutan House as they fluttered their prayers for the late Raja Tobgye Dorji. Jigme Dorji had assumed the duties of his father as the Drukpa (head) of Ha Valley and later became the Prime Minister of Bhutan.

The planning for our trip into Bhutan was a major undertaking for the Dorjis. They were able to travel via a shorter route through a section of Tibet, which was occupied by the Chinese. As Americans it was considered too dangerous for us to travel through the Chinese occupied territory; therefore we had to start from Chamarchi, a small village in India.

It took a sizable entourage to escort us on our five-day trek to Ha Valley, where we would meet the Dorjis. We had servants eager to take care of our wishes, ponies to ride up the mountains, and porters and pack animals to carry all of the necessary equipment. It was the end of monsoon season and leeches were abundant near the lower altitudes of India. Although I had trousers tucked into high rubber boots, one evening the servants removed five leeches from my legs. They dropped off with the application of a wadded salt stick, but they had brought blood and were disgusting.

The "road" was an unbelievable maze of huge rocks, some rounded and some jagged, twisting up and down through the steep mountains. Valleys were virtually non-existent—no sooner did you descend than you had to start up again. The ponies had to be raised in that type of country to be able to cope with the footing. Although we rode the ascents, it was customary to walk the descents because it was considered dangerous to ride an animal downhill in case they might slip. Our thighs began to scream despite a helping staff in one's hand. Servants and porters preceded us to set up a neat and comfortable camp for us every night. They even made a little entrance with pine boughs, which was charming and welcoming. We had a comfortable tent with two cots, a table for our reading material and a kerosene lamp, and a tarpaulin laid down for a rug. They even made an enclosed relief place for us. The Dorji's cook, Matay, was with us to prepare our delicious meals.

I recall our fourth day noon stop, which was on a summit of 10,000 feet. The wind was blowing vigorously, we were up in the clouds, and it was downright cold. We all gathered around the fire and passed the welcomed bottle to hopefully warm our bodies. Burt and I wondered what our friends at home might be doing on that Sunday!

Our three-month stay in Bhutan was fascinating, and I felt very comfortable with Tess-la and Jigme, who were both warm and amusing. We stayed with them in the comfortable cottage next to Ha Dzong. The impressive dzongs were originally built as fortresses in the valleys and now are used for storage, official business, or to house monks. The dzongs vary in size due to the importance of each valley but there is a similarity in their construction. The outer high thick wall protects the inner court with its three- or four-storied building, which is entered by a steep ladder. The Bhutanese scamper up and down the ladders with ease, but they are a formidable obstacle for an outsider. The stone construction is covered by stucco and the brightly colored wooden doors and window openings add to the interest of the building. The Bhutanese are excellent craftsmen and the interiors are brightened with meticulous paintings on the wooden studs and rafters.

Our days were filled with constant activity, and the evenings were spent playing hilarious games of bridge.

In Ha it was enjoyable to ride through the dramatic valley, seeing the people working their fields with oxen, the women flailing in rhythmical unison the wheat and barley crops, the happy children scampering about, and the unusual houses not unlike Swiss chalets. The livestock of pigs, cows and chickens lived on the ground floor, and ladders led to the upper living stories. A stone fireplace with no chimney supplied heat and cooking, but also smoke, and thus a dirty film settled over everything. Understandably with the lack of heat, bathing was not a high priority. As the rapid river twisted through the valley, the bridges supplied a necessary path for the natives to move up and down the valley

I tried to learn to speak Bhutanese, but I only learned words and could not converse. We often visited the local school. The students gave Burt an official signed document of thanks for his donation, and many of those students succeeded in holding important positions in the Bhutanese government. Burt, in his usual fashion mumbled and gargled to the satisfaction of the people. I could understand what he was saying, and by observing the animated expression of the Bhutanese, I thought they got the gist of the conversation.

It was exciting to fish for trout in the fast moving water, but I worried when Namgay, our servant, frequently had to free my line from a rock. He could not swim and could easily have been swept away. The brown trout were not native, but flourished in the waters after being brought to Bhutan as fingerlings. They were carried in earthenware jars by a succession of runners—a truly remarkable feat instigated by Jigme's father, Raja Tobgye Dorji.

Since different delicacies were always welcomed, it was beneficial to go dove shooting in the early evening. The tree area near the river where they roosted at night was very beautiful and afforded easy shooting.

Bears were a problem for the farmers and would come down from the forests and destroy the fields of grain. Despite the loud beating of pans by the farmers, the bears happily lolled through the crop, eating and flattening huge areas. Several nights we were called upon to go bear hunting, but we were only successful in eliminating one bear. When Jigme insisted that the village headmen eat a morsel of bear steak they became violently ill. The steak was tasty, but the meat was apparently taboo for the Bhutanese.

Leopards also proved to be a menace, preying on the farm animals. One night we sat in a granary of a house, with a goat staked out. It was unbelievable that the leopard was so swift that it killed the goat without any of us seeing it. We waited patiently until the leopard made the mistake of returning to his kill—the farmers were very grateful to have the marauder eliminated.

On several occasions we made trips into the mountains to hunt Monal pheasant and search for mountain sheep. The birds were easy prey, especially when they were inebriated after eating wild opium seeds and simply flopped around. Bharal, the blue sheep of the Himalayas, were elusive and the mountains so open that it was hard to get near them. We were up at an altitude of 11,000 feet, where the air was thin, so it took an effort to walk around, and sleep did not come easily.

King Jigme Wangchuk and his bride Ashi Kesang Dorji invited us to visit Thimphu Valley, the site of their summer palace. A lovely tent camp was constructed for us down by the river, amid billowing willow trees. The handsome regal couple was very gracious, but we had to be advised by Jigme and Tess-la to follow the proper protocol.

The king loved to hunt, and a pig shoot was organized. We climbed up a steep mountain and by chance I was near the king when he deliberately catapulted down the tree-studded mountainside. Not to be outdone, I followed, ricocheting from tree to tree. He was amazed to find me with him when a group of pigs marched towards us. Being a gentleman, he let me shoot first and I miraculously dropped one out of the line. In hindsight I cannot imagine how I survived that precipitous run, but it was certainly exciting.

Archery is the national sport of Bhutan. The Dorjis invited the people from a neighboring valley to attend a special competition. There were two competing teams of archers at each end of a 250-yard field, and two groups of female dancers singing and harassing the marksmen by surrounding the small bulls eye target at each end of the field. The men also danced with raised bows and taunted the opposing archers, as they attempted to hit the target. As a guest of honor, Jigs thought I should participate. I had watched the men elevate the angle of their bows but there was no hope I could hit the target. On my second attempt I went through the motions and turned to go to my place when a roar filled the air. By pure chance the arrow flew through the air and lodged in the target. It was positively astounding to everyone, and it would have been interesting to understand the comments that were made.

After the competition a meal was served. All Bhutanese carried in their clothing, their own *po* (a small special bowl) to receive the bountiful rice and curry provided by the hosts. People sat in lines on the ground as the servants passed the food. This custom simplifies entertaining, and eliminates dishes and chairs.

Jigs was always full of fun and ready to try anything. One night the discussion of polo came up and Jigs thought we should organize a game on the playing field. Word was sent out that "polo ponies" were to be tried in front of the dzong. Any creature that would go in a relatively straight line was selected. Miraculously, workable mallets were made from my simple drawing and the date was set. Village headmen were appointed as players and a crowd assembled on the playing field for the big game. With the first toss of the ball, a Bhutanese gamely swung at the ball—but his mule strongly objected and the pair disappeared up the valley. It was far from a scintillating game, with utter confusion for both the players and their reluctant ponies. The good idea was amusing, but it was the beginning as well as the end of polo in the valley.

Burt was intrigued with the stories of the elusive Migu (also known as the Yeti), the notorious Abominable Snowman. Jigs enthusiastically would send a servant out to check on any sightings. One returned with a bunch of hair, which a native claimed that he had taken from a tree where he observed a

Migu scratching. Tess-la and I were present when the servant returned and we were certainly not impressed with the hair collection. I had recently trimmed Burt's hair and we giggled as we added a bit of Burt's hair to the unlikely assortment. We never said a word, but Burt carefully wrapped the assortment. I never confessed until Burt had the hair analyzed in Pittsburgh and his collection was proclaimed as "not human."

The Bhutanese are very religious and follow the teachings of the Yellow Hat Sect of Buddhism. Almost every family sends one son to become a monk. The monasteries play a vital role in the valleys and the monks also become proficient in performing religious, story-telling dances. Prayer flags are seen everywhere, constantly fluttering the peoples' prayers to the heavens. Chortens (rock-piled altars) mark the roads and passes so that travelers can stop and appease their gods. The explanations of their religion were so complex that I found it difficult to fathom. It is also accepted for a husband to have more than one wife, and therefore most of the families are polygamous.

We were sad to leave Bhutan. There was no doubt that we had been royally entertained, enjoying every minute of our stay. Jigs and Tess-la came to visit when our daughter Laurie was christened, and Jigs was one of her godfathers. We later joined Jigs when he visited Sweden to learn how Bhutan could harness the Bhutanese rivers to supply electricity to India. This dream of Jigs' became a reality, and has supplied substantial revenue to Bhutan.

Burt and Jigs thought of another avenue of income for the small country of Bhutan. After a lot of detailed preparation, Burt produced many Bhutanese stamps. The stamp world grumbled about Burt's innovative ideas, but the stamps were highly sought after by collectors around the world. The income and the recognition of Bhutan in the world were very beneficial to the country.

Bhutan has changed from the country that we knew when it did not even have wheeled vehicles. The government has wisely limited tourism, which they felt might endanger their Bhutanese way of life. In 1966 we took our children to visit and we drove into the country from the Hasimarah airport in northern India. It was odd to see the traffic and bustling activity in the once serene valley of Thimphu. Presently with expanded education and communication, the Bhutanese people are having difficulty adjusting to their place in the modern world.

Our return trip from Bhutan included a stop in Ceylon, where Burt nursed a cold and I ventured forth sightseeing, and had the dubious pleasure of riding an elephant. We stopped in Rome, then went north to see Walter and Taitsie Curley, good friends from Pittsburgh. They had spent several years in Italy while Walter was working for Caltex, an American corporation. Later on, Walter became the Ambassador to France, a post that both of them thoroughly enjoyed. Our next stop was London, where Burt had so many friends to catch up with. Besides seeing his best friend, Edward St. George, we were invited to Saltwood Castle near Hythe to stay with Alan Clark and his family—Sir Kenneth Clark and Lady Clark.

The Clarks were charming and received us with warm hospitality. It was a treat to see Saltwood and its fabulous art collection. It was also fascinating to listen to Sir Kenneth, the author and narrator of the *Civilisation* series on television on the subject of art. Saltwood Castle is so ancient that it is mentioned in Chaucer's writings, and supposedly still has active ghosts who occasionally make themselves evident.

We returned to the United States before Christmas, excited about seeing our families again and anxious to start our life in Ligonier. There is no doubt in my mind that going home is the most satisfying part of any trip.

As a postscript, I would like to add that we have had the recent pleasure of getting to know Khandu Om, the granddaughter of Jigme and Tess-la Dorji. She attended and graduated in 2002 from Wooster College in Ohio. Khandu Om is a lovely young lady, intelligent and pleasant. She is a credit to her family and has become close friends with Franny Stewart and family. She has returned to the Far East, so we shall miss seeing her on holidays.

Ligonier

Ligonier Valley has always held a magnetic attraction for me and I love living here. It offers all of the qualities that I enjoy—beautiful country, four seasons, special people, a wonderful friendly town, hunting, skiing, golf, tennis and any other sport that may be of interest. Cultural interests can be found within easy driving distance and Pittsburgh is about an hour away. I actually have a sense of peace as I drive through the gap on my return trip from any excursion. When my parents first brought me to Ligonier, I loved the cool refreshing air—even then I knew I was in a special place. If we spent a night, we stayed at the Fort Ligonier Hotel, now the site of the Ramada Inn. The driveway to the white-framed hotel was lined with lovely trees, creating an air of quiet grandeur. The Rolling Rock Club was reserved for the pleasure of its adult members.

We should all be thankful to R. B. Mellon and his son Richard K. Mellon who were largely responsible for preserving the beauty of Ligonier Valley. When farming was no longer lucrative, the Mellons under the name of Miller Enterprises purchased farms and sold them to people who agreed to keep the land intact and allow the hunt to transverse the property. Thank heavens this was accomplished—the drive along 711 South is still breathtaking.

Richard King Mellon married the lovely Constance Mary Prosser in 1936 and they moved into their new home at Huntland Downs in 1939, where they raised their four children, Crossandra, Constance, Richard and Prosser. Although the Mellons had many close contemporaries in the valley, they realized that it was necessary to attract young families to complete the growth of the community. Connie utilized her excellent organizational skills to start the Valley School of Ligonier and the church, St. Michael's of The Valley. Peter and Nikki Messer did a fantastic job with the school, and Charlie and Betty Price attracted people to the intimate church in Rector.

By the late 1940s, quite a few young couples moved to the Ligonier Valley, despite the necessary long commute to Pittsburgh for the working husbands. They formed car pools, which proved to be rather entertaining in some cases. Richard King Mellon made the commute daily, driven by Ed Burnes, his excellent driver. It was reported that their door-to-door trip took exactly one hour and a half—a clock could be set by their passing. The roads were not as good then as they are today, but this was compensated for by less traffic.

My sister Molly and her husband, Sam Off, moved to Ligonier in 1946. They purchased the Ken Phillipi farm on Jefferson School Road. The Phillipi dairy barn was changed to accommodate their horses and ponies. In the late 1940s, I drove up from Fox Chapel with Weasel Stringer and Diane Osborne to hunt with Rolling Rock. Molly was very kind to let me board my mare, *Marron*, on their farm. The hunting and the people that I met were attractive and very friendly—I was enthralled with life in Ligonier!

After our marriage Burt gave me the choice of where we should live, and my response was "Ligonier!" We arrived home from our honeymoon and in 1954 moved into Parson's farm, "Burnt Chimney" on Route 711 South of Ligonier. I knew it well because Blaine and Caroline Fairless had lived there enjoying its nice house and big barn. The chimney and foundation on the hill were all that remained of the original homestead after it had been burned by raiding Indians. Burnt Chimney is now owned by the D. T. Bennetts and they keep it immaculately, with attractive fences and buildings for their roping horses and Texas Longhorns.

My mother and Mrs. Todd did a lovely job of decorating our new home, and after we settled in, we lived there happily for two years. Our daughters

Laurie and Franny were newborns there. But I was not a good broodmare, and we were fortunate to have help from my wonderful old nurse, Edna Himes, and from Matay, a nice Bhutanese man, who had worked for the Dorjis and cooked for us in Bhutan during our honeymoon. He arrived shortly after we got home. Matay was a big help to us but he was homesick. He was kind enough to stay for two years before requesting his return to Bhutan.

Living in Ligonier does take a certain type of person. You have to be rather self-sufficient with your own interests and an appreciation of its peace and beauty. It was a cultural shock to Burt—a city boy who loves people and constant activity—but he adjusted nicely. He liked the people and loved all the activities that the Rolling Rock Club had to offer.

I hesitated to make up a list of people living in the valley in the 1950s, but Peggy Caves, the reservationalist at the Rolling Rock Club, found a rare 1954 Loyalhanna Register for me to copy. I was thrilled to see all the familiar names. In fact it brought back such warm memories of the people that I felt as though I should call them on the phone. I was pleased to see our names, since we had not moved into our house until late fall. Someone had kindly penciled our names into the book. Those interested in recapturing the names of old friends or relatives, can turn to the list near the end of this book, after the Rolling Rock Hunt chapter.

With many thanks to Stevie Hackett and Lizzie McKay, I was introduced to "The Car Pool Waltz" composed in 1960 by the talented John Gile. It certainly captures the frivolity of the car-pool days. Mrs. A. W. Thompson, in her incomparable style, gave a party with Johnny Gile playing the piano on her terrace, which overlooked the Rolling Rock Farms nestled into the foothills of impressive Laurel Mountain. Many of the car poolers were present and the song was a smashing success, with people singing and dancing well into the night.

The Car Pool Waltz

A finer assortment of fellows
We're certain can never be found

Than those who foregather each morning
For riding the car pool to town.
We come from the forests and mountains
Converging on old Ligonier.
The atmosphere's perfumed on Mondays
With the odor of booze and stale beer.

The Monday trip down to the city
Is known for its absence of talk,
For he who rattles his choppers
Is quickly invited to walk.
A prize is awarded the person
Who has the most weekend remorse.
His feat must be rather spectacular,
Like entering the club on a horse.

The trip to the city is easy.
It's purely a thing of routine.
But once in a while there's a bonehead
Who must stop to buy gasoline.
And then there's the oil executive
Who shocked all the members, alas!
On the day he was doing the driving,
His Mercury ran out of gas.

We've stated that riding the car pool
As a way of commuting is tops,
But then there are bound to be hazards,
Like icy roads, flat tires and cops.
The latter are really obnoxious,
Their presence has wrecked our whole day.
If further details are required,
Just check with Sam Off and McKay.

A Yearly event in the car pool
By our wives is just not understood.
It's our annual meeting at Gebert's
For cocktails served under the hood.
Six rounds of martinis per person,
Make all of us feel very fine,
But our wives are most furious when we
Come home singing "Sweet Adeline."

The car pool's a great institution.
It runs in the snow and the rain.
We're sorry for those individuals
Who wish to commute on the train.
But if you drive down to Pittsburgh
From the valley of old Ligonier,
And put up with us in the car pool,
Then, bub, you're a real pioneer.

To welcome us to the valley, Barbara and Harvey Childs, our Pittsburgh friends, gave a party introducing us to all the neat people that I had not known previously through foxhunting and skiing. There were enough couples with growing families, and a few years later Barry and Sallie Sullivan also moved into the valley. Sallie became a close riding buddy.

People worked hard and blew off steam on the weekends. I must admit that my sister's age group was more excessive in their escapades than our group. In a relatively small community there was a healthy mixture of interesting people of all ages.

There is an amusing story about Caroline and Blaine Fairless. For reasons unknown, Caroline decided to play a joke on her husband. She took his favorite hunter *Graytone* to the Latrobe Railroad Station and tied him to a parking meter. Caroline must have had an accomplice, and they watched as Blaine emerged from the station to find his horse waiting for him. He had no choice but to ride *Graytone* back to Ligonier—despite the fact that he was wearing his good business suit. It was a zany idea but everyone had a good laugh.

This is just one incident among many played by the fun-loving couples. When our age group carried on in later years, our activities seemed like child's play in comparison. We spent harmless times visiting each other while our children had fun playing together. But I must admit that Ladies Monday Bridge was a time to forget one's responsibilities. The ladies of the community took turns supplying cocktails and luncheon, and it was a perfect occasion to catch up on gossip. It was nice to talk to adults and have a respite from our household duties. The husbands were not thrilled with Mondays because often the wife was late getting home, but they did like to hear the latest gossip.

Although we were fortunate to live at Burnt Chimney, I knew that our location was too far away from the hunting country, and I kept heckling Burt about buying property. When our "dream farm" became available in 1956, the Mellons were kind enough to let us purchase it. This was perfection, and I think of our Foxley Farm as heaven on earth.

Foxley Farm

I fell in love with the farm the first time I saw it. It originally belonged to the James Kimmel and the Reininger family and at that time the driveway entrance was on route 711 South (later moved to Barron Road due to the dangers of fast moving traffic). From the highway, I could see the old brick house snuggled amongst the big trees. A black iron fence encompassed the yard, Brown Swiss cows contentedly grazed in the lush pastures around the big red barn, and the large open farm fields completed the inviting scene. I eventually met Bertha Reininger, whose mother was one of the Kimmel girls. She was married to the Reverend Reininger. The house was built in 1832, with the red brick made from clay obtained from the top of the hill behind the house. There is still an indentation in the field where the clay was dug—which today forms a pond after a good rain.

We have added wings on to the typical Pennsylvania farmhouse, but the brick house has been preserved. I was told that the original barn had burned and the present bank barn is in a slightly different place. Originally, the home was a log cabin, which was moved to Zion Church Road. It looks very attractive with its clapboard addition. When we bought the farm in 1956, there was a brick smokehouse next to the house, which we annexed, using it as a den and a guest room. The original kitchen had been in the basement, which also contained the only bathroom. Two second-floor bathrooms were added over an enclosed back porch before we purchased the house.

We loved our little house but we wanted more space—it seemed that the dust never settled with all of the activity. Although we had an architect design our first connection, I made drawings on yellow legal paper for our next addition. We had found a superb contractor, Bob Lundquist—it was a joy to work with Bob and his marvelous crew. The only detriment was that we never have had complete plans for reference. When we added the addition, we made the back of the house into our front entrance to preserve the lovely front yard. By 1962 we had a nice house that would satisfy anyone—other than Burt Todd.

While Burt was passing through Bedford, Pennsylvania, on a business trip, he noticed that the Bedford Springs Hotel had burned but the immense columns were unscathed. He made a deal with the owner and never mentioned it to me. When they were delivered I tried to tell the driver "there must be some mistake." The driver replied, "The man that bought them said you might say that." The virgin pine columns made in Somerset, Pennsylvania, sat in our driveway for two years before we could agree on plans.

It was a challenge to figure out an attractive addition of one hundred feet—which we did not need. The large columns for the porch did set the scale and I could visualize having an interior balcony similar to the one at the Pittsburgh Golf Club. Fortunately, Bob Lundquist was available and we started building in 1972, using my simple drawings and solving problems as they arose. He would figure out the structural details and together we would "eye-ball" the measurements of the interior details. Burt did not have complete faith in my sense of design, especially when he wanted something different. We met an impasse on the design of the double staircase into the big room and he asked an interior decorator to do some drawings. They were nice but impractical due to Burt's request. I solved the problem by tracing my design, including the decorator's signature! I did not confess my deceit until the stairs were completed and Burt was happy. It was a good thing that we were young when we built the big addition because even my cousin, Grant Curry, an excellent architect, was dubious about the outcome.

There was also another charming little frame house within the fenced-in yard. The north wing was carefully angled to preserve this little house, but it looked so silly next to the new structure that we had to move it. We tried to keep the excellent spring under the house but, unfortunately, it proved to be contaminated, probably due to the use of modern fertilizers on the fields. The movers were amazed at the weight of the small building and concluded that there had to be a couple of layers of siding. It was an exciting moment when the building listed to a 45-degree angle during the move. I asked Mr. Abel "Do you have insurance?" The answer was "No." To my next inquiry "What happens if it falls over?" He nonchalantly replied, "You have a lot of kindling." Luckily, the house made it to its new foundation and we renovated the interior to suit its new location. There is no doubt in my mind that "fools are protected."

It took quite a few years to complete this project and at one point we even considered taking the structure down. By 1977 it was complete, and it lends itself beautifully for entertaining any size group. The only problem is that giving parties takes a lot of work and I would rather be doing something else. Burt, on the other hand, would like to entertain constantly and expects it to be done as graciously as his mother would have done in their lovely Nassau home.

I have deviated a bit from my story of living in Ligonier so I will pick up the threads again. Although I rode and hunted very little while the children were small, we had my gray mare, *Marron*, and a bay mare called *Goodwood*. In 1952 Burt had purchased *Goodwood* at the auction sale on Thursday evening of the Rolling Rock race week. For those auctions a tent was erected below the terrace of the clubhouse, and a group of the Mellon's young horses were auctioned. Burt was carried away by the excitement of the evening.

Goodwood was an attractive, small yearling, but not particularly suited to racing. After the bid finally went to Burt, he asked me, "What can I do with her?" I remember saying, "You can feed her carrots and watch her grow." *Goodwood* came to Fox Chapel before we were married, and I eventually broke her and did hunt her successfully at Rolling Rock.

Raising Ponies

Not long after our acquisition of Foxley Farm we decided the farm should become a self-supportive enterprise. At that time, Welsh ponies were the rage, bringing high prices. My friend Barbara Childs and I went to a sale in Virginia, and I bought a yearling black stallion, *Leeway Victor*, and she bought a nice gray gelding for her daughter, Lisa.

I had decided to raise cross-breds, using the Welsh stallion on small horses, to get a more sizable hunting pony. I accumulated several nice mares and it was not long before I had a sizable herd. I tried desperately to make the venture a paying proposition, taking in some boarders, selling manure, and, of course, selling ponies.

I had good help in the house and despite the hard manual labor, I did enjoy the peace of doing the barn work. Our neighbor, Mrs. Hodge, a perfect lady and the mother of Billie Sarosdy, was stunned when she observed me driving the tractor and manure spreader. Later our outside man, Bob (Canonball) Roberts helped me while I was breaking colts. I never had a problem as long as I went about it slowly and did not scare them. The one chore that I did not relish was loading ponies on a van when they were shipped to their new home. It was logical that they trusted me more than the driver but they were nervous and it was dangerous.

Mark Thompson from Uniontown bought one of our ponies and his children had great success with him. Libby Eireman Slaughter from Sewickley bought another that her son Johnny showed very well. Our neighbors, the

Donald McLennan's, bought *Kirkey*, and after filling the bill for their daughters, he went up to Boston and became a superstar pony. While my breeding program was a success, financially it failed to meet the necessary profit to remain a tax-exempt operation.

As a businessman working at Jeanette Glass Company, Burt was not interested in my project. One eventful morning I truly needed his help to breed a mare. My man was absent and the mare had to be bred that day. Burt, dressed in his nice business suit, had to be talked into the task. I coached him to back the mare up to a stall where I would handle the smaller stallion. But Burt was overcome when *Victor's* snorting head came close to him, as he was holding the mare. With nervous fear he patted *Victor's* head, saying "Good Boy"—which abruptly ended the ardor. I was furious with Burt, and yelled, "Does anyone pat you on the head at a time like this?" Needless to say, and to his relief, Burt was banished from future barn activities.

Laurie and Franny graduated from their marvelous beginner ponies, *Santabelle* and *Chocolate*, to *Piper* and *Kirkey*, two of our nice homebreds. They pony-clubbed them, hunted, and rode in the Rolling Rock Horse Show successfully. On one occasion, out hunting, Franny and *Kirkey* whizzed along a stream bank and fell in. When we checked in the next field, Franny and *Kirkey* appeared absolutely covered in mud, but completely undaunted. Thank heavens Sallie Sullivan had been in back with them, and helped put the pair together again.

Sallie Sullivan, a good friend, boarded her horses with me at Foxley Farm. It was nice to have her as a riding buddy, and we had a great time hunting together. When her daughter Kate Sullivan (Scovil) was old enough, I boarded her pony *Rocket*, and then *Jaybird*, at Foxley Farm. The farm was a beehive of activity for children and ponies. Barry Sullivan and my godson Tim were just as disinterested in horses as Burt, but this is often the case with the male gender.

I sold a nice bay mare, *Tammy*, to Bill and Polly O'Neil for their daughter Joannie O'Neil. I had purchased this part Morgan mare from a Virginia dealer, and with a bit of schooling she became a kind, capable animal. Joannie, a lovely girl, was a soft rider and they became an unbeatable pair in Pony Club competitions and horse shows. When Joannie went away to college, I was delighted to receive *Tammy* back as a gift.

Although I spent a great deal of time with my horses, we also had a busy social time on the weekends. In 1962 Kit Bughman, Sallie Sullivan and I gave a surprise birthday party for our respective husbands, Lennie, Barry and Burt, at the Fort Ligonier Hotel. These May birthday boys were amazingly similar in type. Each year the wives would try to think of a different twist for their celebration—it was often the antithesis of what they would have planned. On this occasion we engaged a local band for the affair and offered ample liquid refreshments. For reasons unknown, the band did not wish to play more than three pieces at a time and expected everyone to return to their seats. We could not persuade them to change their custom and it had a devastating effect on maintaining the party spirit. The only solution was for everyone to resort to the open bar—the tempo certainly picked up but not necessarily in the desired way.

It turned out to be a hilarious party. To top off the evening, my sister Molly brought Sally Love's retired hunter, *Angel*, to the hotel in a trailer. Molly led her in through the big doors opening onto the dance floor. Our unsuspecting husbands were hoisted onto *Angel's* ample back—Barry Sullivan with a cast on his ankle was the third to be put on and *Angel* started to lose her hind legs on the slippery floor. It was a tense moment, but *Angel* regained her composure and made a magnificent departure. Thanks to *Angel*—it was a memorable evening.

The Daisy

In 1968 as another offshoot from my interest in horses, Barbara Childs, Sallie Sullivan, Mare Roberts and I started a gift shop in Ligonier called The Daisy. Our husbands were not thrilled with the idea—but we told them we wanted their advice only when we asked for it. We started in a very tiny shop on Main Street (next to the future Daisy building), and after our first buying trip to New York it was decided that we needed more merchandise for the "grand opening." We scoured our attics and opened on time. For a short period Trudy Mellon joined our group, and we moved into 215 Main Street, where The Daisy completed 32 years of supplying nice "wedding-type presents" to Ligonier. In the year 2000 The Daisy closed its doors, and is sorely missed by our customers. It did serve a purpose.

I would like to add a few more things to our great business adventure. We were fortunate to have G. Gray Garland, a friend and an excellent attorney, advise us in the beginning to keep us from making legal mistakes. Gray kindly was on our board for several years but retired when he realized we would call if we needed help.

After a few years of the owners alternating working days, we decided to hire nice Joyce Connally to run the shop. When Joyce got married, Helen Davidson came to our rescue. Helen had great drive and business improved to the point that she needed part-time help. Pam Dovey ably assisted for several years and then Denise Tetkoski took Pam's place.

Towards the end I was the only original owner available to oversee the store. It was also evident that the slight profits for the owners were consumed by salaries and overhead. Sallie Sullivan and I decided that it was time to sell.

Thank heavens for Denise who stuck by to the end keeping everything in order. I could not have done it without her. After surviving the sale, I can honestly say that it is a lot easier to open a business than to close one!

Travel

Travel is a way of life for Burt Todd and I never know when "the little bird is going to take off." After the war he finished his education at Oxford University in England. He made many good friends who later became influential leaders in their respective countries. After graduating Paul Bower, Edward St. George and Burt took a trip around the world. They had a marvelous time, and came back with many amusing stories. They have remained good friends. Edward and Burt are similar types, with avid interests in business deals. They are closer than brothers and talk almost daily on the telephone—they have an amazing relationship. In the spring of 2001 we took our 15-year-old granddaughter, Natalie Stewart, to visit the St. George's at their marvelous enclave in Freeport, Grand Bahamas. Natalie astutely commented to Burt, "I hope that I will have a friend like Edward in my lifetime." Strangely enough, Edward is now married to Lady Henrietta, who is like me and loves the country and horses. Henrietta and their two children spend most of their time in England and vacation in Freeport. Edward is well known in England for his famous string of racehorses.

I used to travel with Burt a great deal, and had very little time for preparation. Ingrid Rea remembers when we were giving a dinner party and I had to say "We are leaving in the morning for a trip around the world." When our children got a little older, Burt would call me with the news that he was taking one of them to Paris or Hong Kong—come home and pack for them. Peter Messer, the head of Valley School, thought the trip would be an educational adventure. We did take Laurie and Franny around the world when they were eight and ten. While Burt was doing business, I would take them to see sights that they would enjoy. We kept talking about the places that we visited so they would remember them. The place that they liked the least was Cairo, Egypt, where in the market place they saw children covered with flies sleeping under the tables. Their favorite place was Hawaii and I must say that I liked it too—the air, the music, the ambience of life makes it a special place.

Among my most favorite trips were those we took to Africa with Barry and Sallie Sullivan. They were great fun to be with and they knew Africa well. I think we went three times and I loved it. To me there is nothing more exciting than watching animals in their natural habitat. I fell in love with giraffes, with their suspended way of moving and their huge, limpid-pool eyes. I really did not like shooting animals, but the others found it thrilling, and I must admit that the hunt itself is exciting. One white hunter tried to convince me that culling was necessary. We did have two encounters with elephants that left me with indelible memories. We had encroached upon their territory and they strongly and unconditionally told us to leave. Laurie came with us on our last trip and she loved it too. On this trip I was fascinated by the silly looking wart hogs. The second white hunter, John Brown, got into the spirit of the chase and we spent a lot of time careening through the bush in pursuit of these creatures. With photographs and memories, I was able to capture in bronze a wart hog charging along with its tail straight up in the air.

Making Bronzes

I have always dabbled in art. As the children were growing up, I would give them presents of art materials that I thought would be fun to try. Regrettably I am not as good an artist as all the equipment I have accumulated would indicate, but I have certainly had fun trying. We did have a great time with Sculpey, a non-drying polyform product that is made permanent by baking in your oven.

Then in the late 1970s I read a book on wax sculpture by Frank Eliscu, and I loved the photographs of his freely moving animals and people. I immediately purchased a block of microcrystalline wax and tried to duplicate his work—with no success. When I had the pleasure of meeting him in Sarasota, Florida, we talked about his omission of a very important step. The working of wax is made so much easier if you soften the material with heat—even a strong lamp will do. In my first attempt my fingers were sore from scraping the wax off the block, and I was unable to recreate his lovely figures. I decided to sculpt something I understood—a pony.

My friends' comments changed from "That's nice" to "That's good." My search for knowledge increased, and I saw in the *Chronicle of the Horse*, a weekly horse publication, an ad for sculpture lessons given by Eugene Shortridge in Sarasota. Laurie was free at that time, and we had a marvelous two weeks with Gene, learning about using wax, and also bronze casting. Gene and his wife were very kind, and we have remained good friends.

I found it hard to accept Gene's advice that when you make something you must leave it without constant reworking. If you are not satisfied, start again—a lesson that also applies to painting. The theory is to make a sketch, working out the problems, and complete the piece when you know what you want. Perhaps my training of animals makes me willing to make constant adjustments to the situation. I still mess around with my art efforts.

I have included in the collection of photographs for this book four of my typical bronzes.

"Cleaning Her Pony" started with my first original wax pony, and then I added the child because it reminded me of the way my own children clambered all over their patient ponies.

"Hurry On" was the first hound that I did. I have observed hounds and I could check on movement with my voluminous photographic files. I envisioned a series of individual hard-working hounds, but I only accomplished three. "Hurry On" was used on a challenge trophy at the Oatland Hound Show.

"Red Hoss" is a self-portrait on my nice thoroughbred. The sculpture made the cover of *The Chronicle of the Horse*, and a man from Ohio bought one for his daughter, and one for a Perpetual Trophy for a horse show. Gene Shortridge cast the first one and applied a lovely multi-colored patina to it. I was advised that this type of patina is not acceptable for bronzes, but I think it is very attractive.

"Mousing" captures a fox in a typical hunting pose. The fox smells a mouse in the grass and pounces to flush his favorite quarry out. When the mouse flees, he is easily caught.

Through the encouragement of Else Tuckerman, Jean Bowman, and Eve Fout, my work was accepted three times in the American Academy of Equine Art Show. These excellent artists were among the founders of the AAEA. I had the honor of becoming a member of this marvelous organization, which has as its purpose the encouragement of equine artists.

There was no doubt that I was a better sculptor than a painter, but the time came when I decided to stop sculpting. Learning the process was challenging and fun. One would think that once you had a mold made, you could simply reorder, but in my case that did not work. Perhaps it was due to the fact that I made small intricate animals that entailed a lot of undercuts, making them difficult to extract from the molds.

I tried five good foundries but the results were always the same. It took one trip to take the original to the foundry. I preferred working in wax and shipping them could cause imperfections. The foundry would make a mold to pour lost waxes and they would clean these lost waxes, removing mold lines, etcetera. It is up to the artist to make the final corrections. This demanded a second trip and I always found things that needed correcting. Supposedly the perfect lost wax will be duplicated when the bronze is poured—not so in my case. The lost wax is encased in a carefully vented ceramic shell that allows for a steady flow of the material. The wax is melted out, hence the name lost wax, and bronze is poured into the ceramic shell. The bronze is poured at a very high temperature and things can go amiss. The ceramic shell is broken away from the bronze and the foundry will clean up the vents and imperfections. I would then arrive for the third time to chase any errors that I might find in the bronze—I always found some. If I needed reins or harness added to the piece, a man would fabricate them for me. This is a highly technical process and the men were excellent in accomplishing what I wanted. The final stage was when I supervised a worker applying the patina that is attained by acids brushed on and heated with a torch. I usually asked them to take the piece out into the sunlight because the lighting was deceptive. Once the proper patina was achieved the bronze would receive a protective coat of wax.

I must say that all of the workmen were extremely nice and capable. I tried leaving a finished piece with the foundry for reference during the various stages, but even then they could not see the necessary corrections needed. I finally became convinced that producing bronzes was not worth all the effort and I stopped doing them.

The Extravaganza

Foxley Farm is the perfect place to entertain. We had lovely weddings for Laurie and Franny, but I think the highlight was celebrating Burt's 70th birthday in May of 1994. He is a World War II addict and with the help of our girls we decided that should be the theme. The date coincided with the 50th anniversary of D-Day and it was proclaimed that the reserve should participate in any worthwhile celebration. The results were a smashing success.

The WWII Airmen's Preservation Society arrived early and set up their authentic encampment in the ring area. It was beautifully done and everyone enjoyed observing all of the detailed collection.

I was unprepared for the arrival of tanks, half-tracks, jeeps, and other gear from the First Battalion, 103rd Armor Division, under the command of Major Preston S. Stape, but Laurie was able to cope with the perfect placement of all of this impressive equipment. Don Guisey, our outdoor man, took over the role of MP at the entrance to "Camp Fox." We had invited friends from far and wide and they made the effort of dressing for the occasion. Many were able to fit into their military uniforms and others were limited to bits and pieces. My costume was a striped pants suit with a "POB" (Prisoner of Burt) sign on my back. I think that we invited 500 people, but the total swelled because of all of the participants. In addition, there were a few uninvited guests who wore uniforms and melted right into the crowd.

One of the most dramatic events was the Flag Folding Ceremony conducted by Major Stape and his men. This awesome ceremony held everyone's complete attention and brought tears to the eyes of many. I treasure the folded flag that the Major presented to me, and I loved the words that were spoken during the ceremony.

Right on cue, and to liven up the party, two old planes did a fly-by over the assembled crowd. I do not recall how it was so perfectly timed, but the next thing that happened was that two parachutists made perfect landings next to the crowd. Cecil B. DeMille could not have orchestrated a better scene.

When it was time to go to the tent for dinner, each person received a decorated mess kit and went through the buffet line. I later learned that we served about 700 people, and the food got pretty scarce. Jack Purcell and his wonderful fourteen-piece orchestra provided excellent music. There was a stage and dance floor inside the tent. Franny and Laurie had a lot to do with organizing the stage production. Eric Widing, Laurie's husband, was an excellent MC and

Charlie Stewart, Franny's husband, assisted by Dave Krantz, did a take-off on the famous Abbot and Costello act of "Who's on first?" Laurie, Franny, and Lisa Kennedy danced and performed to the record of the Andrews Sisters. They were so convincing that many thought they actually were singing. To fill out the program, Michele Flauraud & Company performed two appropriate dancing acts. There was a soloist, Dave Krantz did a Bob Hope take-off, and of course there was a dog act (for me). The show climaxed with everyone singing several of the well-known military songs, the grandchildren getting on stage, and heartfelt thanks given to all the participants who had made the party such a success.

It was an unforgettable time, and we received many thank-you notes that raved about the event. Burt would like to give another big party, but how in the world could we compete with that last extravaganza? With the ingenious minds of the Todd family, it is possible.

Here is just one example of the enthusiastic responses we received from Lisa Rutledge, one of our many satisfied guests:

> Dear Burt and Susie,
>
> What do D-Day and the Todd 40/70 party have in common? Exhaustive planning, meticulous attention to detail, outstanding leadership, inspired ideas, the enthusiastic involvement of masses of people, impressive air support, quantities of equipment and vehicles beyond the greatest imagination, plus the certainty of being discussed and analyzed for decades.
>
> What are the disparate characteristics of D-Day and the Todd 40/70 party? Charming and beautiful grandchildren, a family obviously enjoying and celebrating each other, an army of bartenders and endless libations, entertainment bursting with fun and ingenuity, and dancing to superb nostalgic music.
>
> If I had and tried to imagine what kind of a party could leave 500 party-jaded guests all walking around for hours with their jaws dropping, I could never have conjured up what you did. At the end, I just didn't want to leave, but Mark dragged me to the driveway reminding me that we couldn't be the last to leave. I wouldn't have minded.

How spellbinding the bivouac encampment was. Mark said that it looked just like Korea. I was fascinated that it was all absolutely authentic. The collectors were eager to explain every aspect. I could have spent hours just taking in all the details.

I kept trying to imagine the real reactions of the polite German au pairs. Guess there is more than one benefit to winning a war. No one in Germany is giving parties with a WWII theme.

Think of all those over-contrived charity events in Pittsburgh that take a committee of ladies 12 months to organize. The creative Todd team invents this fantasy by themselves with a regard to particulars unimaginable to any committee.

The new guide to parties: don't even try to emulate in detail, visual impact, attention to detail or pure fun the Todd party of 1994. The Todd 40/70 party set a standard impossible to duplicate.

Mark and I are endlessly grateful to have experienced the Todd 40/70 event. Thank you.

With appreciation and sincerity,

Lisa May 24, 1994

As to be expected, age is creeping up on us. Although I do not hunt anymore, I still ride a bit and still enjoy training. I keep searching for the perfect animal for the grandchildren and I have three ponies, but only one is fairly trustworthy. I do not think there is an equine alive that is absolutely foolproof. If something scares them, their natural instinct for self-preservation makes them react quickly.

Since our grandchildren do not ride often enough, it is hard for them to become accomplished, although they do enjoy riding at Foxley Farm. But I am afraid I have become a poor teacher, because as a grandmother I am too cautious. As you can see in my thoughts about horses, I am always concerned about the different problems that can arise.

Good type

Horses

I have had many horses in my life, some good and some rather mediocre, and I think that I have learned a great deal from all of them. I have always felt sorry that I could not discuss with them their previous experiences. Many of their undesirable defensive quirks were certainly man-made. If I felt that they were basically nice creatures, I would work patiently with them and they usually responded—but not always. I have included just a few of my many horses here because each of these was an interesting project.

Clytie—My First Pony

The J. Crossan Hays family rented for several summers the clubhouse of the Pittsburgh Hunt at Otasaga Farm, and my father bought the farm when the hunt moved to David McCahill's stable and became the Fox Chapel Hunt. At Otasaga Farm my first pony was a dish-faced chestnut and white mare with a saintly disposition. *Clytie* was loaned to the Hays family by the Charles A. Painter family from Sewickley, and was returned to Allie Painter, Mrs. LeRoy Thompson, when the pony's services were needed for other young children. *Clytie* would be proud to know that her tutelage with Allie and the Hays girls ultimately produced three Masters of Foxhounds (MFH is a title that you keep for life).

There was only one habit of *Clytie's* that reduced me to tears. Our house, formerly The Pittsburgh Hunt Club, was up on a hill and my sister, Molly, and brother, Jack, would run down to the stables and procure the only stall cleaning tools before smaller sister Susie arrived. Nine times out of ten, *Clytie* had manure in her feed box. It was necessary to clean the box before I could feed her and, by the time I finished my chores, Molly and Jack had returned to the house. It was a nasty trick of my siblings since, for some unknown reason, I was afraid of being left alone in the barn, especially in the evening. They had a good laugh while I was consumed in tears—definitely not nice of them.

Clytie was a perfect introduction to riding, although I think she was pretty much in charge of the activity. Daddy and I rode in the Family Class at the Pittsburgh Hunt Club Horse Show in 1931. At the age of six, I was happy but not in complete control. When we were asked to trot, *Clytie's* adrenaline flowed and we proceeded to lap Daddy's horse a couple of times before *Clytie* settled down.

One of my most vivid recollections of *Clytie* was our first venture to the Harts Run Junior Horse Show. I cannot imagine what prompted my father but he happily loaded the pony into the back of his huge Packard car, while Molly held the lead line from the front seat. Mother drove behind with Jack and me as a rear guard. Gentle *Clytie* accepted the affair without concern. We must

Clytie approved

have created quite a picture as we drove along with a pony peering out of the window. Of course, in the 1930s the Packard was roomy and built like a tank.

Lucky Boy

Lucky Boy was not a handsome fellow. The horse dealer even tried to talk my father out of buying the small bay gelding, advising him that the horse was not suitable for children. Although he never bit or kicked us, he did have a rather sour outlook on life.

We tried to convince him that he should comply with our desires. When we first asked him to jump over some of the hunt's fences, he would simply quit in mid air. He would just stay suspended on the fence groaning and refused to make any effort to move either direction. The only solution was to break the fence down to release him. Molly and Jack had to cope with all of this while I held the other horses. This happened quite a few times but he finally decided that it was easier to jump. Believe it or not, in time Jack was able to hunt him and even show him. In hindsight, he must have been pretty nice to survive our complete lack of training knowledge.

Titian Blonde—My First Horse

What an exciting present to receive on my ninth birthday in the fall of 1934! *Titian Blonde (Tish)* was a small chestnut Thoroughbred mare with a blaze on her face. She was a very nice mare, but I have to admit that our first few months together were a disaster. It did not take her long to realize that she was in charge. When I tried to ride her by myself, we would get to the end of the hayfield and then she would buck me off, and return to the stable. Since this happened every time that I rode her—I just stopped riding. But my sister Molly insisted that I ride *Tish*, and she rode with me. By spring, I was more confident and would laugh when the mare bucked. This took all the fun out of the game for *Tish*, and she behaved beautifully from that point on. We became a good team and I rode her all over Fox Chapel.

We spent the spring schooling over fences at Johnny Beach's and Dr. Lynch's rings and felt prepared for our debut in June at the prestigious Allegheny Horse Show in Sewickley. It was exciting to take care of *Tish* in her stall in the shed row, and then warm up on the gravel area outside the show ring. I was very proud of my horse, and of being part of the whole scene. She was a bit nervous with all the confusion, so Johnny Beach led us up to the in-gate. As we entered the ring, Johnny suggested giving her a slight tap with my crop while we made our circle. WOW—it was like being shot out of a cannon! *Tish* took off at a mad gallop and we absolutely flew over the eight fences. It took at least two circles to slow down before we could exit the ring. It was not a pretty sight.

Live and learn . . . I never used the crop on her again. Our next show was at Hartwood Acres and *Tish* won the championship of our division. She was wonderful, and we continued to have a very successful career in all the local shows.

Red Robin

This chestnut half-bred gelding was given to us by James McKinney. Mr. McKinney had hunted him successfully for several seasons with Dick Mellon at Rolling Rock. *Red* was a rather rough moving horse with a mouth of cast iron, but he was basically very pleasant and a good jumper.

Red was Jack's horse but of course I rode him too. I do recall one hazardous trip that I had on the horse. I was riding him bareback and on our return home I was enjoying a soft canter up a slight grade. It was too close to home on Hunt Road and at the crest of the grade he increased his pace to a strong gallop. My efforts to stop him went unheeded. We wildly careened down the cinder road, made the turn into the driveway, and luckily he stopped before he took me into the barn. I was thankful that we had not encountered any cars but it was a breathtaking ride that was downright scary.

I really enjoy the nice sensation of riding bareback, but in my experience I have to say that I am not then in complete control. If the horse wishes to give his rider a difficult time, it is pretty hard to change his mind.

Mystic Marron

Although I had enjoyed some previous hunting with Fox Chapel, Rolling Rock and Harts Run, I became truly involved with the latter hunt in 1951 when I was asked to be a whipper-in. It was fun to act as a whipper-in, whose job is basically to keep track of hounds and if necessary turn them back to the huntsman. Fortunately, it was not a prerequisite to be adept with a hunting whip (I failed miserably). The kennels were at Johnny Beach's Boot Hill Farm in Gibsonia. Johnny was the huntsman and Jane Flaccus was the main supporter of the hunt. She varied her role either as Master or Whip, as needed. The hunt attracted an enthusiastic, congenial group of members of various ages and occupations. On Saturdays after an eventful day of hunting, we would gather in the small one-room clubhouse heated by a potbellied stove to enjoy libations and food. Members would take turns providing the "tea" and we were always well taken care of.

The hunt was a drag hunt, cleverly laid by Johnny's sons, Alan and Richard. Instead of hunting live fox, a fox-scented bag was dragged along to allow the hounds to follow the line. A lot of the hunts in the United States are drag hunts and some riders prefer this constant activity to the uncertainty of live fox hunting. The Harts Run Hunt country was pretty open farmland, but other than necessary jumpable fences it was far from polished. The hounds ran well but were not very disciplined and they often pursued deer or sometimes a fox. Needless to say, the field was always entertained with an adventurous ride.

The year that I acted as whipper-in, I rode my small rose-gray mare *Mystic Marron*. She was agile and brave despite her age of four years. We had raised her and I had made the mistake of loving her too much, treating her like a dog. Before I broke her to ride, I would take her for walks and even jump with her over low obstacles. When she fully matured, I realized that I had not created the necessary attitude of respect that a good horse must have.

Marron was fabulous that first year of whipping-in. She was willing to go anywhere and jump anything. As I have said, I was far from adept with my hunting whip, but other than clamping her tail down on the lash as I caught her under her tail, she always forgave me. It was also easy for me to dismount to drop a rail and have her hop over the fence. We handled this "handy hunter test" with great aplomb due to our early training.

Thanks to the service of Chester Sayre's van, I was able to keep *Marron* at home on Hunt Road. I would get her ready for hunting and Johnny Adams, the wonderful driver, would take her out of her stall, load her, and have her waiting for me at Boot Hill's stable. After the hunt, I would take care of her and Johnny Adams would take her home while I joined the party. She was always fed and happy when I checked her on my return home. Those simpler days of trustworthy service are gone but I am thankful that I could enjoy them.

Red Hoss

I bought this small chestnut Thoroughbred from Jack and Joy Kenny in 1976. The Kennys were good horsemen and I had known Joy for years. She was the daughter of Everett Hensley who had taken over Dr. McCague's stable after Johnny Beach moved on. *Hoss* had been raced but he seemed to be sensible, and he was a talented jumper.

I soon found that he had a very strange habit. Even when taking a quiet ride, he would sometimes get frustrated. He would freeze and violently pound the ground with his front legs. The first time that it happened, Sallie Sullivan was riding with me and we were both appalled. It was rather unnerving because he was such an athlete that it was like sitting on a volcano about to erupt. Luckily, he limited this unusual antic to just pawing, but I always distracted him before he blew up. While schooling in the ring, he also let me know if I used my leg aides too strongly. He would pin his ears and even kick out a bit. I learned to abide by his rules and we were both happy.

Hoss had a definite opinion of where he should be in the hunting field. He was excellent in the lead when I became a Joint Master, and for some strange reason he was content leading the second flight. I did have to caution my followers that they were never allowed to get in front of him. I also cautioned them to give him enough space so he would not feel crowded.

I thoroughly enjoyed hunting him. He gave me that wonderful feeling of floating over the ground and effortlessly sailing over all the fences. One early misty morning was particularly memorable as I was taking the field. The moment that the hounds started running strongly I got carried away with the thrill of moving along, forgetting my duty as Master of the field. What a time we had flying through the misty woods and leaping over the fences. It was positively delicious! Fortunately, the hounds did check and the field caught up to us.

On another occasion, *Hoss* and I took the field during a Joint Meet. There were a lot of people out and I wanted to make sure that everyone had a good time. We started in the nice open area of Foxley Farm and Log Cabin Farm, and I had plenty of room to swing the long line of followers. It was like leading a long snake, and I tried to avoid any congestion before a fence. At the end of the day one rider commented, "Everyone had such a lovely hunt. It was always so pleasant and smooth."

Crofton

I was fortunate to acquire *Crofton*, a charming, small, banged-tailed gray gelding. I did not know his previous history, but at that time he was owned by a member of the Rolling Rock Hunt. I liked this 15.2, well-made fellow and he became available when he started a serious campaign of refusing most fences. I had watched him jump many fences well and concluded that all he needed was a bit of patient schooling to restore his confidence. Since I spent a good part of every hunt dismounting to lower rails for my second flight, *Crofton's* size and manners thoroughly appealed to me.

My guess turned out to be right. With the use of cavelleti—a combination of rails and jumps placed in proper distances, to encourage a horse to use himself well—*Crofton* began to feel good about himself. I patiently let him develop this attitude without punishing him in any way if he failed, and

I certainly did not touch his mouth. To the amazement of the previous owners, in a short time *Crofton* would competently jump anything that I headed him into. We were a happy pair.

I have always tried to encourage riders, especially in the hunting field, to grab a bit of mane while jumping obstacles. Little surprises happen frequently and it is devastating to the horse to be hit in the mouth when he is doing the best he can. A rider can be very abusive to his horse when he grabs its mouth or bangs down heavily in the saddle. Men are the worst offenders, probably because they do not have the time or interest to learn to ride properly. I was so pleased to hear Charlie Whitehouse, the MFH of Orange County say, "I take a series of lessons before the start of every hunting season to keep myself in shape." What a wise man. I am sure his lovely horses are very grateful. There is nothing degrading about taking lessons in any sport; it makes sense. Even the fabulous golf pros take lessons to correct their faults and refine their game.

Ducks

Little did I know that the horse I bought was going to be such a "challenge." He was advertised in *The Chronicle of the Horse.* Laurie and I stopped to see him while I was taking her to Wesleyan College in 1973. A young girl rode and jumped him before I got on (this is always a good idea to make sure that the animal is relatively safe). When I rode, I found that he was extremely quiet and stiff as a board. It took me quite awhile, quietly working him, before he even responded slightly. He had fabulously intelligent looking eyes and he was certainly a good mover so there was hope. When he arrived at Foxley Farm, he was definitely a different creature and there was no doubt in my mind that he had been tranquilized when I had tried him out. Stupid me—buyer beware! It was even dangerous to go into the stall to feed him.

Ducks basically was not a mean horse but he definitely had some undesirable qualities. Perhaps he was gelded late in life. He liked to be in control of everything and could be quite threatening, but I must admit that he never bit or kicked a human. He was quite a trial to groom because of his constant fussing, but Milt Selznick attributed this to having boys at the track create this nasty habit.

Ducks did respond nicely during our dressage classes and could have been successful, except for the fact that he flapped his tongue around. Joy Puncher, our very nice teacher, even began to appreciate this talented but wacky horse.

I took him to a clinic that Michelle Douglas organized at Braemar Farms. It was great fun to work with the instructor, Peter Leone, who was extremely nice and patient. *Ducks* blew his stack and was a nervous wreck, but Peter was very kind to say, "I enjoyed watching you ride. You remind me of the group I worked with on the North Shore of Boston." My friend Captain V.S. Littauer had given several clinics there and Peter could recognize his influence on riders. I boarded *Ducks* with Joseph Hardiman one season, and Joseph's comment was, "Never fight with this horse." I knew this to be a fact and if *Ducks* refused to go forward over something, I resolved the problem by backing him over the silly object (like a pool of water or a path of cobblestones). As far as his becoming a good hunter, it was hopeless. He would get so excited that he would lose his sense of preservation. Many people give their horse a bit of Acepromazine to take the edge off, but an adequate amount made *Ducks* too relaxed. It was unnerving to approach a fence, not knowing if he would even make the effort to jump it. I was finally convinced that I should cease hunting him when I had carefully angled him into one particular fence to avoid a tree on the far side. In midair I looked between his ears to see that sturdy tree in our flight path. Miraculously he managed to avoid the inevitable crash. Counting my blessings, I decided to go home.

My goddaughter, Bobbie Childs Off, loved to hack *Ducks* and liked his capricious spirit.

But I often reminded *Ducks* that if it were not for me he would be a candidate for the "glue factory."

Panda

Panda was the cutest little black Quarter Horse you could imagine. He was so appealing with his white star and the white snip on his nose, plus he had gorgeous almond-shaped kind eyes. I don't know how I heard about him, but he belonged to a local farmer. For some unknown reason, there was no saddle available so I rode him bareback. He behaved fairly well in the vicinity of the barn and the farmer suggested we go out for a ride. He hopped on his workhorse and we went out for a pleasant ride. Of course, I bought him.

Things went along pretty well until one day I was hacking with my two daughters. We were on our way home, coming down the Country Club Road. I was in the lead as we walked peacefully along, when for no good reason *Panda* took off at a mad gallop. My efforts to stop him were useless. Fortunately my daughters were smart enough not to pursue and they thought "there goes Mom" as I was headed for the dangerous crossing on Route 711. Luckily, *Panda* broke his stride when he wondered why he was leaving the other horses. I was able to turn him before we crossed the highway but it was definitely a close call.

I boarded him at a stable with a fabulous indoor ring for the winter. He made great progress and everyone admired him. Unfortunately, he became lame with navicular and I gave him to my blacksmith.

Lance

I bought *Lance* in Philadelphia when my good hunter *Hawk* began showing signs of unsoundness. *Lance* was a big-bodied, dark brown horse, an excellent jumper and beautifully balanced.

Although he was a good horse, I have never considered him a nice "person." He was spoiled when he came, with poor respect for people. Perhaps the owner had made the same mistake that I had made while raising *Marron*. I had to ask our huntsman, Joseph Hardiman to straighten him out because my "strong" methods did not even get his attention.

It took a couple of seasons to make him into a good hunter. In the beginning when he was excited he would perform an impressive acrobatic rodeo. My corrections proved useless and I had to resort to spinning him, which made him listen to me. One day he even kicked a hound—most embarrassing! Another day, while we were leading the second flight at a controlled gallop across a lovely field, he made a ninety-degree turn for no good reason—not a trustworthy fellow.

For some reason he and my other horse *Ducks* were very close friends. I don't know why *Lance* accepted the rough treatment that he received. *Ducks* constantly drove him around and often made *Lance* stand outside of the barn in all kinds of weather. To clear my conscience I tried separating them, but they were both miserable. I should have felt sorry for *Lance* but frankly I was jealous of *Ducks'* control over him.

I finally ironed out *Lance's* difficulties and he gave me several seasons of good hunting. I even lent him to an out-of-town guest to hunt and he behaved beautifully. Despite my friend Helen Davidson's love for *Lance,* I did not share this emotion for the horse. Perhaps there was a conflict of personalities, but I might add, "he did not have a kind eye." Despite the fact that he was a good horse, he was not a favorite.

Recent Ponies at Foxley Farm

Now days I have been forced to limit my riding due to arthritis. Therefore I no longer have horses, but I do keep ponies. Ostensibly they are for the grandchildren, but, since they are not perfect, I have to admit the ponies are for me. I love having them, watching them, playing with them, and training them.

Twinkle is a matriarchal white mare and comes closest to being a child's perfect pony. For reasons unknown, the children do not seem to appreciate her.

Clyde is a winsome fellow with great charm. He resembles a small Clydesdale with innocent, almond-shaped eyes. He is a willing learner and tries so hard to please. The person who broke him did a great job, but *Clyde* must have been previously abused in his youth. If anything frightens him, he moves very fast. This fault makes him limited to someone who knows how to ride.

His other detriment is that he is allergic to black fly bites and for the past two summers it has taken a real campaign to treat him. The medicine called Swat works well on open sores. My latest attempt is using Curel, a therapeutic moisturizer obtained at the Giant Eagle. It is perfect for my dry skin in the winter months, so I decided to try softening his scabs and itchy tail. I also have *Clyde* on a regime of homeopathic remedies. At the moment, we are having success. I will share this with my vet if it cures him.

My latest acquisition is *Coco*, a small chestnut gelding. I found him through a newspaper ad and although he presented problems, I found him intriguing. He looks like a cross between a standard-bred and a pony—not too well made but charming. He is intelligent and honest, but something in his past told him to hurry. In the beginning I even had to put a small chain over his nose to make him pay attention while I led him around. I am basically too big for him, but he is willing and we are making progress. It was exciting when my eight-year-old granddaughter, Elsie, was able to walk him around the ring with no problem.

Then disaster struck—critters pulled corn from the crib and *Coco* foundered. For the non-horsey person, this condition creates a severe inflammation in the feet. He is a marvelous patient and loves the attention he receives. The blacksmith is working with his feet and the pony is improving. Hopefully, *Coco* will recover to be a useful fellow.

I will continue to search for the perfect animal for the grandchildren. In the meantime I am enjoying my equine friends and maybe someday the children will be able to ride them.

Tips on Hunters

It is always a challenge to find a good horse to hunt. The breeding is immaterial—the suitability to the rider is most important, plus the adaptability of the animal to the terrain. For example, a big strong-going horse may not be the best choice for hunting trappy country. Someone must take the time to train a hunter since it is a "heady" experience for the animal. It is foolish and even dangerous to ride a horse that is so excited that he is not thinking or listening to you.

If you are introducing a horse to the hunting field, it is wisest to start them slowly by hill-topping (following the hunt at a discreet distance) or keeping them in the back of the field. I am a strong advocate of a hunt having a second flight. It is the perfect way to introduce a newcomer to hunting, whether it is a rider or a horse. The second flight offers a slower controlled pace with smaller fences. When comfortable, the rider may ask permission to move up to the next flight. The slow approach will pay big dividends! If there is not a second flight, ask a friend with a quiet horse to accompany you while hill-topping.

It is always nice to have control in setting your own pace and being able to stop without running into the horse in front of you. I am afraid that the latter is quite a common occurrence and unpleasant for all concerned. Brakes are important and can be acquired with education. I feel sorry for horses and riders who are having a tug of war—neither one of them is having a good time. It is a mistake to let a horse get fully extended and leaning on the bit, unless you are confident that he will come back to you—keep him light. The horse is better balanced to cope with changes if he is not heavy on his forehand. I will not ride a horse that pulls—I will spend more time schooling and if unsuccessful I do not hunt the horse. In the past, I enjoyed training hunters. With a few exceptions, we worked out a good relationship with patience, flat work, and building up their confidence over low fences. There is always room for improvement, and riders miss a lot by not taking lessons to improve their seat and the schooling of their horse. It is so pleasant to be in sync with the animal that you ride.

The young riders of today are fortunate to have so many good teachers available. There is also The United States Pony Clubs (USPC) that is an inspirational source of developing knowledgeable young horsemen. It is a well-run organization offering strict but intelligent guidelines for the local District Commissioners to follow. The USPC was founded in 1954 by a group of fox-hunting enthusiasts and much of the leadership is still drawn from the fox-hunting community. In 1996 there were more than 12,000 Pony Clubbers and 600 clubs throughout the United States and the Virgin Islands. The children have a lot of fun and are guided in the safest way possible to learn about horse care, competition at all levels and foxhunting.

I would like to add just a few other practical suggestions for the novice foxhunter that may be helpful.

- Put a red ribbon on your horse's tail if he is a potential kicker. Keep him in the back of the field.

- Be sure to be well turned out—hair must be in a net or braids (flowing hair is unacceptable). Your horse should be clean and his mane must be short. If you like long manes, then you will have to braid him for hunting. His fetlocks should be trimmed. If you are hesitant to clip him, consider an Irish clip. (My horses were perfectly happy with this clip during the fall even when they just had run-in sheds to get out of the weather.)

• If you cannot stay with your horse over a fence, either grab the mane or have a stirrup leather properly placed on his neck for you to hang on to. It is so wrong to punish his mouth when he is doing a good job!

• When you are hacking to the meet, stay on roads—do not take the chance of disturbing a covert.

• If your horse is too nervous to stand still, keep him walking instead of fighting with him.

• If you have a refusal—give your horse more leg and encouragement before resorting to a stick.

• A horse cannot rear if he is moving forward. (A Kentucky mountaineer told me a good trick to cope with a horse who rears or will not go forward—spin him.) Caution—get some instruction because you may pull him off his feet.

• Be sure to run your stirrups up or cross them over the saddle while dismounted. (I will never forget having my first Thoroughbred getting the stirrup caught behind her front teeth. She could have been seriously hurt when she spun and fell. I had to pull her head back to release her.)

• A death grip on the reins is not as effective as give and take. A pulley rein also is good—put one hand on the neck with a snug hold and pull strongly with the other hand. (While at Chatham Hall School, I rode a marvelous little horse, *Rummy*, for the game of spearing rings. He would get so excited approaching the starting gate that he would lunge uncontrollably; no one else wanted to ride him. The problem was eradicated by keeping him light with little checks and we became unbeatable.)

• The most ideal way to ask your horse to slow down is to cue him with soft legs and a definite shift of your weight back. A horse that is trained will be nicely sensitive to this signal.

• Circling is very good for regaining control but many times there is insufficient space.

• When wishing to pass a horse, alert the other rider with "May I pass on your [left or right]"—do not rush by. I learned the hard way and luckily only received a bent stirrup!

• If you find the pace too fast, drop back in the field as soon as possible. It is rude and disruptive to detain the rest of the field.

• Juniors should not hunt in the front of the field unless invited. It is a matter of respect and manners, not competency! A parent should accompany his child in the back of the field until the child can safely ride with the other juniors.

• Make sure that you allow enough time to cool your horse out before returning to the stable or trailer, even if you will have help awaiting you. It is your responsibility!

Most of the things that you are taught are well founded but you must always keep an open mind. The horse "has not read the book," and you must use your intelligence. If your horse is misbehaving then you have to outsmart him. Correct, but do not start a fight unless you are going to win. It might be best to avoid making an issue of the situation for the moment. If you like your horse but cannot resolve your problems, get help from a good professional.

With all of this advice, I must admit there were two horses in particular that did not comply with my "marvelous" training methods. Although a potential hunter may have most of the desirable exterior qualities, you will not know about the quirks he might have from previous experiences until you have owned him for a while. The story of *Max* might amuse you. I kept looking at him in the pasture of a small horse dealer, and the horse appealed to me. After conversing with the dealer (and learning nothing), I took the horse on trial for a week.

Max was a fairly attractive sturdy bay horse, but he did have a broken ear (*Clue number one*). It is not uncommon for horsemen to twist a horse's ear to make him stand still for treatment, etc. It does get his attention and it is seldom traumatic. I found *Max* to be comfortable and athletic, so I bought him.

One day we were having a fine ride and I popped him over a small fence along the trail. Explosion! He started bucking hard as we landed, and I eventually went off, taking his bridle with me (*Clue number two*). Luckily I was not far from home, and I arrived unscathed as people started looking for me.

The next occurrence happened while hunting. It was a chilly day and we were standing in an open field when Alison Walters offered me a nip of sherry from her hunting flask. We had just been discussing how hard it was to find a proper fitting replacement for your sandwich case. A woman carries a leather case, containing a silver sandwich box and a small flask, attached to the right side of her saddle seat. A man has a leather-encased flask (larger, of course) attached to his saddle near the roll of his right knee. These are the proper hunting appointments and they serve a good purpose on a long, cold day of hunting. Well, *Max* objected to my taking the flask, and he took off at a mad, bucking, gallop. He was going so fast that he could not buck very hard, and the cultivated field was large enough for me to decide where to drop the precious but offending flask. Once I dropped the terrifying object, he stopped his charade and I was able to retrieve the unharmed bottle (*Clue number three*).

The final experience (*Clue number four*) came while exercising *Max* on a lovely day. I cantered up the wide, grassy strip on Rector Road near Braemar Farm. *Max* started bucking, and I knew that I would not be able to stop him to turn into the fence opening near Richard Jamison's woods. The vision of careening down the paved Rector Hill Road did not appeal to me, so self-preservation told me to bail out. As I tumbled I broke my wrist . . . but I was able to walk. A nice young man had observed the performance from his car and offered to drive me home. We met *Max* as he was about to cross Route 711 into Barron Road, and I was able to catch him and lead him home. It was definitely time to get rid of *Max*.

I called a dealer in Altoona and explained the horse's quirk. The dealer said he had a good boy who could ride anything. Everything did go fine for a time, until *Max* did his act and unloaded the roughrider. The sequel to this story is that *Max* was purchased by a rodeo group . . . and became a famous bucking horse!

I tried another dun-colored horse belonging to a reputable dealer. The horse was very comfortable and talented, but seemed to lose his marbles when galloping across a field. Maybe he reminded me too much of *Max*, so I decided to return him. The lady who picked him up was very pleasant, and as she led him to her van she said to him, "You idiot, you had a chance to live in horse heaven." I thought it was such a nice compliment to Foxley Farm.

There is hardly a better introduction to foxhunting than William P. Wadsworth's pamphlet *Riding to Hounds in America*. If you absorb this material, you will have a good start in understanding what to expect in the hunting field. Copies may be obtained from *The Chronicle of the Horse*.

Alert

Foxhunting

It is fascinating to find how early foxhunting was established in the colonies. A large percentage of immigrants then were English and they brought hounds and horses to their new home. Due to its early settlement, the Castle Hill Hounds in Virginia was founded in 1776.

Many immigrants brought their hounds or dogs to help them seek game, providing food for their families. When it was not necessary to hunt for food, the intrepid hunter found other ways to enjoy his hounds. Hunting is a way of life with many people. There are still many night hunters who gather around a friendly fire to listen to the lovely voices of their hounds running a fox or other quarry through the darkened countryside. The owners know their hounds' voices so well that they are aware of exactly how the chase is progressing. The night is passed with jocular verbal competition among the hunters until it is time to call their hounds in. If you are ever invited to join one of these groups, you will spend an enjoyable evening.

There are many people more qualified than I to write on the subject of foxhunting. I can present only my version. The Masters of Foxhounds Association (MFHA) was formed in 1907 to register hunts, their territory, and the breeding of their foxhounds, and by 2000 the MFHA had registered or recognized 166 hunts in the United States. Run by a fine group of individuals, the MFHA is dedicated to keeping foxhunting a well-established sport, conducted in a sportsmanlike manner while adhering to rules and standards. A new hunt must prove through correspondence, recommendations, well-kept records, a good pack of hounds, and an inspection, that it is worthy of recognition by MFHA. Establishing a hunt and developing a hunt territory is not an easy task, and we should be grateful to those who have made hunting accessible to us. Many of the hunts started as private packs, but with escalating costs most hunts are now by invited subscriptions.

I feel there are three different types of foxhunters—the foxhunters who ride primarily to be with the hounds, the riders who enjoy hunting their horses, and the riders who like the comradeship of the hunt. I have to admit I fall into the last two categories. Despite these different interests, a day out with hounds is stimulating and fun for all hunters.

The membership of a hunt *often* changes. It takes complete dedication to participate fully, especially if the rider maintains his own horse. The horse must be kept in top condition, which requires many hours in the saddle. Also it is no small chore to prepare your horse for a day of hunting. This entails cleaning the horse and tack, early feeding, and often trailering the horse for some distance. At the end of the day, the horse has to be properly cared for—a labor of love that may become too constricting. Even if your horse is boarded at a hunt stable, the owner must still be sure that his horse is fine. Running a good hunt stable is a huge responsibility, and costly.

Generally speaking, the hunting season is October through March, but each hunt establishes its own season. Cubbing season may start in August, and is primarily for entering the puppies into the pack. It is one of my favorite times of the year. There is something special about riding through the early morning mist, greeting old friends, enjoying the tranquility of the silent woods, and experiencing short bursts of activity. The opening meet in October is a colorful event with riders turned out in their formal hunting attire, which is worn for the rest of the season.

For many years the Todds at Foxley Farm have offered the traditional Stirrup Cup of port or sherry for the opening meet of the Rolling Rock Hunt, and many people come to enjoy this active scene of assembled riders and hounds. It is a colorful occasion with riders dressed in their formal attire and a special effort is made to have their horses beautifully groomed. After the traditional blessing of the hounds, the huntsman blows his horn and the field moves off briskly as they ride up through our open fields. Some people rush to their cars to follow the hunt to enjoy intermittent sounds and sights as the hunt progresses. Throughout the rest of the season it's not uncommon for landowners to offer a Stirrup Cup when the meet is on their land. After the official opening of the season, the traditional hunt teas on Saturdays provide a delightful time to recapitulate the experiences of the day. Usually limited to weekends, the hunt teas vary in size and grandeur, and hunt members take turns hosting the parties.

Many hunts are limited to drag hunting, primarily due to restricted terrain. To lay a facsimile line of a fox, a scented bag is dragged by a person either walking or on horseback. If well laid, this drag-line is challenging to a pack of hounds and provides wonderful gallops for the field. Generally speaking, a drag hunt assures an active day, but plans can still go awry—the scent can be poor, live quarry may be encountered, hounds may overrun the line, or the drag person may have been too creative, and so on. Most hounds that are accustomed to hunting live fox are usually not interested in running a drag. I prefer hunting live fox, and am willing to accept blank or slow days. Anticipation plays an important part of any kind of hunting, and the thrill of hearing hounds striking off on a live fox is truly exhilarating! The foxes at Rolling Rock have little to fear since they have many places to go to ground. They often seem to enjoy outwitting the hounds in a lengthy chase, when they could have gone quickly to ground.

It is a sad occasion, but there are many reasons for disbanding a hunt: the loss of the dynamic leaders, the development of the hunting country with houses and highways, and the lack of dedicated people willing to accept the large responsibility of running the hunt. Although there is prestige in acquiring the title of Master of Foxhounds, the position demands a great deal of time, effort, and financial support. The Masters are responsible for the hunt staff, hounds, horses, coordinating the hunt committee, and for keeping the landowners happy. The latter is perhaps the most important of all! It is only through their kind permission that the hunt is able to traverse their property, and the landowners' wishes must be strictly adhered to. A hunt is doomed without ample country. The field should be very cognizant that they are guests of the landowner and should act accordingly. Most hunts have a professional huntsman, but some Masters hunt the hounds; if they do not have a Joint Master, they appoint a Field Master.

Hunting the hounds demands full concentration and it is absolutely essential to have someone in charge of the field. It is not uncommon for riders to get carried away with the thrill of the chase, and pass the Field Master, who will quickly remind them of their manners! The Master is responsible for giving the huntsman and hounds adequate room to hunt—pushing or overrunning the hounds is not acceptable. I love the story of Squire Osbaldeston, who said in his 1906 *Autobiography* that he simply took his hounds home when the field became too pressing and unruly. This occurred in England in the 1800s. The Squire left a field of over one hundred astonished riders, but he cared about his hounds, and he could not control the overbearing thrusters (some of them were his good friends).[1] A Master has the right to excuse from the field anyone who is out of line—the safety of the hounds and that of the entire field of members is of paramount importance.

A good huntsman plays a vital role in making a hunt successful. Most of them possess a rare gift with hounds. Besides this, he (or she) must oversee the kennels, have a breeding program, train puppies, work on the hunt country, be on friendly terms with the farmers, keep up the hunt horses, be nice to the members, and answer to the Masters. It takes a dedicated person, and it is not a five-day-a-week job. Foxhounds are strong individuals—competitive, keen, independent and intelligent—but they must learn to work as a pack and be biddable to their huntsman. This invisible thread between the

1. *Squire Osbaldeston: His Autobiography*, London: John Lane, the Bodley Head Limited; New York: Charles Scribner's Sons, March 1906

huntsman and his hounds can only be obtained by acquiring the hounds' respect and willingness. To watch a good huntsman working a fine pack of hounds is awesome.

While hunting his hounds, the huntsman requires the aid of whipper-ins. They may be professionals or honorary members but they have to know the country well and have a good working knowledge of hound work. At this point in time, two-way radios are widely used and are very beneficial to the safety of the hounds. In hilly country it is extremely difficult to hear hounds and the radios truly are helpful in keeping track of their line, often preventing a potential disaster at a highway.

In the case of a subscription hunt, it is run by the Master or Joint Masters, a President and Hunt Committee, a Secretary and a Treasurer. Sometimes the latter two offices are combined, but both offices demand time and dedication. These officers deserve a great deal of appreciation and respect for a hunt cannot exist without them.

There are many breeds of foxhounds in the world. For hundreds of years they have been meticulously bred for their suitability to a terrain and to a desired style of hunting. An expert like Benjamin Hardaway III, MFH of the Midland Hunt in Georgia, gives you the feel of the breeding process. Ben Hardaway is famous in the United States as well as England. I met this delightful man at the colorful Georgia–Florida Field Trial for shooting dogs, and was fascinated by his "Reflections On Some Of The Best Foxhounds at Midland" (in *Covertside*, March, 1997—the fine periodical published by MFHA Educational Foundation). Hardaway discusses his 50-plus years of breeding hounds at Midland, and reflects on ten of his most outstanding hounds. All were exceptional, but his description of *Watchman* is particularly appealing:

> *Watchman* inherited the solid red color and conformation of his July sire, but the biddability and deer-resistance of his cross-bred dam. The trait that made *Watchman* stand apart was his magnificent voice. Of all the hounds that I have raised and run, I have never had one that gave me the thrill running a fox that *Watchman* did. Not only did he have a

> thunderous, booming roar, but he ran up at the head of the pack giving tongue with every breath. It was something to hear. My hunting companions would ask why I even bothered to bring the other 59 hounds, and I would tell them that *Watchman* needed some background music.

It is interesting that *Watchman* inherited such wonderful genes, but there is no mention of his littermates. Breeding the top of the line does not necessarily produce superb individuals, but the percentage for achieving a high standard is better with selective breeding.

I have listened to many foxhunters extol the merits of their hounds, and I envy their experience! I can understand how thrilling it is to hunt your own pack of hounds. I wish that the members of the field would be more respectful of and interested in the hounds. Each member of the pack, whether young or old, contributes something that is cherished.

I had the pleasure of hunting with C. Martin Wood III, MFH of the Live Oak Hounds in Georgia. It was so impressive to observe Marty handling his biddable pack. On one occasion the hounds worked a fox through a veritable swamp and after about twenty minutes of lively going, Marty called in his hounds to proceed to a different area. There he was in a small clearing with all of his hounds, waiting for the field to catch up! His infectious love of the sport produces a stimulating conversation with him about foxhunting. Marty, a past president of MFHA, and his wife, Daphne, who has become the first lady President of the MFHA, are extremely knowledgeable about hounds, and have a superb hunt. They share their knowledge by being active in the MFHA and by judging hound shows. The Woods are very fine people, and will long be remembered for their contribution to foxhunting.

When Richard K. Mellon was MFH of the Rolling Rock Hunt, he sent out the following suggestions to his members to remind them of some of the basic tenets and traditional requirements of foxhunting. He emphasized that hunting is not to be considered a competitive sport. The "Suggestions" were given to him by Harry T. Peters and Harvey D. Gibson, Joint Masters of the Meadow Brook Hunt. I was surprised to read their comment about the "ever-present" complainers: "When anyone feels like complaining, he might well first ask himself what he has done to help, and how much he gives in time, and real interest, quite apart from his financial subscription, to promote the sport."

To remember when hunting the fox that the sport is dependent on hounds alone. Therefore, everyone should be quiet, and do nothing to disturb hounds, if it can possibly be avoided.

To stay each in his proper place well away from hounds, and not crowd or be over anxious to go on.

To offer no assistance to or interference with the hunt staff; they know their job perfectly, and any help offered is more than likely to be a hindrance.

To give the Huntsman room at all times to hunt his hounds; he should always be considered right in the hunting field, and his judgement accepted as is the judgement of the captain of a ship at sea.

To keep well away from a member of the staff who is listening to find hounds, so that nothing will interfere with his hearing.

If a member of the field inadvertently finds himself ahead of hounds, or to one side, with hounds running toward him, he should stop his horse and keep perfectly still until hounds and staff have passed.

In jumping, the rider in front should be given plenty of time to get well over. Also, a rider about to jump should not be cut off. In case of a refusal, place should be yielded to those coming on before another attempt is made.

Children should not ride up with the leaders of the field. This is particularly important when it is necessary for grooms to ride with them. Parents should accept the responsibility for observance of this rule.

Grooms who have been given permission to hunt must be instructed by their employer to keep to the rear of the field.

Anyone who is not a regular subscriber should present himself to the Master at the meet. A subscriber who is accompanied by a guest must present his guest in the same way.

In 1998 I had the pleasure of visiting Charlie and Janet Whitehouse in Marshall, Virginia. Janet (Ketchum) is a very dear old friend from Pittsburgh. She is nice, beautiful, and intellectually brilliant—and we laughed about the time she thought she was stuck in a stall, but kept on pulling the sliding door the wrong way! Charlie (who died in 2001) and Janet were a very attractive couple, and they worked hard to preserve their community. At that time the Honorable Charles S. Whitehouse and James L. Young were Joint Masters of the Orange County Hunt in Middleburg, Virginia, which has an excellent reputation. While visiting the Whitehouses, Janet and I went to the meet, giving me a chance to say hello to Mark Stickley, former huntsman at Rolling Rock Hunt. Charlie praised Mark for his horsemanship and subtle handling of the handsome, beautifully marked pack of hounds. It was such a pleasure to see the well turned-out field and admire the gorgeous hunting country. An avid foxhunter, Charlie's eyes sparkled when he said, "It gets in your blood." I asked him if he would write about his feelings about foxhunting and the following comments were his response.

The Magic of Hunting

> Reflecting on the aspects of foxhunting, which make it such an intriguing sport, I conclude that the diversity of almost any day of hunting is what gives me the greatest pleasure.
>
> I enjoy the tranquility of riding to a meet down a wintery Virginia lane. There is the anticipation of the unknown excitement that lies ahead, and the sense of well-being which comes from riding a fit, well-groomed horse, and of being appropriately dressed.
>
> I enjoy the conviviality of a meet. It is fun to joke and laugh with friends and neighbors and, as MFH, to discuss plans for the day with the huntsman.
>
> I enjoy watching and listening to a pack of hounds drawing through our beautiful countryside. I like the purposeful way in which hounds traverse our woods and fields. There is a special magic to their growing cry as the whole pack closes on the hounds that spoke first, and in the bursts of sound continuing from the pack as it works out the line.
>
> Like everyone else in the Field, I enjoy the excitement of a run—the cry of hounds—the encouraging calls of the huntsman—the thrill

of galloping on twisting trails and across the fields. This thrill is heightened by the horrid sense that there are groundhog holes everywhere, and that tussock in front of you may well be concealing one! The thrill is enhanced even more by the fact that everyone is braver when hounds are running, and jumps which loomed so menacingly in the past suddenly become just part of the landscape and obstacles to be met boldly.

It is, of course, particularly enjoyable to participate in a memorable run, and foxes are so plentiful in Virginia that blank days almost never occur. But many runs, perhaps most, are over in about fifteen minutes when the fox goes safely to ground. I recall with special delight, however, a number of runs of an hour or more; runs in which the staff and a very small field galloped on and on through woods and fields, returning to our trailers and vans only after a long, cold walk in the gathering darkness of a winter afternoon.

A part of the magic of hunting is that one does not know when one sets off—so bright and shiny—whether one is going to have a pleasurable day, or whether one is about to be part of a thrilling adventure, the memory of which will stay with you forever.

—Charles S. Whitehouse
(1921–2001)

Raingear

Part II

Foxhunts in Western Pennsylvania

ST

Preface

I have included the 12 recognized foxhunts in Western Pennsylvania, recording their history up to the year 2000. With the exception of Chestnut Ridge and Rolling Rock, all of the hunts were primarily drag hunts. As I have previously stated, Sewickley and Rolling Rock are the only hunts that remain active. Other than records obtained from the MFHA files, most of the documented material has vanished. I have gathered as much information as I could find, and I am indebted to many people who have supplied me with enlightening details.

G. Gilbert (Mark) Thompson was extremely helpful in supplying me with material about the Chestnut Ridge Hunt. Without Mark's help I don't think I would have ever gotten started on the long search for the elusive material. Stite and Janie Vipond lent me photographs and printed material about the Frankstown Hunt. J. C. Dovey also lent memorabilia from this hunt, collected by his mother, Jean Dovey. George Weidlein, the son of Libby McNary Weidlein and the grandson of George McNary, gave me invaluable information on the Westmoreland Hunt. George did a marvelous job of writing about the Westmoreland Pony Club. Kathy Watson, the daughter of Bobbie Watson O'Dell, lent me the priceless collection of her grandmother, Mrs. A. C. Martin. Bobbie O'Dell also sent me the fascinating handwritten diary of Torrence Miller, MFH of Westmoreland. Ruth Robinson Warner, the daughter of Lucius W. Robinson, wrote about her early recollections of the Indiana Hunt. Nancy Campbell Fales gave me some invaluable photographs of Jane Flaccus and Johnny Beach. Peggy Skinner helped with the Harts Run Hunt. The list of helpers from Sewickley is extensive—Bill Boyd, Joe and Helen Roberts, the entire Semple family, Dick Smith and Alie Painter Thompson. All of these people were (and some still are), involved with the various hunts and I appreciate their contributions.

Another invaluable source of information has been *Baily's Hunting Directory*, published by Vinton and Company, LTD: Chancery Lane, London E.C.4 (now published by Pearson Publishing, Ltd., Chesterton Mill, French's Road, Cambridge CB4 3NP). Wherever I have made use of information gleaned from these texts, I have noted the year of publication so that those who are interested can pursue further investigation.

Some of these chapters are more detailed than others. Despite my lack of personal knowledge about each hunt, I am sure that the members enjoyed every minute of their hunt's existence. I wish I could adequately describe the camaraderie and excitement they must have shared. I have included as many names as possible to allow the reader to refresh his memory, even if the references are to the names of forbears or friends. Due to the lack of hunt rosters, I have added some other horse-related lists at the end of some hunt chapters.

There is a similarity to all registered hunts. The necessary attributes for success are available capital, good leaders, enthusiastic members, and suitable country. The most important roles are the Master and the Huntsman, who maintain the spirit of the hunt and provide good sport for the members. The Secretary and the Treasurer also play key roles in keeping the system running smoothly.

Each of the hunts will have its own chapter, which will clarify the basic evolution of the Pittsburgh Hunt, which can be a bit confusing. The Harkaway Hunt did spin off in 1903 from the Pittsburgh Hunt Club under the leadership of Frank Lowrie, but lasted for only six years. The Pittsburgh Hunt (dropping the name Club) was not recognized by the MFHA until it moved to Fox Chapel in 1927. Later the Fox Chapel Hunt and the Harts Run Hunt evolved from the Pittsburgh Hunt due to changes in leadership. When the Hart's Run Hunt disbanded, E. P. Moriarty started his own private pack, calling it the Saxonburg Hunt.

It is not advantageous to guess why there were so many changes in these hunts. The changes in most hunts are generally for any of the following reasons: lack of financial support, a play for power amongst the members, loss of open country due to highways or development, or the loss of leaders. Any of these situations can cause a hunt to become inactive.

Anytime that you have a group of intelligent people making decisions, there is room for dissention. This is particularly true of foxhunters, who are often strong-minded, assertive types. While they are likeable people and they share a common interest, foxhunters like to express their opinions. Many of them are successful in their own lives and are accustomed to assuming leadership. This trait can be exasperating to Masters, and I appreciated Buss Moriarty's solution with his Saxonburg Hunt—a private pack. It does make a difference if one person is footing the bills, giving him the right to make the final decision.

I have purposely avoided any controversies. I have my opinion of what may have transpired in many cases, but the important thing is that the hunt continued and that it provided a great deal of pleasure to many people. I find it almost impossible to recapture the unique flavor of each hunt. How can one adequately describe "Having a good time?" I do not know of anyone who has been a member of a hunt who did not thoroughly enjoy the experience. It is a very special sport.

To the meet

Pittsburgh Hunt

Est. 1926

1927–1932

Uniform: Hunting. Evening dress: Scarlet, green collar.
Foxhounds: 25 couples English.
The country hunted is rolling to hilly, mostly uncultivated. Jumps: post and rails with some worm fences (Baily's Hunting Directory, 1927).

The above data applies to the Pittsburgh Hunt when it attained recognition in 1927. The official location was Otasaga Farm on Mauer's Lane (Hunt Road) in Fox Chapel Borough. The farm was owned by H. G. Lytle and later purchased by my family and Uncle Grant Curry. J. Crossan Hays called their place Twin Oaks and the address became Hunt Road.

It may be of interest for the reader to understand a bit of Pittsburgh's early history. Its location at the confluence of the Allegheny, Monongahela and Ohio rivers made it the key to the west from the times of the early settlers. This favorable location provided river transportation that also contributed to its later growth in commerce and industry. After Fort Duquesne was taken from the French, it was renamed in 1758 by General John Forbes in honor of William Pitt, the Elder. The area was primarily settled by people from England, Scotland, Ireland, and Germany. To encourage the settlement of the land west of the Allegheny Mountains, the Virginia Commissioners authorized land grants of four hundred acres to settlers who would build a cabin and grow some corn. If they could survive the rigors of the unsettled times, they were entitled to an additional thousand acres of adjoining land if it was vacant. Pittsburgh officially became part of the Commonwealth of Pennsylvania in 1784 when the Mason-Dixon Line established the boundaries between Virginia, Maryland and Pennsylvania.

One of the earliest recorded foxhunters in Pittsburgh was Dr. Nathaniel Bedford living "in the style of an English nobleman, at the northwest corner of Seventh and Liberty Avenues" where he maintained a stable of hunters and a pack of hounds. He married Jane Ormsby, the daughter of John Ormsby, a leading Pittsburgh merchant. Besides being a practicing physician, Dr. Bedford was civic-minded. He laid out the town of Birmingham, now the Southside of Pittsburgh and he was one of the original incorporators of the Pittsburgh Academy, founded in 1787. It was the beginning of the University of Pittsburgh (1806). It is interesting how early the people felt the need in their lives to establish churches, seats of learning, and the pleasures of racing, hunting, and other gaming pursuits.

It is uncertain whether the Pittsburgh Jockey Club was established in 1788 or 1801, but the seventh issue of *The Pittsburgh Gazette* published a notice of The Jockey Club's horse races to be held on October 19, 1786. Pittsburgh's first official race course was located on the "plain or common" between Grant's Hill and the Allegheny River.

An account of the meet written by an observer beautifully captures the bedlam:

> Every business or pursuit was neglected during their continuance. The whole town was daily poured forth to witness the Olympian games, many of all ages and sexes as spectators, and many more, directly or indirectly, interested in a hundred different ways. The plain within the course, and near it, was filled with booths as at a fair—where everything said, and done, and sold, and eaten or drunk—where every fifteen or twenty minutes there was a rush to some part to witness a fisticuffs—where dogs barked and bit, and horses trod on men's toes, and booths fell down on people's heads!

> All at once the cry, to horse! To horse! suspended every other business or amusement as effectually as the summons of the faithful. There was a rush toward the starting post . . . on a scaffold, elevated above the head's of the people, were the judges of the race, and—but I am not about to describe the races: my object was merely to call to mind the spot where they executed.

Prior to the invention of the car, horses and carriages were the mode of transportation and it was very natural for men to take a great deal of pleasure and interest in horses. It is understandable why harness racing was such a popular sport in the early days, since everyone who could afford it owned a horse and buggy and was proud of them. The Homewood racing track held various races in 1883 and became the Pittsburgh Driving Park, underwritten by Captain S. S. Brown. In 1885, the Gentleman's Driving Park was built near the Manchester Bridge. It was very popular with many businessmen who would allow enough time to stop there for an exhilarating spin around the oval. What fun they must have had! The Schenley Oval was built in the 1800s and the Brunot's Island track became famous for having some of the best trotters and pacers in America raced by amateur drivers. Harry Darlington, a Pittsburgher, became Vice-President of the National League of Amateur Driving Clubs. Some of the other enthusiastic men mentioned as good drivers were J. D. Callary, J. G. Bennett, Captain Harry S. Denny, H. N. Van Voorhis (later a member and leader of the Pittsburgh Hunt and the Sewickley Hunt), H. Oliver, W. J. Chapman, R. H. Boggs, and G. T. Braden.

The riders of Pittsburgh formed the Pittsburgh Riding Club in 1895, which later became the Pittsburgh Hunt Club in 1898. The fashionable Schenley Riding Academy was established in the 1890s, located where the University of Pittsburgh now stands. A capable horseman named Mr. Howe conducted classes and people enjoyed the organized riding that could continue the year around due to the indoor ring. The Riding Club, headquartered at the Academy, even imported European masters to teach them the fine art of riding. Attractive trails were accessible in Schenley Park. Charlie

Arensberg (later a member of the Harts Run Hunt) remembered riding with his father from the McClean stable located behind Forbes Field.

The Riding Club was exposed to its first foxhunt when Joseph Holloway brought his hounds to Sewickley, twelve miles west of the city along the Ohio River. It was a huge success. Some 200 people joined the hunt and it was recorded in the *Pittsburg Leader* of October 12, 1897.

Thrilled with their new riding activity, they established themselves as the Pittsburgh Hunt Club in Sewickley in 1898 with Frank M. Lowry as the MFH. By 1900 they moved their operation to the Pittsburgh Country Club on Beechwood Boulevard. The area was quite undeveloped at that time and they amused themselves with hunting, paper chases, music rides, and horse shows. They even scheduled some meets at Kennywood Park. As mentioned in the previous chapter, Frank M. Lowry took a group of members with him to start the Harkaway Hunt in 1903. This did not deter the remaining riders and in 1906 there was a fantastic four-day horse show held at the Duquesne Gardens. It was a great success attended by prominent citizens and exhibitors from near and far.

As the city began to develop, it was time to move to Fox Chapel and the club established itself as the Pittsburgh Hunt at Otasaga Farm. William J. Almy, Jr. was the Huntsman and MFH. In 1928 he was succeeded by George Paull, an excellent horseman. He had come to Pittsburgh through his association in the coal business and was an attractive, well-liked man.

My good friend Bill Bickel was the only person I knew who remembered riding in the Pittsburgh Hunt. He wrote to me of his memories of the Pittsburgh Hunt in the 1920s. His family had purchased 72 acres on Squaw Run Road (East). At that time they summered in "the country" (before it became known as Fox Chapel). Every summer a horse was rented for Bill from McClean's Stable near Schenley Park in Pittsburgh, and he rode all over the countryside. Bill remembers:

> This was the Pittsburgh Hunt country—an open agricultural country then. Where today the hillsides are covered with trees and dotted with houses, then it was mostly open fields with grazing cattle. Old man Ri-

ley next to us pastured about 35 head of crossbred dairy cattle. The McRoberts brothers had the same, plus a goodly number of pigs and chickens. They all still farmed with horses, and their crops were mostly wheat, corn and hay.

In 1929 my parents built a year-round place, "Glen Laurel," and bought two horses and a pony. I got around entirely on horseback, and that fall I became part of the Pittsburgh Hunt. My parents got me a Junior Membership. In the excitement of my first hunt, because of my ignorance of the rules, I had to be reminded to stay in the back of the MFH. The bug really bit me about that time, and my parents bought me a three-quarter-bred hunter-jumper, a chestnut mare named *Taxaway*.

In that open country the roads were of slag, unpaved, and one could canter right down the center of the road. The fields were nearly all bordered by barbed wire fencing, and the Pittsburgh Hunt "paneled" the countryside. They removed three or four panels of wire and installed post and rail panels, or most commonly used a "chicken-coop" overlay. We also had a few "Aiken" brush-and pole jumps, one of them being at least four-plus feet high and a good challenge. My *Taxaway* never refused a jump on me.

The Pittsburgh Hunt headquarters was on the old Lytle-Hays place on Old Hunt Road. Here we kenneled the hounds, and we also kept a nice, smiling red fox in a large run. His bed was a pile of burlap sacks. Before each hunt the huntsman would reach in and get a "beautifully" aromatic burlap sack, tie a line around it, and tie the other end of the line to his saddle. He would take off across the field and thus lay the "drag" for the hounds to follow, but every so often he would pick the drag up, which would allow for a check, or breather.

Only once in my memory did we run a real fox to ground. It was out by a deserted barn, upstream from the millpond. I didn't get the brush, but I was awarded one of the paws.

Later on the hunt headquarters moved to McCahill's place above the polo field on Squaw Run Road.

Some of the people I remember in the hunts were Colonel Cherrington, MFH, Mr. and Mrs. John Lawrence, Mr. and Mrs. Rex Flinn, the Ralph Lynch family, the McCague family, Homer St. Gaudens,

E. C. Bothwell, Jules Sunstein, Molly Hays, Dave McCahill, his father and two sisters, and Charles, Bliss, and Jane Flaccus.

On one hunt Miney McCague was knocked off her horse and injured when she struck a guy-wire that she did not see. My mare galloped right over her so deftly that Miney was not even touched—but the event was scary.

I would hack *Taxaway* to wherever the hunt was that week, and I also hacked her over to Kelly's Blacksmith Shop on Dorseyville Road at the head of Hart's Run Road. That was a magic place, and the one place where it was thoroughly enjoyable to wait one's turn. Off-season I would ride around the entire countryside—out as far as Hartwood. Jane Flaccus was a pretty girl, and I would occasionally ride with her, meeting at some agreed-upon spot. Her parents always sent a groom along—I guess to make sure their little girl was properly chaperoned. The groom's name was Fletcher, and the trouble with Fletcher was that he was always there.

Another trouble that befell me was that the football season and the hunt season were one and the same. As I got into my senior years at school, football became all-important. I played on a championship team—but that was the end of my hunting career.

However, I still stand tall in the saddle, and as every horse-person knows, "The world looks different from the back of a horse."

Respectfully submitted,

Bill Bickel (1918–2002)
January 28, 2000

Although I was only four or five years old, I vividly remember the Pittsburgh Hunt Club with its barn and kennels, which offered intriguing summer investigation for the Hays children. During one summer I lost the tip of a finger while I was feeding a horse who was stabled in an aisle standing stall. I obviously offered a tidbit without carefully extending my fingers properly. It was my fault, and it did not daunt my enthusiasm for horses. In the Fox Chapel chapter there is a complete description of these wonderful buildings that became part of our family home.

The Pittsburgh Hunt
MFHA Data

1927 Master and Huntsman: William Almy, Jr. Hon. Sec.: Lawrence Grinnell, Esq. Whippers-in: M. Pettey and F. Carrier.
1928 Master: George Paull. Hon. Sec.: Herbert G. Lytle. Huntsman: Ben K. Carr. Whippers-in: Herbert G. Lytle, Edward K. Davidson and Bliss Flaccus.
1929 Hon. Sec.: J. Raymond Price. Huntsman: B.C. Cence. Whippers-in: Edward K. Davidson and Bliss Flaccus.
1932 Joint Masters: George H. Cherrington and G. Bliss Flaccus. Hon. Sec.: G. Bliss Flaccus. Huntsman: G. Bliss Flaccus. Whippers-in: Edward K. Davidson, Charles L. Flaccus, Jr. and Charles L. Flaccus.
1933 Name changed to Fox Chapel Hunt.

Pittsburgh Hunt Horse Show

Reported in *The Fox Chapel Country* periodical: Vol. 1, December 1929, Number 2, is a list I found interesting, since there is no membership list available for the Pittsburgh Hunt. Some of the people listed on the committee were not riders but were willing to assist in the community venture. The ring committee also demonstrates how other hunt members willingly interacted. This quality was particularly true of the times. You will find many of these horsemen playing key roles in the other contemporary hunts in western Pennsylvania.

Committee Members

Bothwell, M/M E. C.
Cherrington, George H.
Diebold, A. J.
Flaccus, M/M Charles L.
Flinn, Mrs. Ralph E.
Gray, George P.
Hamilton, Wm. Barry
Heinz, Howard
King, Mrs. Gordon C.
Leslie, Dr. E. C.

Lynch, Dr./M Ralph
Lytle, Mrs. L. C.
McCague, Dr./M. E. J.
McCahill, David I.—Chairman
McCook, M/M George L.
Mellon, Richard King
Moreland, Thomas B.
Page, F. LeMoyne
Patterson, Mrs. Simon T.
Paull, George
Price, M/M J. Raymond
Steitz, J. G.

Ring Committee

Paull, George—Joint MFH of Pittsburgh Hunt—Chairman
Bughman, Jr., Henry Clay
Burgwin, John O.—Joint Master of Sewickley Hunt
Flaccus, Charles L.
Jack, William J.—MFH of Indiana Hunt
Lynch, Dr. Ralph
McGiffin, Malcolm
May, Herbert A.
Mellon, Richard King—MFH of Rolling Rock Hunt
Miller, Torrence—MFH of Westmoreland Hunt

Exhibitors not previously mentioned

Beach, John W.
Flaccus, Bliss
Flaccus, C. L., Jr.
Flaccus, Jane Louise
Kaufmann, M/M Oliver M.
Kelly, Woodruff T.
McCahill, Jr., David O.
McCahill, Marguerite
McCahill, Marie
Peebles, Lt. Harry B.
Phillips, Winnie A.
Rodgers, Mrs. D.
Walter, Howard K.

Harkaway Hunt

1903–1911

Masters: Frank M. Lowry, 1898–1911. Formally the Pittsburgh Hunt, and relocated in McDonald, Pennsylvania. Established 1898 as the Pittsburgh Hunt with kennels at Sewickley. Moved to the Pittsburgh Country Club in 1900. Moved to McDonald and reorganized as Harkaway in 1903. Recognized by the NSHA 1903. Not recorded by MFHA but registered hounds in volume 2 of the MFHA studbook. Given up about 1911.

Sources NSHA: 1903 (Pittsburgh), 1905–1911. Higginson 1908.

The above data is all that I could find in the MFHA records. I would not be able to contribute any further information without the following found in J. Blan Van Urk's *The Story of Rolling Rock*. Frank M. Lowry was the MFA of the Pittsburgh Hunt Club in 1898 when it was established in Sewickley. He must have been a good horseman and a well respected man amongst the influential riders in the Pittsburgh area. The book has a picture of Frank M. Lowry captioned with, "Pittsburgh Hunt Club, 1898–1903; Harkaway Hunt, 1903–1909."

The officers of the Pittsburgh Hunt Club were Robert D. McGonnigle, President; E. Roger Kemp, Secretary and Treasurer; and Frank M. Lowry,

MFH. The Board of Directors included, besides these men, James R. Tindle and Reed Knox.

They certainly were leaders of an enterprising group and the November 17, 1900 issue of *Rider and Driver* reported on a unique hunting tour under the title of "A Fox Hunting Festival." The Club hired two steamboats to take them up to Carmichael's, Greene County on the Monongahela River. One boat carried the large group of members and the other accommodated the horses, grooms, hounds, and provisions for their two-week holiday of hunting. In addition to the above mentioned officers were H. N. Van Voorhis, Edward Groetzinger, Jr., Herman Straub, A. M. Jenkinson, J. Seam Atterbury, W. H. Wasson, Daniel O'Day, Sam Pickering, J. P. Murphy, W. L. Elkins, E. R. Braden, J. B. Chapman, John Chapman, J. A. Davidson, D. L. Gillespie and Dr. Bean.

They had exclusively engaged the Flanagan Inn for their stay and even took along a well-known group of vocalists for social entertainment. Obviously, they knew how to do things well and their sojourn was a huge success. They planned to hunt daily and one particular day took them across the border into West Virginia. Only a few followers had the stamina to stay with Lowry and the hounds on that memorable hunt.

It appears that the location of the Pittsburgh Hunt Club at the Pittsburgh Country Club in Schenley Park was inadequate for this energetic group. Frank Lowry took his group of followers to McDonald, Pa. in Washington County about twenty miles southwest of Pittsburgh. They established the Harkaway Hunt with Frank Lowry as MFH. The Hunt officers were Walter Lyons, President; Addison M. Irwin, Secretary and Edward McDonald, Treasurer.

The open, rolling country was panelled with post and rail and snake fences. Jack Caffrey was Huntsman, and Arthur Cregan, the professional Whipper-in. The Hunt's Honorary Secretary was F. H. Richard. The surrounding farmland was excellent except for the occasional hazards of oil companies digging wells. There were barely visible telephone wires, which were just about the height of a horseman's neck, and also abandoned coal mines where a fox easily took refuge. Despite these encumbrances the hunting was considered excellent.

Jack Caffrey, the huntsman, was also very talented in teaching young people about horsemanship and hunting. Among the young ladies who were his proteges were Winifred and Rebecca Jones and Mary Flinn (later Mrs. John W. Lawrence). Edith Flinn (Mrs. Simon T. Patterson) also hunted a bit.

George Wiedlein remembers that his grandfather George McNary started hunting with the Harkaway Hunt, as did several other members of the future Westmoreland Hunt.

Unfortunately, the Harkaway Hunt disbanded in 1911 when Frank M. Lowry moved to Buffalo.

Who spoke?

Well done

Fox Chapel Hunt

Est. 1926

1932–1940

Uniform: Scarlet, canary yellow collar. Evening: Scarlet, canary yellow collar and facings.
Foxhounds: 21 couples; 11 American, 10 English.
The width of the country East to West is approximately 10 miles. The length North to South is approximately 12 miles; rolling and hilly, mostly uncultivated; post and rail, board fences, chicken coops, with some worm fences (Baily's Hunting Directory, *1933*).
Formerly Pittsburgh Hunt. Name changed in 1932. Established 1926. Moved to Allison Park about 1933. Country recorded by MFHA January 1927. Recognized by NSHA 1928. Disbanded 1940. Part of country subsequently hunted by Harts Run Hunt. Sources: 1928–1932 (Pittsburgh) and 1933, MFHA: 1927–1932 (Pittsburgh) and 1933–1939. Span: 1926–1940.

Although the Fox Chapel Hunt was a continuance of the Pittsburgh Hunt, it had to re-register its officials and country with the MFHA. The members had voted to change the name of their hunt to one more appropriate to the community. As Master of the Pittsburgh Hunt, George H. Cherrington followed the necessary paper procedures, and registration was granted in 1932 to the Fox Chapel Hunt.

Something happened and for reasons unknown, the hunt was asked to leave the McCahills. At this time George Cherrington also resigned his mastership to John W. Lawrence to insure the future of the Fox Chapel Hunt. G. Bliss Flaccus and John W. Lawrence became Joint Masters and the Fox Chapel Hunt was relocated to the Charles L. Flaccus estate on Kittanning Road (now Dorseyville Road).

Many of the former members of the Pittsburgh Hunt continued to hunt with Fox Chapel and a large number of junior members joined as well. Ben and Helen Carr were responsible for the added interest among the young riders. They were excellent teachers and promoted cross-country riding with their students. The Carr Stable was located on Middle Road (now the site of the Winchester Thurston School) and the Carrs had previously received written permission from the Pittsburgh Hunt to use part of their territory to conduct paper chases and junior hunts. The Carrs developed paths and jumps with some financial support from the hunt since it would be beneficial to both parties. The Carrs named their children's hunt the Harts Run Junior Hunt.

I had forgotten about the existence of this "hunt" until I talked to Tommy Hilliard one morning at breakfast, in 1998, while we were staying with Audrey and Tommy. Perhaps this was due to the fact that I was too young to hunt at that time. With a little research it was verified that Thomas J. Hilliard, Jr. was indeed Master of the Harts Run Junior Hunt in 1932. Tommy had told me:

> I rode my 14.2 white pony *Lila*, a gift from my Aunt Lila Thayer. She would jump anything in the hunting field but not in the ring. Jack Potter was our huntsman and competently displayed his ability when we were invited to hunt at Rolling Rock. The junior hunts were on Saturdays and I remember Homer Saint Gaudens and John W. Lawrence often participating. The juniors were Joe and Steele Roberts, Helen Shaw, Nancy and Isabel Patterson, Mary Stevenson, Rita and Betty Laughlin, Mary Louise Flinn, Peggy Gould, Kassie Nimick, Molly Hays, Miney McCague, Ann Teal, Anne Berger, Phyllis Kiester, Virginia Robinson, Louise McKinney, Janet Oliver, and Jane Flaccus.

I would like to say that both George Cherrington and Homer Saint Gaudens were fine men who contributed more than their share to the evolution of the Pittsburgh Hunt. Colonel Cherrington had been a Master and Mr. Saint Gaudens served as Honorary Secretary on several occasions. Devoted to the sport, these men had enthusiasm and gentle ways that made hunting appealing to both young and old. I was a bit younger so I did not really hunt until later, when I joined the Harts Run Hunt, but I do have fond memories of these two gentlemen. I certainly remember all of the juniors that Tommy Hilliard mentioned and as the years have dissolved the age differences, they are now my contemporaries.

Mary Louise Stevenson (Hackett) also writes about those memorable days of the Fox Chapel Hunt. "The Lawrence's Hartwood Acres gave us a pristine challenge to hunt in their gorgeous woods and the many untouched fields. There were stunning hunt teas and breakfasts. The members agreed that those hunting days were the most tolerant, healthy, worthwhile times that any teenager could spend."

John W. Lawrence, an insurance broker, was married to Mary Flinn and was MFH of the Fox Chapel Hunt in 1934. They had two boys, Johnny and Billy. Mary's sister was Edith Flinn Patterson, who had three children: Nancy, Isabel, and Reese. Mrs. Patterson kept a lovely stable on her place on Middle Road, filled with show horses and hunters. The Family House Polo Matches are presently held on this property. The Rex Flinns were good friends of my family and we *loved* going to their house in Fox Chapel to swim. Mary and Edith's brother was A. Rex Flinn, who had a charming wife called Dolly. Mrs. Flinn was warm and friendly with people of all ages. The Flinns had Bill and Mary Louise (Weasel) who were contemporaries of my sister Molly.

Ralph Flinn was the father of Rex Flinn, and the owner of the beautiful Beechwood Farms. I find it impressive that the highly respected Flinn Construction Company was responsible for making the famous Holland Tunnel that passes under the Hudson River, connecting the state of New Jersey with New York City. Not only were the Flinns successful in business, they were all ardent foxhunters, including their wives and children. The A. Rex Flinns were good friends of R. K. Mellon and were early members of the Rolling

Rock Hunt. In later years their daughter Mary Louise (Stringer, Knapp, Davidson) played a key role in the Rolling Rock Hunt.

By 1934 John W. Lawrence moved the hounds from the Flaccus estate to the Carr Stable on Middle Road. In 1935 Mrs. George M. Laughlin, mother of Betty (MacDougall, Douglas) and Rita (Blair), replaced Homer Saint Gaudens as Honorary Secretary. Disaster struck in 1936 when the Carr Stable burned to the ground and many horses were lost. My father took us to see the ghastly sight—a horrible memory that remains indelible in my mind. The hounds and the outer buildings survived and somehow the hunt managed to continue.

In the spring of 1940 the members held a meeting at the Pittsburgh Golf Club and the Fox Chapel Hunt was dissolved. I do not know the reason for this decision, but in accordance with a former agreement Mr. and Mrs. John W. Lawrence assumed the responsibility of covering any outstanding bills. Present at that meeting were Mr. and Mrs. John DeWees, Mrs. A. Rex Flinn, Homer Saint Gaudens, Mrs. George M. Laughlin, Mr. and Mrs. John W. Lawrence, Mrs. Ralph Lynch, Dr. E. P. Moriarity, and Mrs. Albert Wells.

As you will see the Harts Run Hunt was quickly formed and hunting continued in the fall of 1940.

Fox Chapel Hunt
MFHA Data

1926–1930 Master: George Paull.

1930–1931 Masters: George Paull and George H. Cherrington.

1931–1932 Master: George H. Cherrington.

1932–1933 Joint Masters: George H. Cherrington and G. Bliss Flaccus. Hon. Sec.: Homer Saint Gaudens. Huntsman: (prof.) John Potter. Whippers-in: (prof.) William Ridley.

1934 Master: John W. Lawrence. Hon. Sec.: Homer Saint Gaudens. Whippers-in: (prof.) William Ridley and John Ridley.

1935 Hon. Sec.: Mrs. George M. Laughlin III. Whippers-in: John Beach and Harold Ridley.

1940 Disbanded

Harts Run Hunt

Est. 1940

1946–1976

Uniform: Green, scarlet collar and waistcoat. Evening: Scarlet, green facings.
Foxhounds: 8 couples American.
Country: Approximately 10 by 25 miles, extending from the Fox Chapel district north to Bakerstown. Later extended north of the Bakerstown area toward Butler, Pennsylvania, east of Route 8. A rolling country, heavily wooded, but with a great deal of open country. Paneled with post and rail and chicken coops, board fences and Aikens (Baily's Hunting Directory, *1949*).

The Harts Run Hunt, formerly the Fox Chapel Hunt, continued to hunt the registered country and kept most of its members. The Fox Chapel Hunt disbanded in the spring of 1940 and the Harts Run Hunt continued to hunt that fall. Unfortunately Homer Saint Gaudens is not here to tell us what really transpired with the cessation of the Fox Chapel Hunt and the immediate organization of the Harts Run Hunt. As President of the new hunt, he started the necessary paperwork to gain new recognition. Through his superb effort the hunt became registered in 1941 and recognized in 1946. Homer Saint Gaudens was the Director of Fine Arts at the Carnegie Institute of Pittsburgh and was well versed in organizational skills.

The 1940 records for the Harts Run Hunt show Mary D. Hays MFH (my sister Molly); Hon. Whippers-in: Jane Flaccus and Helen Shaw; Huntsman: (prof.) John W. Beach. Officers: Homer Saint Gaudens, President; Blaine Fairless, Vice President; J. L. Roberts, Secretary; J. C. Dewees, Treasurer; Helen Shaw, Corresponding Secretary. Other members on the committee were Dr. Ralph Lynch, Dr. V. E. Beldham, A. Cass Sunstein, and Alice Walton.

I find it amusing to see Blaine Fairless as Vice President, and somewhere else T. Coleman Ward is mentioned as an officer. At that time Blaine was a beau of Jane Flaccus, and Coley was squiring my sister Molly. It is not uncommon for the opposite sex to participate in a sport to please their pursued quarry. Later on Blaine married lovely Caroline and they lived in Ligonier, where he was active in the Rolling Rock Hunt. Coley and his bride Bobbie also moved to Ligonier. Both of these families were in residence when Burt and I moved there in 1954.

Mr. George Walton, the father of Alice Walton (Mansmann), acting as an agent had rented to John W. Beach the rebuilt stables on Middle Road in Fox Chapel, where the previous stables of Ben Carr had burned. The Harts Run Hunt took over this lease and Johnny W. Beach was appointed Huntsman. This provided a perfect place for the hunt to have stables, kennels, and a clubhouse. Homer Saint Gaudens described Johnny Beach in a letter written in 1941:

> We have found ourselves most fortunate in our huntsman, John Beach. We have come to believe that he is half horse and half hound. Last winter, after the mud became too deep for drag hunting, some of us went with Beach on occasional foxhunts. To my surprise, on each occasion we viewed fox . . . we plan to hunt live fox on Thursdays.

In 1945, due to increasing development, the hunt moved its kennels to Boot Hill Farm in Gibsonia. Johnny Beach owned this farm, and it was during the late 1940s and early 1950s that I hunted with Harts Run. In 1951 I was delighted to be invited to be a whipper-in. There was a great group of people of various ages and interests. I became good friends with Bill and Jean Stirling, who later moved to Ligonier. During that time A. W. Kennedy was a Joint Master with Jane Flaccus. He was a handsome, tall man with a very soft way about him. I also remember the colorful Charley and Jimmy Arensberg brothers, who were amusing and filled with hunting enthusiasm. I hesitate to name more of the members because I surely will omit some names. Fortunately many of the people will be listed in the official data. We had a fine time hunting, and the Saturday teas were delightful as we crowded into the small clubhouse heated by a pot-bellied stove.

Most hunts have an annual horse show to help defray expenses. Having attended a very successful Horse Show and Lawn Fete in Philadelphia, I decided we could duplicate a similar scene at Harts Run by enlisting the charity of the Fox Chapel Day School. We had an impressive list on the committee, but the real worker was Charles F. Lloyd. Chuck and I worked hard at amalgamating all kinds of vendors, and it seemed like a great idea. But it rained, and frankly the day was pretty much of a flop. Chuck and I laugh about our venture now, and he claims that the hunt and the school did very well financially due to advertising and pre-sales.

My friends Joe and Helen Shaw Roberts were "long time riders" and we have enjoyed a lasting friendship. They appear in many places in this hunting record of western Pennsylvania. Besides holding other positions in the Harts Run Hunt, they were the Joint Masters in 1948. Before the war, Helen had worked at Friendship Hill with Evie Thompson, helping her run the farm, plus enjoying the hunting with Chestnut Ridge. Both of the Roberts are efficient, pleasant people willing to take on responsibility. They have helped me considerably by filling in many dates and events. The Roberts resigned from Harts Run when they moved to Sewickley in 1959. Their three girls Melinda, Jean and Christine were raised in the hunting tradition. Jean is now Huntsman for the New Market Middletown Hunt in Virginia, and as of the year 2000 Joe is still active in the Sewickley Hunt.

It is hard to imagine what would have happened to the Pittsburgh, Harts Run, and Fox Chapel hunts through the decades without the interest and support of the Charles L. Flaccus family. Mr. Flaccus had been instrumental in forming the Pittsburgh Hunt. Their children, Charlie, Bliss and Jane, at different periods were equally involved in their father's guiding interest.

While I did not know the boys well, I certainly knew and respected Jane. She was a beautiful girl with many admirers, but horses were her life. She was quite shy, but she had found a perfect foil in Johnny Beach. Together they accomplished miracles, to the constant enjoyment of everyone involved in horses and hunting. The hunting was primarily drag but given the opportunity the hounds would run a live fox. You could always count on an active day filled with fun, comradeship, and good humor. Jane could easily have retained the Mastership of the Harts Run Hunt, but she actually preferred whipping-in. With her strong support and interest, the hunt always had an easy, friendly atmosphere that encouraged people of all ages to participate.

When Jane Flaccus and Johnny Beach decided to spend more time with racehorses, George Bancroft became the MFH in 1959, and his daughter Kitty was the Huntsman. George and Barbara Bancroft were fine people, and they instilled in their children their dedication to the Harts Run Hunt. In 1960 the hounds were moved to their new kennel on the Bancroft farm. The kennel was built as a gift from Charles O. Rall from Greensburg. His daughter Vivian was involved in the hunt and enjoyed laying the drag. The whippers-in were juniors and they found time to work the hounds after school hours.

Because of the increased development in the Fox Chapel area, on Saturdays the hunt alternated between the local area and the northern country in Butler County. The members would van their horses to either the Moriarty's or the Pietz's places in the north country, and then hack to the meet. The Tuesday hunts were always held in the local area around Allison Park.

In 1975 George Bancroft had a heart attack, and his wife Barbara took over. When she suffered a paralyzing spill, the hunt was left without leadership, and it was disbanded. It was sad that no one was able to take over the responsibility, but Buss Moriarty started his own Saxonburg hunt in 1978, acquiring some of the Harts Run hounds.

In the 1950s I hunted with Rolling Rock so I rather lost touch with the activities at Harts Run. I am indebted to Peggy Skinner who has provided many of the details. Peggy was devoted to Harts Run and she duly praised the parents for all the work and support they gave to the hunt. Her letter to me ended with the heartfelt sentiment about the hunt becoming inactive, "It is the excitement of the hunt and the sharing of experiences that seems such a loss." Peggy was devoted to Harts Run, but she was able to continue hunting with Saxonburg.

Although there were many changes in leadership and names of the hunts, it is interesting to note that Pittsburgh area hunts continued over the period from 1927 to 1976.

Harts Run Hunt
MFHA Data

1940 Master: Miss Mary (Molly) Hays. Hon. Sec: J. L. Roberts. Huntsman: (prof) John W. Beach. Whippers-in: Hon. Miss Jane Flaccus and Miss Helen Shaw.

1943 Joint Masters: Mrs. S. W. Off (Molly Hays) and Miss Helen B. Shaw

1944 Master: Miss Helen B. Shaw. Hon. Sec: Miss Betty Michel. Whippers-in: Hon. Miss Jane Flaccus, Miss Alice Walton and Dr. V. E. Beldham.

1944 Pres: George Bancroft. Treas: Jules Polachek. Hon. Whippers-in: Miss Alice Walton and Dr. Ralph Lynch.

1947 Whippers-in: Miss Susan Bancroft and Miss Jane Carter.

1948 Masters: Mr. and Mrs. Joseph L. Roberts, Jr. Hon. Sec: William Stirling Jr. Huntsman: temporary (prof) John Romanofski. Whippers-in: Miss Alice Walton and Dr. V. E. Beldham.

1949 Masters: Miss Jane L. Flaccus and A. W. Kennedy. Hon. Sec: Mrs. William Stirling, Jr., Pres: Hugh L. Ruffner. Vice Pres: Verne Miller. Treas: Jules J. Polachek. Huntsman: (prof) John W. Beach. Whippers-in: Hon. Miss Susan Bancroft.

1951 Whippers-in: Hon. Miss Susan Bancroft and Miss Frances (Susie) Hays.

1952 Hon. Sec: Miss Alice Haas

1954 Masters: Miss Jane L. Flaccus and William Stirling, Jr. Whippers-in: Mrs. William Stirling, Jr. and (prof) Merle Brown.

1956 Hon. Sec: Miss Margaret Skinner.

1957 Field Master: William Stirling, Jr. Hon. Sec: Mrs. Robert Kiehl. Whippers-in: Mrs. William Stirling, Jr., Miss Barbara Kraeling and (prof) Merle Brown.

1958 Field Master: George Bancroft. Hon. Sec: Miss Alice Haas.

1959 Master: George Bancroft. Hon. Sec: Mrs. James Douthitt.

1960 Whippers-in: Miss Barbara Kraeling, William Hartle and (prof) Merle Brown.

1962 Hon. Sec: Mrs. Anthony Susan. Whippers-in: Miss Barbara Bancroft, Miss Karen Campbell, Mrs. John Voight and (prof) Merle Brown.

1963 Whippers-in: Miss Barbara Bancroft, Miss Katharine Bancroft, Mrs. John Voight and (prof) Merle Brown.

1966 Whippers-in: Miss Barbara Bancroft, Mrs. John R. Voight, F. Carl Anderson, G. Thomas Bancroft and (prof) Merle Brown.

1967 Whippers-in: F. Carl Anderson, Miss Susanne Bahnson, G. Thomas Bancroft and (prof) Merle Brown.

1968 Whippers-in: F. Carl Anderson, G. Thomas Bancroft, Miss Pata Wylie, Miss Lynne Tooke and (prof) Merle Brown.

1970 Hon. Sec: Mrs. Iris Susan. Hon. Huntsman: Katharine B. Bancroft.

1972 Hon. Sec: Lois Burtoff. Whippers-in: Miss Peggy Skinner and Robert Stiles.

1973 Masters: George Bancroft and W. Guy Pietz, V.M.D. Whippers-in: Miss Marjie Gregg, Miss Lisa Maguire and Miss Peggy Skinner.

1974 Hon. Sec: Mrs. James L. Ferson.

1975 Whippers-in: Miss Marjie Gregg and Miss Peggy Skinner.

1976 Inactive

Harts Run Hunt Members —from the memory of Peggy Skinner

Anderson, F. Carl
Arensberg, Charles
Armstrong, Betty
Bahnson, Dr. Henry
Bancroft, Katharine
Bancroft, M/M. George
Clokey, George
Flaccus, Jane
Fort, Ms. Judith
Haas, Alice
Haas, Mrs. Robert
Henderson, William
James, Ms. Mary
Kennedy, A. W.
Kiel, Ms. Harriet
Kraeling, Barbara
Kraeling, Sue
Lawrence, Mrs. J. W.
McKelvey, Nancy
Moore, Dick
Moriarity, E. P.
Patterson, Mrs. Simon T.

Pietz, Guy VMD
Pietz, Weesley
Roberts, M/M John
Spink, M/M Jack
Stirling, M/M. William
Susan, Ms. Iris
Wiley, M/M. J

Junior Members
—with accolades to the very supportive parents.

Armstrong, George
Armstrong, Jim
Bahnson, Barbie
Bahnson, Susie
Bancroft, Barbie
Bancroft, Tom
Campbell, Karen
Campbell, Melanie
Campbell, Nancy
Christner, Carol
Cosgrove, Sally
Daily, Brooke
Daily, Sue
Donaldson, Anne
Gregg, Marjorie
Gregg, Sarah
Grunagle, Susie
Hannon, Mike
Hannon, Patty
Hannon. Kerry
Henderson. Matt
Hensley, Joy
Kraeling, Barbara
Maguire, Lisa
Mansmann, Patty
Mansmann, Barbara
Mansmann, Richard
Mustard, Barbara
Pietz, Julie
Pietz, Rhoda
Pietz, Wess
Rall, Vivian
Rickey, Barbara
Rickey, Nancy
Robinson, Missy
Sherman, Cindy
Shurko, Greg
Shurko, John
Susen, Barbara
Tausky, Billy
Tausky, Peggy
Vechek, Donna
Wiley, Peata
Woods, Bill
Woods, Connie

Sewickley Hunt

Est. 1922

1924–Present

Uniform: Scarlet and pearl gray. Button: Gold, with monogram S.H.
Foxhounds: 25 couples of American foxhounds.
The country is approximately 12 miles by 15 miles, hilly and rolling country in the neighborhood of Sewickley, Pennsylvania. Post and rail and worm fences with panels in wire (Baily's Hunting Directory).

Sewickley is a very attractive town on the Ohio River approximately twelve miles southwest of Pittsburgh. The name is derived from the Indian word *Seweekly* meaning "sweet water," used to describe the local sap-producing maple trees. In 1783 Daniel Leet secured a large portion of the bottomland through Certificates of Depreciation awarded after the Revolutionary War. At that time he sold land for $2 an acre. The area grew steadily and by 1851 the village had the service of two trains a day, plus available boat service. The town and the Sewickley Heights attracted many people who wanted an alternative residence westward of the smoke-belching, steel-producing city of Pittsburgh.

In the late 19th century, Harvey N. Van Voorhis, an ardent horseman of the Sewickley community, decided to introduce hunting. He helped import the Joseph Holloway hounds from Chevy Chase, Maryland to hold a hunt in

1897. The hunt attracted the attention of *The Pittsburg Leader*, which reported that 200 people would follow the hunt by road. Fifty people enjoyed riding the eight-mile drag course over the McKean Shooting Club grounds. The thrill of hunting was established, and by 1899 members of The Pittsburgh Hunt Club held regular meets in the Sewickley Valley. By 1900 the Pittsburgh riders moved their club to the Pittsburgh Country Club.

The desire to hunt continued in Sewickley and in 1922 the sporting couple, Mr. and Mrs. J. O. Burgwin, had their own private pack, kenneling the hounds at their farm "The Paddock." In 1925 the Burgwins donated their hounds to the Sewickley Hunt Club and the hunt has continued to grow with a succession of highly dedicated people. The Sewickley Hunt is the 36th oldest hunt in the United States, and it is also the seventh oldest active recognized drag hunt.

It was not long after Sewickley attained its stature as "the place to live" that Fox Chapel began to develop. My family built a lovely house in Fox Chapel near the Allegheny River, but they had many dear friends living in Sewickley. At that time, since there was little traffic, it was only about a 30-minute drive across country to visit Sewickley. Even at an early age I was thoroughly impressed with Sewickley. The magnificent estates, the charming people, the Allegheny Country Club with its sporting life and its horse activities were extremely appealing. The Hays children made many friends there and participated in the sports and attended most of the fantastic parties.

The attractive, enterprising people of Sewickley knew how to do things well and their annual horse show at the Allegheny Country Club was sensational. It was not only a big social event, it attracted some of the finest horseflesh in the East. There were classes for breeding stock, gaited classes, hackney ponies, hunters, jumpers, ponies, juniors, family class, and the popular costume class. The family class at the Allegheny Horse Show was a pleasure to watch since the families of various sizes were always beautifully turned out. The costume class created a fantastic sight because the participants went to great lengths to complete the vivid picture of their theme. The winners could range from colorful medieval finery to pioneers in Conestoga wagons or any-

My father Crossan Hays, with a trio of his good friends, Annie, Spot and Trixie. Pittsburgh, 1904.

Bert Cence, Huntsman, with Pittsburgh Hunt hounds. George Paull MFH on the gray horse. Otasaga Farm driveway, Fox Chapel, 1929.

Publicity for Harts Run Junior Horse Show. Molly, Susie and Jack Hays. Twin Oaks Farm, Fox Chapel, 1938.

Susie overzealous, *Tish* unconcerned. Harts Run Junior Horse Show, 1938.

Milt Selznick showing off with nice *Nat Bragg*. Schenley Oval, Pittsburgh, 1939.

Hunt Team Class. Susie Hays on *Lawn Fete*, Betty Blackburn on *Charcoal*, Maddie Blackburn on *Meadow Lark*. Harts Run Junior Horse Show, 1941.

A typical switchback on the road into Bhutan. Susie on a trusty mule. Honeymoon, 1954.

Interior court of a dzong. Bhutan, 1954.

"Cleaning Her Pony," bronze by S. Todd, 1979.

"Hurry On," bronze by S. Todd, 1982.

"Red Hoss," bronze by S. Todd, 1981.

"Mousing," bronze by S. Todd, 1982.

Jane Flaccus MFH and great benefactor of the Harts Run Hunt. Fox Chapel, 1945.

Talented horsemen, Johnny Beach on *Duhallow Lass*. Westmoreland Hunt Horse Show. Bothwell Farm, Greensburg, 1936.

Peggy Skinner, a member of both the Harts Run and Saxonburg Hunts, 1980s.

Buss Moriarty and Barbara Mansmann, 1980s.

Parading the Saxonburg hounds at the Family House polo match, 1980s.

Indiana Hunt Team at the Rolling Rock Horse Show. From left to right: Blair " Red" Gibson, Whipper-In, on *Flint Rock*; Lucius W. Robinson Jr., Master, on *Last Penny*; and Alfred Fletcher, Huntsman, on *Reformed*, 1930s.

Valley View Farm barns and house on hill (built in 1922). Residence of Lucius W. Robinson Jr., 1930s.

What a memorable group of people! From left to right: Harry Black, Huntsman 1950–1972; Phyllis Semple (Mrs. Harton S.), MFH 1950–1954; Bud Richardson (Mr. Frank E. Jr.), acting MFH 1943–1944, MFH 1950–1988; Alie Thompson (Mrs. LeRoy) MFH 1955–1992; Tad Marshall (Mr. C. Taylor) MFH 1968–19947. Sewickley.

Sewickley Hunt, Joint Masters. From left to right: Cherry Semple White (Mrs. Raymond B.), MFH 1995–present, Huntsman 2001; Andy Komer (Mr. A. F.), MFH 1989–present; Ann Metcalf (Mrs. William A.) MFH 1991–present. 2001, by Richard V. Thompson.

The originators of the Sewickley Hunt, a true sporting couple. Adelaide Burgwin (Mrs. John O.), MFH 1924–1938 and John Burgwin, MFH 1924–1934. 1925, by Richard V. Thompson.

Happy riding sidesaddle, Eugenia Hill Binney (Mrs. George), grandmother of Ann Metcalf. Sewickley, 1930s.

The Frankstown Hunt with "Old Frank's" hunting horn adorning the wall behind them. Front row, from left to right: Fred Stormer, Dr. Pellman Gluver, Dan Lenehan. Back row, from left to right: Paul Vipond, Ben Levine, Charles Maloy, George P. Grable. 1940s.

A fun filled group. From left to right: Paul T. Winter, Benjamine Levine, Hans Kloepter, Charles E. Maloy, George Pomeroy, and George Gable. Missing from the photo is Carl Davies. 1939.

Beautiful country. Ned Malloy with the Frankstown hounds. In the background is Plank Road, near the old cavalry stable. 1930s.

Well turned out. John and Jeanne Dovey with Jeanne's father, William Burd. Frankstown, 1930s.

Illustrious MFH's celebrating the 50th anniversary of the Westmoreland Hunt. From right to left: Abbie Hunt, Bobby Watson, Alice Mansmann, Dr. Ralph Lynch, Frank Richardson, Evie Martin, George Bancroft. Greensburg Polo Club, 1975.

Libby McNary Weidlein , a mainstay of the Westmoreland Hunt, showing at Sewickley. 1942.

Bobbie Watson, MFH, displaying a splendid smooth ride at the Westmoreland Hunt show. 1950.

Preparing to unload the Chestnut Ridge hounds at Red Barn. Chestnut Ridge can be seen in the background. 1960s.

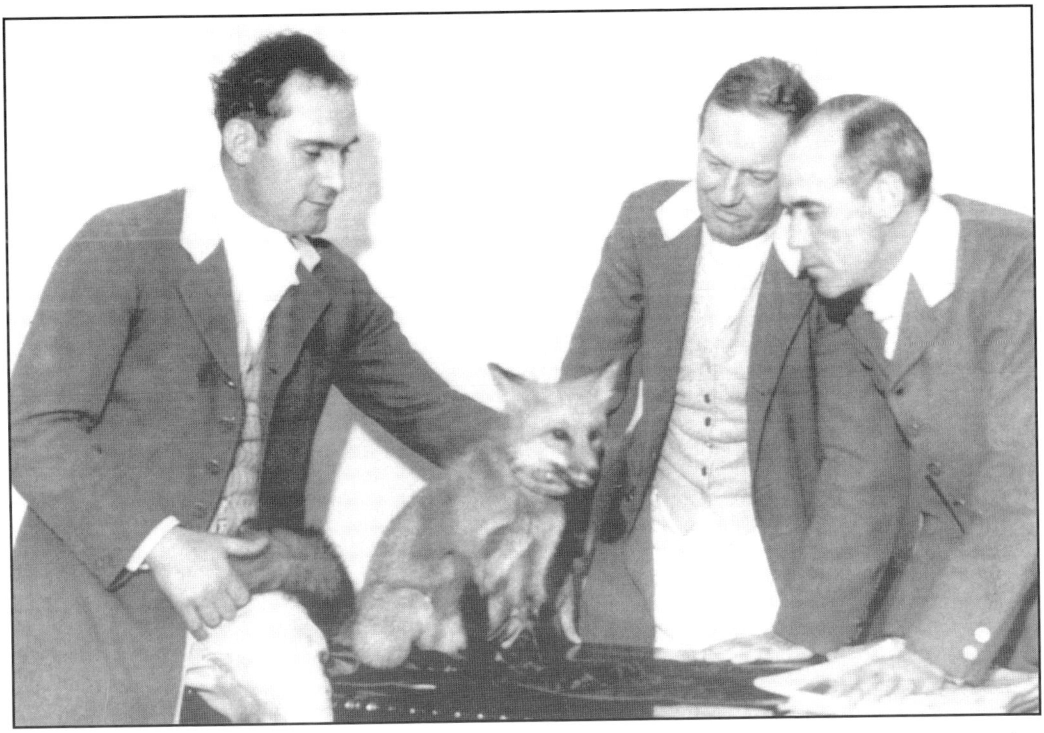

Bert Cence, Huntsman; Andrew Thompson, Jt. MFH; J. Lester Hawkins, Jt. MFH. Chestnut Ridge Hunt Club, 1932.

Blessing the hounds at Friendship Hill. From left to right: John Slaughter; G. Markel Thompson, Jt. MFH; Linda Crow; Bill Hanley; Alfred Hunt; Mrs. Sherwood Martin, Jt. MFH; Linda Jenkins. New Geneva, PA, 1953.

A handsome couple, Mr. and Mrs. Richard King Mellon. Rolling Rock, late 1930s.

Katy Jones (standing) and Laura Jennings (center), car followers at Rolling Rock.

A fabulous hunting trip to Belvoir Vale and Quorn. From left to right: George Laughlin, Harry Bovard, R. K. Mellon, Sarah Scaife, Rex Flinn and Alan Scaife. Not pictured are Dolly Flinn and Paul Mellon. 1930s.

A. Rex Flinn and Dolly Flinn at Rolling Rock. 1930s.

The Rolling Rock Polo Association Committee. From left to right: Charles M. DuPuy Jr., Leonard W. Bughman, Gordon Thompson, Richard K. Mellon and John R. Bigelow. Not pictured are George R. McNary and Blaine T. Fairless. 1941.

The Ligonier Valley Polo Association Team. From left to right: Mark Thompson, Bill Hanley, Jack Kenney and Roy Bates. 1941.

Fox Chapel members at the Rolling Rock Hunter Trials. From left to right: Maggie Hillman, Freddi Berger, Weasel Flinn, Mary Louise Stevenson, Betty Laughlin, Isabel Patterson and Peggy Gould. 1936.

Pony Clubbers and Future members of the Rolling Rock hunt. From left to right: Marjorie Bale, Shirley Wallace, Elise Clement, Barbara O'Neil, Gilpin Oliver, Lorraine MacDougal, Toni Freeland and Polly McKenna. Not pictured are Timmy Borntraeger and Laney Rogers. 1958.

Three fine winners of the Hunt Team Class. From left to right: Mary Louise Stringer, Jeanne B. Dovey and George C. Clement. Rolling Rock, 1957.

The opening meet at Braemar. From left to right: Janet Replogle, Alison Walter, Jeanne Dovey, Mark Saxman and Morrie Morrison. 1956.

Having fun in New Jersey. From left to right: George Clement, Perk Oliver, Abbie Hunt, Anne Clement and Barbara Kraeling. 1950s.

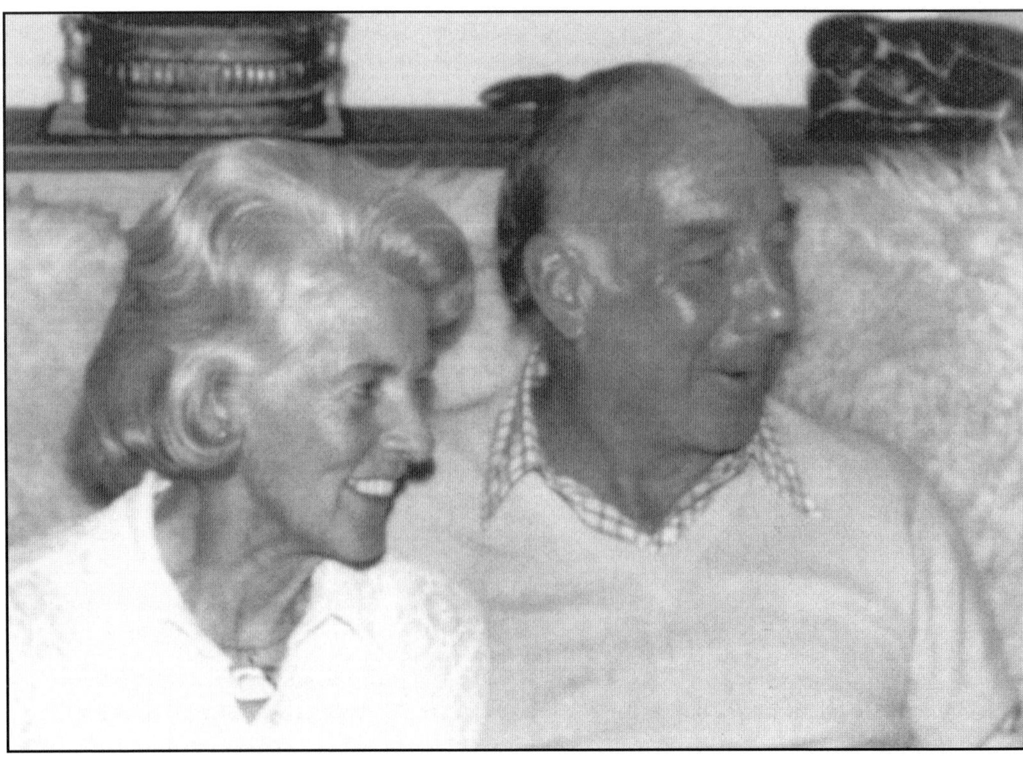

Kit and Lenny Bughman. Rolling Rock, 1960s.

The Todds attend the Rolling Rock Family Class. From left to Right: Susie on *Laurel*, Burt on *Tammy*, Laurie on *piper* and Franny on *Kirkey*. 1960s.

The Rolling Rock Race Committee. From left to right: Alfred Hunt, Lewis Murdock, Alex Stokes, Jack Cooper, Jack Tierney Jr., P. S. Oliver, Bill Robinson, Frank Powers, Herb May, General Mellon, Lenny Bughman, Phil Fanning, Barry Sullivan, Mark Thompson, Bill Stirling, Frank Richardson and Frank Richardson Jr. 1960s.

Opening Meet at Braemar. New MFH's from left to right are: Stite Vipond on *Ransom*, Perk Oliver on *Wintertime*, and Susie Todd on *Goodwood*. Rolling Rock, 1977.

Crossing Rector Road. Tom Slater, MFH; Dan Connally; Stite Vipond, MFH; Greg Suppes; Danny Berger; John Frazier. Ligonier, 1981.

Carolyn Rizza; Susie Todd, MFH; Georgia Smith, Betty Kelsey. 1983.

Rev. James Simons blessing the hounds as John and Joseph Hardiman look on. 1995.

Stite Vipond, age 80, jumping *Matthew* from Foxley Farm into Log Cabin Farm. Ligonier, 1990s.

Portrait of Mrs. Burt K. Todd, Jt. MFH, by Minnett Bickel. 1994.

thing in between. This was an annual challenge to the creative people of Sewickley, and the results were marvelous.

The fabulous old wooden grandstand added immensely to the grandeur to the scene. I can still remember the clatter of the wooden boards as people paid their respects to the well-dressed box-holders while others climbed the tiers of benched seating. It was grand and exciting. The audience was attentive and respectful to the events in the show ring. Occasionally, the dignified atmosphere was shattered with exclamations from Mrs. Edith Flynn Patterson, an ardent horsewoman who supported many horse events. She would make people gasp with her vociferous comments, but she somehow got away with this unusual conduct. There were also parking places for a select few on the other side of the ring. I always found it a problem to put names to the many familiar faces—a smile and perhaps a handshake had to suffice.

I think the first time I showed there I took my chestnut mare *Tish*. It was fun taking care of her in her appointed stall, and warming up in the congested gravel area outside the ring. As far as I was concerned, we were in the big time! Unfortunately Johnny Beach suggested that I give her a tap with my crop as we made our preparatory circle in the ring. Well, *Tish* took off like a bat out of hell and we flew around the eight fences. Needless to say our debut was disgraceful.

When I became more proficient, I was asked to ride an "out-of-town" horse in the Hunters Under Saddle class. The class was scheduled immediately following the lunch break and the trainer requested that I be there early to get acquainted with the horse. It was a reasonable request but somehow the luncheon at the club lasted too long. I just had time to get a leg up, adjust my stirrups and enter the ring. The horse went like a dream and stood like a rock when the class lined up to have the riders dismount and remount. Since I am short, it was a painful performance remounting but the nice big bay horse never flicked an ear. We were awarded first place, and were greeted by a grinning trainer as we left the ring. He hastily told me that we would have been in real trouble if I had picked up the reins. In those days it was acceptable to perform on a loose rein and that was my style anyway. How lucky for all concerned that it worked out well.

I have such fond memories of most of the key members of the Sewickley Hunt. They were such great people that we became good friends despite our age difference. W. C. Robinson MFH and his sister, Mrs. C. S. Richards MFH (Althea Richards now Mrs. Paul Gorman) impressed me tremendously. They were always so well turned out, gracious, and in full control. Bill was more gregarious, but Althea was popular, a competent horsewoman, winning many ribbons on her good gray mare *June Holliday*.

Mr. and Mrs. James O. Flower were very attractive and friendly. He loved hunting and played an important part in the functions and congeniality of the hunt. Alie Painter Thompson recalled the time that Jim held onto Sweetie George's coat tails, saving her from her inevitable fall. Once she was safely back in the saddle, he exclaimed "Now you just stay there." The Charles Painters were good friends of my parents and had lent their marvelous pony, *Clytie*, to the young Hays children. Alie (Mrs. LeRoy Thompson) grew up riding and became a Joint Master of the hunt (1955–1992).

Frank (Bud) E. Richardson MFH (1950–1988), although diminutive in stature, was a giant in the hunt. He and his gracious wife, Rosie, were highly regarded by everyone and contributed so much to hunting in western Pennsylvania. They were attractive and added a great deal with their presence at most horse events. It was always a pleasure to see Frank Richardson on his gray hunter as they participated in joint meets at Rolling Rock. The Richardsons also invited the Todds to join their table at the prestigious Masters of Foxhounds Dinner in New York City. It was my first attendance there, and it was nice to be with friends. It was a sad day for us to go to his funeral, which was well attended by his many admirers. Tears were shed when the huntsman blew with his hunting horn "Gone to ground." It was an inspired tribute to a very fine man.

Bill Boyd kindly lent me the hunting diary of his sister Posey, from which I gleaned more information about the Sewickley Hunt. In the 1940s she was a hunting fanatic. It made me tired just to read her schedule. Posey hunted regularly with Sewickley, but also helped her friend Evie Thompson at Chestnut Ridge on Sundays. To top off this schedule, she often joined Helen Roberts and Johnny Beach for some informal hunting at Harts Run. Posey was a popular girl and also an accomplished artist. I cherish the pencil portrait she did of my mare *Tish*.

In Posey's hunting diary there was a poem by Francis (Red) M. Stifler, one of the active foxhunters in the 40s. The verse was presented at the Master's dinner, and captures the fun and closeness of the Sewickley Hunt members, and their love of hunting the often hilly country.

The Roller Coaster Hunt

A stranger free from the rolling grass
    Of Leisestershire would hack
The hills above Sewickley
    With a sigh and an "Alack,
"You could only hunt this country
with a roller coaster pack."

    Then fill your glasses who dare ride
    Across these hills—in front
And down a bumper to the brave
    Of the roller coaster hunt

To gallop and gallop down
    A horse must have a knack
To stay with him requires some skill
    Of the rider on his back
Some fortitude or alcohol
    Or the zeal of a maniac

        Then here's a toast to those who ride
        With a zeal demoniac
        And the hardy, daring souls who fall
        With the roller coaster pack.

To lead the field o'er hill and dale
    And the fences high attack

Requires a nerve of toughened steel
    That the Robinsons don't lack
Against the finest in the land
    Their handsome grays will stack.

Then doff your hats to masters twain
    Who bear the awful brunt
    Of leading 'cross a wild terrain
    The roller coaster hunt.

A huntsman keen rides at the top
    A man of Ken and knack
Who knows that following Bud and Jim
    Will turn each skirter back
Those two and Will perform a task
    On an undulating track.

    Then three times three in rousing cheer
    Or if you're hoarse just grunt
    A greeting to this able staff
    Of the roller coaster hunt.

At dawn a bag of anise seed
    In weather fair or black
Is drawn by Quigg o'er field and wood
    From the find to the kill and back
His ingenuity excels
    Even a fox's track.

    Then cheer again and ring it loud
    For the lonely dragman's sack
    In laying the terrible, tumbling course
    For the roller coaster pack.

Before we leave celebrities
    We must observe the crack

Of all the known hunt secretaries
Wise as an almanac
How quietly he tools his horse
Confederate's rein is slack.

A courtly bow and curtsy too
The open a pipe of sack
This bachelor, barrister, learned one
Of the roller coaster pack.

Let's turn aside a moment from the staff so prominent
And look about the tidy field to see how each one went
First in affection and loved by many
Is our ablest rider, Mrs. George Binney
We must not compare for fear of bad slips,
And the honors are even between the Holdships.
There's Posey on *Touzy* and Frank on *Big Ben*
And Drayton and Andy, those young sporting men,
The Bells and the Painters, the Walkers and Kipps,
The Walkers who share together the meet trips,
Judge Dithridge on *Charley Boy*, Johnny on *Chief*,
Morgan on *Billy* safe from all grief,
Adelaid on *Frosty Night*
Jim McCready holding tight
Where else is there such a sight?
In such sportsmen we delight
When the hounds get a disease
They just call on Justin Lees.
Colonel Cherrington on his big bay
Shows the smaller Cherry the way.
Rare are the riders who smile at a spill,
But Janet and Phyllis are in at the kill.
Bebe Leonard gallops like sin;

Then Mrs. Hill and Susie Burgwin.
Elizabeth Campbell's a girl; you can't shake well
Jumping abreast of the Valkyries Bakewell.
Dr. Kastlin's among the first flight;
Closely behind him following tight
Is Carlotte Lyon and Willison's Bobby,
Then Bill Sweet returned to his hobby.
Here at a check are the camera fans:
Georges, Robinsons, Joneses and Hanns;
Jaunting along in their motors so sleek,
Picking up hounds exhausted or weak.
These and others, score by score,
Carry on this sporting chore,
Taking nature as they find it—
Not a word to show they mind it.

Your patience has been tried enough
    Now end this long symposiac
A verse like a horse may need a rub
    Bill Masters, will you take the tack
And I shall hand the verse to Chubb—
    Before my rhyming gets the sack.

Then have your glasses filled again,
And cheer them, mild or blunt,
The masters that we love
Of the roller coaster hunt.

—*Francis M. Stifler*
Hon. Secretary 1942–1943

Starting in 1948, the dedicated Harry Black was Sewickley's popular Huntsman for 22 years. Harry and his wife Chris were also very helpful in running horse shows for other hunts. Harry would be ringmaster and Chris was a very efficient secretary. They retired to Thomasville, Georgia and I had the pleasure of seeing them there at a horsy event.

C. Taylor (Tad) Marshall was an enthusiastic MFH from 1968–1994. Tad still hunts and he has done a thorough study of the Sewickley Hunt, which will be printed one day. Tad also hunted the hounds a bit before John Tabachka became Huntsman in 1982. John was extremely well liked and, sadly, died of a heart attack in the field in 1998.

I cannot omit Joe and Helen Roberts who moved to Sewickley in 1959. They have been good friends of mine for many years and you will find them mentioned with their involvement in other hunts, namely Harts Run and Chestnut Ridge. They instilled a love of foxhunting in their three daughters Jean, Chris, and Melinda. In fact, Jean is the Huntsman for the New Market, Middletown Valley Hounds in Maryland. The Roberts have loved their life in Sewickley and Joe still hunts.

I do not recall John Burgwin but I certainly recall his wife Adelaide Burgwin. She was a small, soft-spoken woman with twinkling blue eyes. I had the pleasure of riding her good horse, *Vodka*, in the local series of point-to-points. He was a tall, thin bay horse with nice manners and great stamina. Frank Vescio was his excellent groom and kept the horse in perfect condition, so all I had to do was ride. We never should have lost a race but in my first attempt I cut a flag at Rolling Rock. Utterly chagrined, I solved the problem by painting my right hand with red Mercurochrome, reminding me to leave the red flag on my right, and we never lost another race. I treasure the beautiful jeweled compact that is inscribed *Vodka* 1947.

Mrs. Burgwin was a great lady, vitally interested in horses. In her later years, she established a very successful breeding program for flat racing. Barberry Farm produced high quality horses that brought big prices at the auction sales of Keenland and Saratoga.

Another lady that I became involved with was Miss Katherine Walker, the sister of Mrs. Kipp. Both of these ladies were active members of the hunt. Miss Walker had raised a gorgeous small chestnut mare called *Lawn Fete*. The mare was not only attractive but she was talented. It was like riding a perfect machine and we won the championship in numerous horse shows. The tribute to her success should go to her wonderful groom, but I was overcome when a young girl at the New Kensington Horse Show asked me for my autograph.

For many years, George Chubb ran an immaculate stable at the Allegheny Country Club. The old green building was unusual with a small indoor riding area surrounded by box stalls, two places for grooming and living accommodations upstairs for the Chubbs. There was also another small stable plus shed rows of box stalls to accommodate the in-coming show horses. Their daughter, Ethel, was successful with gaited horses and harness ponies. She later ran an excellent riding department at Gimbels Department Store in Pittsburgh.

Daniel P. Lenehan and his young riding family succeeded Mr. Chubb at the Allegheny Country Club. Sewickley was very fortunate to acquire this attractive, soft-spoken Irishman who was an unbelievably talented horseman. He had come to Friendship Hill from New York State, then went to the Frankstown Hunt with Mr. Paul Vipond, but found his niche in Sewickley. Danny favored showing and among his many clients, Bill Hanley acquired an excellent string of show horses. Bill was a good rider and under the tutelage of Danny they were very successful showing throughout the East. After his fine wife Eileen died, Danny moved to Virginia, married again and became a prominent judge in the horse show world. Unfortunately, he died before receiving the news that he was inducted into the Horse Show Hall of Fame, a well-deserved tribute to this remarkable horseman.

Phyllis Keister (Mrs. Harton Semple) was MFH from 1950 to 1955. Phyllis and her sister, Jean, became ardent members of the hunt when their family moved to Sewickley. Phyllis was closer to my sister Molly in age but we were all good friends. She had many talents—a rider, an accomplished harpist and a fantastic golfer. This attractive, unpretentious lady has passed her abilities to her children. As you will see in the listings, Mrs. Cherry Semple White is a Joint Master with Mrs. William (Anne Binney) Metcalf and Andrew Komer, and she is currently hunting the hounds. Carol Semple Thompson also hunts, but her true love is golf. As an amateur she has won many tournaments and she was awarded the 2001 Dapper Dan Sports Woman Award.

Several people had helped me with information about the Sewickley Hunt, and I am indebted to Alie Painter Thompson, Dick Smith, and Joe and Helen Roberts for their kindness. I still needed updated material and I had appealed to Cherry Semple White for pictures and lists of the Sewickley Hunt members. Her mother Phyllis called to invite me to see their marvelous collection of photographs. When we met at the Allegheny Club, Phyllis, Carol Semple Thompson and Cherry Semple White were there to show me around.

Although I had not driven to Sewickley for years before my visit in 2001, I felt like a "homing pigeon" when I went to meet the Semples at the Country Club. Blackburn Road carried me past many familiar properties, despite the fact that only their location and handsome stone walls were recognizable. Most of the magnificent old estates have been developed. Just before I turned into Country Club Lane, I had a close call with a deer that jumped a wall but safely crossed the road.

It was such a pleasure to revisit the charming Allegheny Country Club, since it awakened so many memories of the marvelous times that I had there. The ladies recently had the myriad of hunting pictures reframed and placed attractively on the walls. Besides some breathtaking Frank Voss paintings of various old friends, there were two delightful large canvases done by Dick Smith portraying a homogenous group of key Sewickley Hunt people, with the Country Club in the background. It was thrilling to see the fantastic display of the history of the Sewickley Hunt.

In a cavalcade we went to visit the Sewickley Hunt Club and Kennels on Little Sewickley Creek Road. We passed the "huntsman's house," the newly renovated kennels, and wound up to the clubhouse on the hill. The walls of the warm, friendly clubhouse were festooned with a multitude of wonderful photographs. Carol Thompson volunteered her husband's ability to make some copies for this book. I am indebted to Dick Thompson for his excellent copies of the old photographs.

It is sad to report that the old stables and impressive grandstand are gone. The fabulous Allegheny Country Club Horse Show has been replaced by the two-day Western Pennsylvania Horseman's Association Shows in May and June. These shows are financially beneficial and well filled with exhibitors seeking to add to their point system in the WPHP division championships awarded annually.

I was interested when Cherry told me that she is now hunting the hounds, and that the 30 couple of crossbred hounds had responded to her after she had spent the summer walking them. She also commented on the effect the winds can play on moving the scent of a drag line and that a wind from the south was devastating to scenting. I recalled having Lewis Murdock from Far Hills, New Jersey telling me that an easterly wind caused bad scenting in their area. Scenting is mysterious and not thoroughly understood due to nature's variables.

As a result of several busy highways, Sewickley has lost a lot of good hunting country. It has been difficult for Cherry to get to the hounds when they find a fox or coyote. The quarry inevitably sneaks through the fences that guard the highway, which creates a hazardous situation. I did not know that coyotes had appeared in their country and their presence is not welcome. In big country the coyote can provide a fabulous long run, but in the hilly area of western Pennsylvania they are a problem for the foxhunters when they cannot stay with their hounds. Coyotes are also likely to kill the fox population, since they both hunt the same prey.

There has always been something special about the Sewickley community. The people are dynamic and pull together. Although the hunt is now curtailed by land development, the enthusiasm of the members and the community holds the tradition together. Rolling Rock and Sewickley are the only two surviving hunts in western Pennsylvania.

Sewickley Hunt MFHA Data

1926 Masters: Mr. and Mrs. J. O. Burgwin. Hon. Sec.: Mr. H. C. Bughman, Jr. Huntsman: Percy Trafford. Whippers-in: H. C. Bughman, B. F. Jones, III and J. C. Cappeau.

1930 Huntsman: Michael Cullinane. Whippers-in: Frank Richardson, Jr., J. O. Flower and William C. Robinson, Jr.

1935 Masters: Mrs. J. O. Burgwin and Mr. W. C. Robinson, Jr. Whippers-in: Frank E. Richardson, Jr. and J. O. Flower.

1936 Hon. Sec.: Charles A. Wood, Jr.

1937 Huntsman: Kenneth Smith.

1944 Masters: W. C. Robinson, Jr. and Mrs. Snowdon Richards. Acting Joint Masters: J. O. Flower and Frank E. Richardson, Jr. Hon. Sec.: Justin D. Lees. Huntsman: (prof) William Leverton. Whippers-in: Frank E. Richardson, Jr., J. O. Flower and Mrs. Harton S. Semple.

1946 Masters: W. C. Robinson, Jr. and Mrs. Snowdon Richards. Hon. Sec.: C. A. Woods, Jr. Whippers-in: Frank E. Richardson, Jr. and J. O. Flower.

1947 Whippers-in: F. E. Richardson, Jr., J. O. Flower, Mrs. Harton S. Semple and (prof) Harry Black.

1948 Huntsman: (prof) Harry Black. Whippers-in: J. O. Flower, F. E. Richardson, Jr. and Mrs. Harton S. Semple.

1950 Master: Frank E. Richardson, Jr. Whippers-in: James O. Flower and Christine Metcalf.

1951 Huntsman: (prof) Harry B. Black. Whippers-in: James O. Flower, Christine Metcalf and Ann Binney.

1953 Masters: Frank E. Richardson, Jr. and Mrs. Harton S. Semple. Whippers-in: James O. Flower, Mrs. William Metcalf, III and (prof) Mickey Koval.

1954 Whippers-in: James O. Flower and (prof) Mickey Koval.

1955 Whippers-in: James O. Flower and C. Taylor Marshall.

1956 Frank E. Richardson, Jr. and Mrs. LeRoy Thompson. Hon. Sec.: J. O. Flower. Huntsman: (prof) Harry B. Black. Whippers-in: C. Taylor Marshall.

1957 Whippers-in: C. Taylor Marshall and Frank E. Richardson, III.

1960 Whippers-in: C. Taylor Marshall, Frank E. Richardson, III and Junior Whip Susan F. Fifer.

1961 Whippers-in: C. Taylor Marshall and Junior Whip Susan F. Fifer.

1962 Masters: C. Taylor Marshall and Mrs. LeRoy Thompson. Hon. Sec.: William A. Tauskey. Whippers-in: C. Taylor Marshall and Junior Whips Jean Roberts and Jo Ann Kolesien.

1968 Whippers-in: C. Taylor Marshall.

1969 Masters: Frank E. Richardson, Jr. and Mrs. LeRoy Thompson and C. Taylor Marshall. Whippers-in: LeRoy Thompson.

1970 Masters: Frank E. Richardson, Jr., Mrs. LeRoy Thompson and C. Taylor Marshall. Hon. Sec.: Michael F. Fifer.

1971 Whippers-in: LeRoy Thompson, Jr. and Mrs. David Knapp.

1973 Masters and Huntsman: Frank E. Richardson, Jr., Mrs. LeRoy Thompson and C. Taylor Marshall. Whippers-in: Mrs. David G. Knapp and Mrs. William H. Stevenson.

1975 Hon. Sec.: Mrs. Joseph L. Roberts, Jr. Whippers-in: Mrs. David Knapp, Cherry Semple and Mrs. Elaine Stevenson.

1976 Masters and Huntsman: Frank E. Richardson and Mrs. LeRoy Thompson. Whippers-in: Jean Roberts and Cherry Semple.

1977 Huntsman: (prof) Patrick Wright. Whippers-in: Jean Roberts, Mrs. Cherry Siefert, Harvey Rickert and Mrs. Molly Herring-Bell.

1979 Masters: Frank E. Richardson and C. Taylor Marshall. Whippers-in: Jean Roberts, Mrs. Cherry Siefert and Harvey Rickert.

1982 Whippers-in: Hon. Jean Roberts, Mrs. Cherry Siefert, Harvey Rickert and Mrs. James Edson.

1984 Huntsman: (prof) John Tabachka.

1985 Whippers-in: Mrs. Cherry Siefert, Harvey Rickert and Mrs. James Edson.

1986 Whippers-in: Mrs. Cherry Siefert, Harvey Rickert, Mrs. James Edson and Andrew Komer.

1988 Whippers-in: Mrs. Cherry Siefert, Mrs. James Edson and Mrs. Raymond Schuerger.

1989 Masters: Mrs. LeRoy Thompson, C. Taylor Marshall and Andrew F. Komer.

1990 Hon. Sec.: Mrs. James P. Edson. Whippers-in: Mrs. Cherry Siefert, Mrs. James Edson and Mrs. Raymond Schuerger.

1991 Masters: C. Taylor Marshall, Andrew F. Komer and Mrs. William A. Metcalf, III.

1994 Hon. Sec.: Mrs. Andrew F. Komer. Whippers-in: Mrs. R. B. White, Mrs. Raymond Schuerger, Dr. Raymond Schuerger and Floyd Wine.

1995 Masters: Andrew F. Komer, Mrs. William A. Metcalf III, and Mrs. R. B. White.
1999 Huntsman: (prof) Ms. Bryony O'Connor.
2000 Acting Huntsman: Mrs. R. B. White. Kennelman: (prof) Tammy Radu. Whippers-in: Carolyn Smith, Lynn Whitmore and Floyd Wine.

Sewickley Hunt

Active Members, 1947

Burgwin, Mrs. J. O.
Flower, J. O.
Heard, Drayton
Holdship, Miss Federicka
Jones, B. F. III
Kipp, Mrs. Eugene
Lees, Justin D.
Painter, Mrs. C. A., Jr.
Park, Mrs. Lewis A.
Richards, Mrs. C. S.
Richardson, F. E., Jr.
Robinson, W. C., Sr.
Robinson, Mrs. W. C., Sr.
Robinson, W. C., Jr.
Rugg, Dan M.
Semple, Mrs. Harton S.
Stoner, Frank R., Jr.
Thompson, Mrs. LeRoy
Walker, Miss Katherine
Woods, Charles A., Jr.

Associate Members

Alexander, Mrs. Maitland
Auch, Mrs. John L.
Bell, John A., Jr.
Bell, Reynolds
Blair, Mrs. William H.
Brown, Lawrence
Buffington, Joseph
Burgwin, Miss Susan
Chapin, Mrs. Newton
Clarkson, Mrs. Newton
Potter, Miss Susan
Cherrington, Edison
Clarkson, Mrs. W. F.
Richards, Mrs. R. S., Jr.
Clause, R. L.
Davies, Miss Marian
Donaldson, Dr. J. P.
Flower, Mrs. J. O.
George, Mrs. W. D., Jr.
Hann, George R.
Holdship, Miss Margaret
Horne, Josep
Jones, Mrs. B. F., III
Jones, W. L., Jr.

Lees, Mrs. Justin D.
Leonard, Miss Mariette
Lermann, Dr. Wm. W.
Lyon, Miss Charlotte
McGrath, John H.
McCune, Miss Mary
Mellon, Richard K.
Metcalf, Miss Christine
Oliver, John C., Jr.
Perkins, Mrs. Coleman
Rea, Henry O.
Richardson, Mrs. F. E., Jr.
Robinson, Mrs. A. L.
Robinson, Mrs. W. C., Jr.
Schoonmaker, Mrs. J. M., Jr.
Snyder, Wm P., Jr.
Stoner, Marcus W.
Stuart, James L., Jr.
Tener, Hon. A. C.
Tener, Mrs. George E.
Tener, Kinley J.
Vant, M/M Clarence H.
Willison, Dr. Robert W.

Sewickley Hunt

Members 1958

Burgwin, Mrs. J. O.
Flower, Mr. James O.
Hanley, Mr. William H.
Hazzard, Mrs. William
Heard, Mr. Drayton
Holdship, Miss Fredericka
Hunt, Mr. Alfred M.
Jones, III, Mr. B. F.
Kipp, Mrs. Eugene
Lees, Mr. Justin D.
Marshall, Mr. C. Taylor
Marshall, Mr. R. M.
McCargo, Mrs. Grant, III
Metcalf, Mrs. William B, III
Morison, Mr. Samuel N.
Okie, Mr. Fred
Pursglove, Mr. Joseph, Jr.
Richards, Mrs. C. Snowden
Richardson, Mr. F. E., Jr.
Robinson, Mr. W. C.
Robinson, Mrs. W. C.
Robinson, Mr. W. C., Jr.
Semple, Mrs. Harton S.
Stoner, Mr. Frank, Jr.
Thompson, Mrs. LeRoy
Vant, Mr. Clarence
Walker, Miss Katherine
Woods, Mr. Charles A., Jr.

Associates

Barker, Mrs. Wayne
Bell, John A., Jr.
Bell, Reynolds
Blair, Mrs. William R.
Brown, Mrs. Robert G.
Buffington, Mr. Joseph, Jr.

Chapin, Mr. Newton, Jr.
Cherrington, Mr. Edison
Clarkson, Mrs. W. F.
Clause, Mr. R. L.
Craig, Mrs. George, Jr.
Fifer, Mr. Michael
Flaccus, Miss Jane
Flower, Mrs. James O.
George, Mr. W. D., Jr.
George, Mrs. W. D., Jr.
Gross, Mrs. John
Hall, Mrs. Elizabeth
Hann, Mr. George R.
Holdship, Miss Margaret
Jones, Mrs. B. F., III
Lees, Mrs. Justin D.
Lermann, Dr. W. W.
McCune, Miss Mary
McMaster, Mrs. Joseph, Jr.
Nevin, Mrs. Hugh
Pursglove, Mrs. Joseph, Jr.
Ratcliffe, Mrs. George, Jr.
Rathbun, Mr. John
Rathbun, Mrs. John
Rhodes, Mrs. Thomas E.
Richardson, Mrs. F. E., Jr.
Robinson, Mrs. Alexander
Robinson, Mr. Alexander, Jr.
Robinson, Mrs. W. C., Jr.
Robinson, Miss Elise
Schoonmaker, Mrs. J. M., Jr.
Schurko, Mr. John
Stevenson, Mrs. Frederick
Tener, Hon. Alexander C.
Walker, Mrs. S. P.
Wright, Mrs. Donald

Sewickley Hunt

Juniors 1958

Beall, Judy
Cramer, Mrs. Paul
Cross, Mrs. Charles
Culbertson, Tingle
Deane, Stephanie
Fifer, Barbara
Flower, Sarah E.
Floyd, McDaniel
George, Althea
George, Madelaine
Holbrook, Sarah
Irwin, Constance
Jackson, Mary
Kenyon, Mrs. Marshall
Lees, Jane
Lees, John
Lenehan, Michael
Lenehan, Sheila
Magee, Mrs. Robert
McClintock, Mary
Millard, Ann
Nimick, Mrs. Howard
Ratcliffe, Dorothy
Ratcliffe, Stephen
Richardson, Beth
Richardson, Frank E., III

Richardson, Thomas F.
Ruffner, Hugh L.
Ruffner, Jay
Rugg, Sally
Schurko, Gregg
Schurko, John
Standish, Ann
Standish, Mrs. Peter
Standish, W. L., IV
Stoner, Barbara
Stoner, Doris
Semple, Harton
Trainer, Mardi
Willard, Sally

Sewickley Hunt

Members 2001

Allyn, Mary
Barry, Barbara
Bartlett, Jennie
Bell, Carol
Blier, Rocky
Block, Karen & Henry
Bradley, Carol
Brennan, Dianne & Dick
Bronson, Pam
Coll, Joan
Connelly, Marc
Courneen, Ann
Craig, Emily
Curry, Henry
Divosevic, Debby
Eichleay, Haven
Giles, Cindy
Gladstone, Ginny
Gorman, Althea
Guilot, Meg
Hall, Bonny
Haushalter, Susan
Hencher, Eileen & Dennis
Hennon, Kim, MD
Holland, Susan Gaudio
Jakacki, Regina, MD
Johnson, Robin Hummel
Kirsch, Katie
Kitner, Jack
Komer, Ginny & Andy
Komer, Kristin
Lantzsch, Christian
Larkin, Lana
Lemp, Father Joseph
Marshall, C. Taylor
McCullough, Cindy & Bob
McCullough, William
McFarland, Jessica
McGarry, Tom
Metcalf, Ann
Montaganese, Tony, DDS
Mullin, Karen & Mike
Murphy, Jane Allen
Pfaeffle, Gwen & Hugo

Phelps, Jeffrey
Pivar, Gerry
Rassiga, Ann, MD
Renkes, Katie
Richardson, Mrs. F. E., Jr.
Roberts, Joe
Schreiber, Carolyn
Schuerger, Ray, VMD
Seifert, Fraser
Seifert, Holly
Semple, Heather
Semple, Phyllis
Semple, Harton
Sidel, Dennis
Smith, Richard
Smith, Carolyn
Sponseller, Dan
Sullivan, Luke
Sullivan, Mary Cotton
Thompson, Alice
Thompson, Carol Semple
Thorbeck, Sonya
Torrence, Lisa
Vance, Marge
Volk, Jane
White, Cherry Semple
Whitmore, Lynn
Wine, Donna & Floyd
Wine, Sarah
Yates, Tony, MD

Sewickley Hunt

Master

Mr. J. O. Burgwin	1924–1934
Mrs. J. O. Burgwin	1924–1938
Mr. W. E. Robinson, Jr.	1935–1949
Mrs. C. Snowden Richards	1939–1949
Mr. J. O. Flower (acting)	1943–1944
Mr. F. E. Richardson, Jr. (acting)	1943–1944
Mr. F. E. Richardson, Jr.	1950–1988
Mrs. H. S. Semple	1950–1954
Mrs. LeRoy Thompson	1955–1992
Mr. C. Taylor Marshall	1968–1994
Mr. A. F. Komer	1987–1988
Mr. W. A. Metcalf	1991–Present
Mrs. R. B. White	1995–Present

President

Mr. H. N. Van Voorhis	1924–1932
Mr. B. F. Jones III	1933–1935
Mr. J. O. Burgwin	1936–1938
Mrs. J. O. Burgwin	1939–1949
Mr. W. E. Richardson	1950–1963
Mr. J. O. Flower	1964–1967
Mr. J. Pursglove, Jr.	1968–1973
Mrs. H. S. Semple	1974–1986
Mr. J. Markey	1989–1993
Mr. A. F. Komer	1989–Present
Mr. J. L. Roberts	1994
Mr. F. Wine	1995–Present

Huntsman

Mr. P. G. Trafford	1926–1932
Mr. Michael Cullinane	1933–1937
Mr. Kenneth Smith	1938–1945
Mr. Will Leverton	1946–1949
Mr. Harry Black	1950–1972
Mr. Tom Jackson	1973–1974
Mr. Patrick Wright	1975–1981
Mr. John Tabachka	1982–1998
Ms. Bryony O'Connor	1999
Mrs. R. B. White	2000–Present
Mrs. Edson	1991–1992
Mrs. A. F. Komer	1993–Present

Secretary

Dr. A. C. Howell	1924–1925
Mr. H. C. Bughman	1926–1935
Mr. C. A. Woods, Jr.	1936–1941
Mr. Francis M. Stifler	1942–1943
Mr. Justin Lees	1944–1945
Mr. C. A. Woods, Jr.	1946–1955
Mr. J. O. Flower	1956–1963
Mr. W. A. Tauskey	1964–1968
Mr. F. Fifer	1969–1973
Mr. J. L. Roberts, Jr.	1974–1990

Treasurer

Mr. G. A. Hann	1924–1929
Mr. J. O. Burgwin	1930–1932
Mr. H. C. Bughman	1933–1935
Mr. C. A. Woods, Jr.	1936–1965
Mr. J. Pursglove, Jr.	1966–1967
Mr. J. L. Roberts, Jr.	1968–1990
Mrs. P. Dreisbach	1991
Mrs. L. Schuerger	1992–Present

No brakes

Indiana Hunt

Est. 1925

1928–1936

Uniform: Scarlet coat, green collar, yellow piping. Button: brass button, standing fox with I.H.
Foxhounds: 17 couples half-bred English: American cross foxhounds.
The country is approximately 18 miles long and 12 miles wide. Rolling farmland with wooded hills, mostly natural fences, post and rail and worm fence (Baily's Hunting Directory, 1928).
Indiana Hunt, Indiana, Pennsylvania. Established 1925. Country recorded by MFHA April 1928. Recognized by NSHA 1929. Discontinued 1936. Sources: NSHA: 1929–1933. MFHA: 1928–1935. Span: 1925–1936. (Information from John B. Glass 1996)

My closest connection with the Indiana Hunt is through a contemporary friend, Ruth Robinson Warner, the daughter of Lucius W. Robinson, Jr., who had been an officer in the hunt. When I contacted her in Nashville, she kindly sent me some photographs of their beautiful farm in Indiana, Pennsylvania and snapshots of visiting hunting guests. They all seem to be beautifully dressed and having a good time but I cannot identify them. Ruth's recollections of the farm and the hunt are limited to "loving her visits to their beautiful farm."

I am indebted to Ruth for writing her charming memories of the Indiana Hunt at their Valley View Farm:

> I was very young when the hunt was in its heyday at our farm in Indiana, Pennsylvania. My memories are few and vague, probably dating sometime after 1930. Valley View Farm, as it was called then, was where we spent summers and we children loved it more than anything. My younger sisters have no memory of that magical time. Sally was too young, being born at the farm in August, 1930. The youngest, Lucia, was not born until 1937 and by then the hunt was history.
>
> My strongest memory of hunting is probably that of a Joint Meet with riders coming from other Hunts such as Greensburg, Ligonier and Pittsburgh. As the day of the hunt approached there was an air of excitement as the household was busy with preparations for the arriving guests. I was kept out of the way, but I remember peeking eagerly out of the windows, straining to catch sight of the exotic riders in their colorful "pink" coats and handsome riding outfits as they gathered on the terrace below for pre-hunt libations. Of special interest and wonder were several women in riding skirts who always rode sidesaddle.
>
> My father was a superb horseman, but suffered from childhood with an allergy to horse dander. I seem to recall that sometimes he even rode with a mask over his nose! His riding clothes were always kept in a small hall cupboard, well away from his other clothes. I remember how handsome he was dressed in his riding attire and his beautifully polished boots. The bootjack was especially fascinating to me. I loved to watch him use it to remove his boots after he came in from riding. He was truly a figure of wonder to a small child.
>
> A few memories remain of being taken in the car to follow the hunt, as best we could, over the narrow, rough dirt country roads. We strained with excitement to catch a glimpse of the horses in the distance, galloping across the fields and disappearing out of sight. We always listened for the baying of the hounds and the sound of the hunting horn telling us that the riders were near.
>
> The foxhounds were kept in a kennel some distance from the stable, across the field at the edge of the woods where they were out of sight but not out of hearing. We loved to visit them and hear about

their care. They were fed a mixture of cereals cooked for them in big pots. The only ingredient was oatmeal, something that I did not care for very much! As one approached the kennel the odor was overwhelming. Since the hunts were all drag, a fox was kept in a pen with burlap sacks that were dragged along the ground to lay the course of the hunt. The fox pen was well away from the kennel and other farm buildings as the odor was so pungent, even stronger than the hounds. I always felt sorry for the fox because he was all by himself.

To this day, if I should hear the haunting sound of the hunting horn, either at a local equestrian event or even on some BBC television program, I am instantly transported back to that early childhood time on our farm in Indiana.

—*Ruth Robinson Warner*

Lucius W. Robinson, Jr. moved to Indiana in 1917 soon after his marriage to Harriet Overton of Nashville, Tennessee. His father had extensive mining interests in Western Pennsylvania and Lucius, Jr. went to work for him in the Coal Run Mining Co. of Indiana. Later this was absorbed by a subsidiary of the Rochester & Pittsburgh Coal Co. After residing in Indiana for some years, the Robinsons moved to Pittsburgh in 1932, keeping the farm, called Valley View, primarily as a summer residence. The Robinsons kept the farm until 1947 and their four daughters, Virginia, Ruth, Sally and Lucia, learned to ride at an early age. The Robinsons were a very attractive couple who were well liked and made many friends in Pittsburgh.

While living in Indiana, the Robinsons became close friends with William (Bill) Jack and his wife Martha and other hunting enthusiasts. Lucius (Lou) was helpful in getting the Indiana Hunt recognized and in 1928 he became the Honorary Secretary. Mr. Robinson was an excellent rider, often winning prizes on his big hunter *Last Penny*, who, it was said, never refused a jump. In 1931 Mr. Robinson became the MFH and managed to continue in this position until 1936 despite moving his family to Pittsburgh.

Burt and I tried to research information about the Indiana Hunt at the Historical Society in Indiana but, even with help, we were not very successful.

Fortunately, the people there were able to give us directions to the former farm of Lucius W. Robinson.

Indiana, which is about 50 miles northeast of Pittsburgh, is an attractive, well-preserved town. It is the site of the county seat, the birthplace of Jimmy Stewart (the famous actor) and the home to Indiana University of Pennsylvania, the state's fifth largest university. The surrounding countryside is absolutely beautiful and when we found the old Robinson farm, now known as Claypoole Manor, we were so impressed with the awesome view of the valley below the house. What a thrill it would have been to hunt that rolling country when it was all farmland.

It bothered me that I had no knowledge about William J. Jack, who instigated the Indiana hunt, other than data obtained from the MFHA and the fact that he was a good friend of the Robinsons. I wrote to Christine Jack Toretti, who presently owns the Robinson farm, assuming that she was a relation. She replied with a very nice letter stating that she was not related but gave me the name of Mrs. John Simpson.

Elizabeth Musser Simpson graciously provided me with the following information that she found in Clarence D. Stethenson's *History of Indiana County*, Vol. IV.

The father, Summers Jack, was an attorney and a Congressman from 1890 to 1912. His son, William Jack (1883–1936) was a graduate of Exeter and with a B.A. and M.A. from Yale University. In 1906 he began teaching Greek and Latin at the Indiana Normal School, now Indiana University of Pennsylvania, and continued to do so until 1917. He also earned a Ph.D. from Harvard. When he retired from his teaching position, he established a very successful automobile business.

William J. Jack was a very erudite man of many interests and talents. He was highly regarded locally and was descended from old families of social importance. He organized the Hunt Club in 1925 and started hunting twice a week in 1926. His committee consisted of Alex M. Stewart, Pres., Dr. F. B. Stevenson, V. P., L. T. McQuade Sec. Treas., Wm. Bennett, Dr. F. J. Kellam, Dr. J. M. Torrence, Vernon F. Taylor, L. W. Robinson and Wm. J. Jack MFH. The hunt was recognized in 1928 and Lucius W. Robinson became Master in 1931 with Mr. Jack becoming the Hon. Sec. Unfortunately Mr. Jack died of a heart attack in 1936 while hunting at Rolling Rock.

During its brief existence the Indiana Hunt enjoyed a great time in their beautiful expansive country. Both Alfred Fletcher and V. C. Lewis, formally employed by Rolling Rock, helped them along their way.

The Indiana Hunt with its energetic membership instigated two hound pack trials, which were successful and well attended. *Polo Magazine* (April, 1933) recorded:

> The hound trials run over the rolling country of the Indiana Hunt in western Pennsylvania late in January of 1933 had several unusual features. Five couples each were entered by the Rolling Rock, Sewickley, Fox Chapel, Westmoreland, Harts Run and Indiana Hunts, and six drags some three to four miles long were laid, the order of their running being decided by lot.
>
> The judges were instructed to score 10 points for speed, 40 for general work as a pack without the leadership of any one hound. Sewickley placed first, Indiana second and Harts Run third.
>
> (Information supplied by G. *Markle Thompson* 1996)

Mrs. Elizabeth Simpson wrote a second letter to me saying that her older sister, Helen Musser Thorne, was a member of the hunt. Because of this, Elizabeth was allowed to take riding lessons from Lewis at the Robinson's stables, which was large enough to hold many hunt horses. She hunted once as a young teenager about 1929, and remembers that she always rode the same horse—a mare with the unimaginative name of *Martha*. "During the hunt I was reprimanded for finding myself ahead of the Master—a real gaucherie."

I was grateful to Mrs. Simpson for sending me her valuable information about William Jack and her singular hunting experience. Only through the kindness of people such as Elizabeth Musser Simpson is it possible to fill in the missing pieces that are so essential to the whole picture. I assured her in my thank-you note that she was not alone in making the mistake of getting ahead of the Master.

Indiana Hunt
MFHA Data

1928 Master: William J. Jack, Esq. Hon. Sec.: Lucius W. Robinson, Jr. Huntsman: (prof) Alfred Fletcher. Whippers-in: (prof) V. C. Lewis and Doyle Sprankle.

1929 Whippers-in: (prof) V. C. Lewis and Paul Anderson.

1931 Master: Lucius W. Robinson. Hon. Sec.: William J. Jack. Huntsman: (prof) Alfred Fletcher. Whippers-in: (prof) Blair Gibson and Paul Anderson.

1935 Whippers-in: (prof) Blair Gibson and Lloyd Gibson.

1936 Discontinued.

Snug

Frankstown Hunt

Est. 1933

1938–1955

Uniform: Scarlet coat, yellow collar, yellow waistcoat.
Foxhounds: 12 couples American.
Country is approximately 10 by 11 miles; rolling hills, some high ridges with steep slopes, considerable wooded country in parts; about 40 percent waste lands and pasture; considerable wire but country well paneled, mostly with post and rails, some original fences (Baily's Hunting Directory, 1937).

The Frankstown Hunt was located in Hollidaysburg near Altoona. It is about a two-hour drive east of Pittsburgh on Route 22 to Route 220. Hollidaysburg on the Juniata River is steeped in the history of its early involvement in canal and railroad travel, which was essential in connecting Pittsburgh with the east. The construction of the portage railroad over the mountain in the early 19th century was a remarkable engineering feat. The Historical Society has done an excellent job of preserving much of this fascinating history. It was not until 1852 that the Pennsylvania Railroad established rail service between Philadelphia and Pittsburgh.

The former country that the Frankstown Hunt enjoyed is now unrecognizable. The site of the old Hunt Club on Plank Road is obliterated by a complex of shopping malls and most of the surrounding countryside has been developed.

There was a great riding interest in the area and the parent organization of the Frankstown Hunt was the Blair County Riding and Hunt Club. It was formed in 1932 and used the old 104th Cavalry Stables as its center. The first officers were Benjamin I. Levine, President; H. Foster Bollinger, Secretary; and Paul T. Winter, Treasurer.

In 1933 the club was reorganized as the Frankstown Hunt Club, aptly named after Stephen Franks, a fur trader who had hunted the country from 1748 to 1785. "Old Franks" would blow his long hunting horn to alert the community to assemble for an exciting day of hunting—the quarry ranged from wolf, gray fox, a herd of wapitis, or an occasional black moose. After the hunt there would be a great outdoor feast with everyone welcome to indulge in drink, food, and song.

The Frankstown Hunt was fortunate to obtain the marvelous horn of "Old Franks" which they hung in their restored clubhouse on the farm located across from the Cemetery. They had a group of enthusiastic members and hunted on Thursdays and Sundays. They would go out on Thursdays in the afternoon and return to their clubhouse for a good party and a delicious dinner provided by their caretakers Anna and Paul Woods. Thursdays became a well-attended social evening enjoyed by the members and their wives. Major Hans Kloepfer, the member most knowledgeable about hunting, would always give a dissertation on the subject that was well received by everyone. It was a new sport and the riders wanted to learn. There is a list of the early members at the end of this chapter that the residents of the area might find interesting.

George P. Gable became the first Master of the Frankstown Hunt in 1933. His family had established an impressive department store in Altoona. He was a popular man, philanthropic and civic minded. With the help of his wife Floss, his home was the center of a lot of activity.

I am indebted to Stitler (Stite) and Janie Vipond for describing the Frankstown Hunt and lending their collection of material about the area. His father Paul S. Vipond was a Master from 1939 to 1944. Janie Vipond's eyes light with merriment as she recalls the lively parties following the Thursday hunt meets.

The Paul S. Vipond family lived in a lovely old brick house, built in 1790 with an addition made in 1840. The place was known as Old Home Farm, R.R., Hollidaysburg, and, at one time, Fort Fetter stood on the property. The Viponds had two boys, P. S., Jr. (Juny) and Stitler A. (Stite), who both inherited their love of riding from their father. Later my life became more involved with Stite because we, with Perk Oliver, became joint masters of the Rolling Rock Hunt in 1977. Stite has my complete admiration; at the age of 83, he was still hunting and going with the best of them. His energy and daring is unbelievable. He loved racing and between that career and hunting, he has had some horrendous spills and was advised (to no avail) to stop riding. It is also a challenge to keep up with him on the dance floor or on the ski slopes. He is an incredible man. Stite was in college during Frankstown's heyday, but his comment was "It may not have been the best hunt around but we certainly did have fun."

The Frankstown Hunt was active as you can see in the following report from the *Middleburg Chronicle*, October 6, 1939:

> Frankstown Hunt est. 1933 rec. 1938
> Paul S. Vipond—Master 1939
> George P. Gable—Hon. Sec.
> Orpheus Newell—(prof) Huntsman
> William Thompson—Whipper-In
> Major B. J. Levine—Whipper-In Drag and fox
> Foxhounds—American and English Hounds went out 40 times
> Annual horse show—Labor Day
> Hunter trials—Decoration Day

Mr. Paul Vipond was extremely fortunate to engage the young Irishman Daniel P. Lenehan to help him with his horses and the hunt. Danny was a tall, thin, dark young man with a phenomenal knowledge of horses. He could recognize the potential of a horse and develop it to its ultimate ability. He had a fine wife, Eileen, and four children, Brian, Sheila, Kevin and Daneen, who all became excellent horsemen. When the Lenehan family ran the Frankstown Hunt Stables on the R. P. Good farm, I asked if I could spend a few days with them, in hopes that I would absorb some of his fantastic knowledge. Everyone was so nice to me, but my experience was limited to having the privilege of working some of their excellent horses. In the 1950s Danny was offered the position of managing the stables of The Allegheny Country Club in Sewickley, Pennsylvania. He had clients who were interested in showing, one of the most avid being Bill Hanley, and with their beautifully schooled horses they were hard to beat on the show circuit. Danny went on to become a most noted judge, his services being sought by all the finest horse shows. Danny was a soft-spoken man with a delightful sense of humor and I feel privileged to have had him as a friend.

I am also grateful to J. C. Dovey who let me borrow things from his mother's archives. Jeanne Burd Dovey had hunted with her father William H. Burd. Since I never hunted with Frankstown, it was a pleasure for me to see pictures of the beautiful hunt country available to them. Jeanne married John C. Dovey and later Jeanne introduced their son J. C. to hunting at Rolling Rock. I distinctly remember J. C. on his gray pony giving some reluctant hunters a lead over a sizeable post and rail fence. J. C. later married Pamela Bughman, the daughter of Kit and Lennie Bughman and they made their home in Ligonier.

Among the photographs lent to me by J. C. was an article by George Swope that I found delightful. I checked with Stite Vipond, who said, "George was a most talented man and a great whip." I have appropriated some poignant passages from his writing that well describe his pleasure of hunting in the 1940s with Fred Stomer MFH and acting huntsman.

From *The Frankstown Hunting Notes* by George E. Swope, Honorary Secretary, published by the *Middleburg Chronicle*:

> *November 17, 1944* . . . With Mr. Stomer and his hounds were: Fieldmaster Mr. Paul S. Vipond, Mr. George P. Gable, Dr. Charles Brown, Mr. William C. Kline, Mr. Boyd Cassidy, Mr. L. F. Crouse

> of Revloc, his daughter Miss Frances of Washington, D. C., Mr. Ned Maloy, Mrs. Fred A. Stormer, Mr. Stitler Vipond, who acted in Dr. John G. Shaffer's stead as Honorary whipper-in, Mr. Hunter Swope, Dr. John G. Shaffer, Dr. Louis P. Glover, Mr. Roy Mauer, Mr. Blair Guyer, Mr. Earl DeShong and Honorary whipper-in, Mr. George E. Swope.
>
> Thoughts out Hunting: Looking down on the undulating backs of ten-and-a-half couples of Frankstown hounds this early morning, October 13th, 1946, A. D., that familiar thrum of the west wind on the back of your ears, stately white cloud ships sailing in the azure sea of the sky, the creak of your leather and the smell of huntin' horses sharp in your nostrils. One can't be held too conceited to conclude that he must have been a pretty nice lad at that to deserve all this. . . . A hound speaks there, now two, now all—and away to the north they roll, bearing into the West Loop Country. . . . Across the hilltop, over a post and rails—another post and rails, down the steep hillside into Stiffler's Wood and can we hear that music. . . . Keep your feet, *Parson* and keep your noggin down . . . there's your kill Mr. Stormer. . . . Beginning to think about that ham and eggs a jolly twelve miles away. . . . The Blue Juniata flows silkily here; no clouds now, just mellow sunlight.
>
> *October 17, 1946* . . . How's a man live without Foxhunting—never want the answer to that one. We hack home through the site of Stephen Franks' Indian Trading Post—Frankstown; his fox horn hangs in our game room. . . . Good to ride into the paddock of The Frankstown, good to see George Gable grin around his pipe, good to hear his wife, Floss' low-pitched friendly voice, good to smell the yeasty grill, good to jam up against your friends at the table, good to grab and stuff and laugh and brag; GOOD (you've guessed it) to be alive.

As you can readily see from George Swope's descriptions, the hunt provided a lot of enjoyment for its members. The Frankstown Hunt continued until 1955, then a few people tried to keep it going until it was permanently disbanded in 1958.

Blair County Riding and Hunt Club
1932

Due to the great interest in riding, the Blair County Riding and Hunt Club was organized in 1932. The officers were Major Benjamin I. Levine, President: H. Foster Bollinger, Secretary, and Paul T. Winter, Treasurer.

Walter W. Ackerman
*Lt. Col. Theodore Arter
*William C. Bashore
*Richard E. Beeler
Krebs Benchoff
Frank E. Biser
John Buchanan
William H. Burd
Sven H. Chelstead
*Paul T. Cline
Harry L. Cohn
Sam M. Cohn
L. F. Crouse
*Carl E. Davies
Lt. J. Clyde Davis
John B. DeBarber
Andrew J. Ford
*George P. Gable
*Dr. L. Pellman Glover
*David Goldberg
Thomas C. Grier
Lt. Col. Benjamin C. Jones
*Dr. David Kaufman
*Phil Klevan
Major Hans E. Kloepfer
J. Donald Lafferty
Frank J. Lawson
*Emanuel S. Leopold
*Major Benjamin I. Levine
Charles E. Maloy, Jr.
Harold E. March
Lester March
James W. Morgan
Mitchell MacCartney
Lt. Warren L. McKinney
John A. Notopoulos
Lt. Charles W. Roberts
*Dr. John G. Shaffer
John L. Stine
William J. Thompson
Paul S. Vipond
*Paul T. Winte

* *charter members*

Frankstown Hunt
MFHA Data

1933–1934 George P. Gable
1934–1935 Joint Masters: George P. Gable and Major B. I. Levine

1935–1936 Joint Masters: Major B. I. Levine and Major Hans E. Kloepfer

1937 Masters: Paul T. Winter, Charles E. Maloy, Jr. Hon. Sec.: B. I. Levine. Huntsman: Charles E. Maloy. Whippers-in: Carl E. Davies, Richard Shaffer and B. I. Levine.

1938 Masters: Paul T. Winter and Charles E. Maloy, Jr. Hon. Sec.: B. I. Levine. Huntsman: Charles E. Maloy. Whippers-in: Carl E. Davies, William J. Thompson and Arthur Hesford.

1939 Master: Paul S. Vipond (1939). Hon. Sec.: George P. Gable. Huntsman: (prof) Orphus Newell. Whippers-in: Hon. William Thompson, Richard E. Shaffer, Major B. I. Levine and (prof) Arthur Hesford.

1943 Master and Huntsman: Paul S. Vipond (1939). Hon. Sec.: George P. Gable. Whippers-in: Hon. Stitler S. Vipond, F. F. Crouse and Dr. John Shepper.

1944 Master and Huntsman: Fred A. Stormer. Hon. Sec.: George E. Swope. Whippers-in: Hon. Dr. John G. Shaffer and George E. Swope.

1946 Master and Huntsman: Fred A. Stormer. Hon. Sec.: George E. Swope. Whippers-in: Hon. Dr. John G Shaffer, George E. Swope and Stitler Vipond.

1947 Master and Huntsman: Fred A. Stormer. Hon. Sec.: George E. Swope. Whippers-in: Hon. George E. Swope and Robert Parks.

1948 Masters: Paul K. Vipond and Daniel P. Lenehan. Hon. Sec.: George E. Swope. Whippers-in: Hon. George E. Swope, Robert Parks and Dr. Glover.

1949 Masters: Paul K. Vipond and Daniel P. Lenehan. Hon. Sec.: George E. Swope. Whippers-in: Hon. George E. Swope, Robert Parks and Dr. Glover.

1950 Masters: Dr. L. Pellman Glover and Daniel P. Lenehan. Hon. Sec.: Charles E. Maloy, Jr. Huntsman: The Joint Masters. Whippers-in: Hon. George E. Swope, Robert Parks and (prof) Richard Franks.

1951 Masters: Hon. Sec.: Charles E. Maloy, Jr. Huntsman: The Joint Masters. Whippers-in: George E. Swope, Robert Parks and (prof) Richard Franks.

1952 Masters: Dr. L. Pellman Glover and Daniel P. Lenehan. Hon. Sec.: to be appointed. Huntsman: The Joint Masters. Whippers in: George E. Swope, Robert Parks and (prof) Richard Franks.

1953 Masters: Mrs. Fred Stormer, Mrs. P. K. Vipond, Mrs. Wesley McCann. Hon. Sec.: to be appointed. Whippers-in: George E. Swope, Robert Parks and (prof) Richard Franks.

1954 Master and Huntsman: Roy L. Maurer. Hon. Sec.: George R. Gable. Whippers-in: Hon. Mrs. Wesley McCann, Stitler A. Vipond and (prof) Richard Franks.

1955 Disbanded

Westmoreland Hunt

Est. 1916

1923–1974
Merged with Rolling Rock

Uniform: Melton gray coat, purple collar.
Foxhounds: 17 couples of American foxhounds.
The country lies in the western section of Westmoreland County, over a good farming district. Fences: post and rail principally; some board fencing and an occasional worm fence of the old type. Considerable wire has been put up in the past two years and some paneling will be necessary this spring and summer. Country hilly, fairly well wooded and a fair amount of pasture land (Baily's Hunting Directory, 1924).

The above description of the area around Greensburg must have excited the imagination of the early foxhunters, but now most of the land is developed. Greensburg is 27 miles east of Pittsburgh and is the county seat of Westmoreland County. The town developed from a stopover on the road to Pittsburgh into a thriving city because of the development of coal in the surrounding area. Fine farmland surrounded the city, and the country itself was rough, with hills of considerable size and large coverts, and open areas used for intensive farming—which meant wire fencing. The hunting country was located north of Greensburg (along and between routes 119 North and 819 North).

The brothers Julian B. Huff and Burrell Huff came to Greensburg to work for the Keystone Coal and Coke Company with the Coulter family. Julian was an attractive, enterprising young man and was responsible for promoting the various horse activities in Greensburg. With the rising coal industry many industrious young men moved into the area and were more than receptive to the pursuit of polo, paper chases (a riding sport without hounds), and hunting. Some of these equestrians were former members of the Harkaway Hunt in MacDonald, Pennsylvania. They were George R. McNary, William S. Moorhead, George M. Laughlin, Jr., Alex Coulter, B. H. Rader, Arthur C. Martin, William Murphy and Torrence Miller. Most of these people were friends of my parents and I remember them well because of our mutual interest in riding. George Weidlein still recalls his grandmother's (Mrs. George McNary) remark; "Our men would be do better if they spent their Sundays in church rather than playing games with their horses."

In 1911 the Huff brothers created an interest in polo. The most regular players were George R. McNary, William S. Morehead, George M. Laughlin, Jr., Alex Coulter, B. H. Rader, Arthur C. Martin and William Murphy. In the fall this enthusiastic riding group filled their riding activity with active paper chases. They purchased a house on the corner of Kenneth and Walnut Street where they could comfortably change their clothes. The Westmoreland Polo and Hunt Club was enlarged over time, and is still a very popular club which offers to its members an intimate place to party or dine.

Kathy Watson, the granddaughter of Arthur C. Martin, lent me a rare program of The Westmoreland Polo Club, Saturday, June 12, 1915. The day included a Horse Show, Polo, and Gymkhana Games, and the price of admission was 25 cents. The most impressive part of the program was the number of prestigious companies, even from Pittsburgh, who purchased ads. It had to have been an unusual but very successful day.

In 1916 Julian Huff acquired a pack of 20 hounds and kept them at his place, Cabin Hill, now the address of *Tribune Review* newspaper. The Cabin Hill Hounds was a private pack and its enthusiastic followers had a great deal of fun drag hunting. This was the predecessor of the Westmoreland Hunt.

In July 1920, Julian Huff married and moved to Haverford, Pennsylvania. In his absence he appointed Torrence Miller as Deputy Master and financially supported the 16 couple of hounds, four horses, and staff until the end of the year in 1920.

The foundation stock of the pack was composed of drafts from the Middlesex, 16 couples, and four couples from the Cheshire, plus a few American hounds bred locally. In the spring of 1920 the hunt had the great misfortune to lose almost their entire pack through a bad epidemic of distemper. Not discouraged, Mr. Miller went to Virginia and purchased a new pack of American hounds. After that time he adopted the policy of hunting crossbred hounds, sired by English hounds bred to American bitches. Miller considered this the best type of hound suited to their hunt country.

In 1921 Henry Coulter and his sister Margaret Coulter accepted the maintenance of the hunt with Torrence Miller as Master. They continued to be staunch supporters of the hunt for many years to come. In 1922 the name was changed to Westmoreland Hunt and was recognized by the MFHA in 1923.

When Julian Huff turned his Cabin Hill Hounds over to Torrence Miller, he could not have made a better choice. Mr. Miller was a dedicated Master of the Westmoreland Hunt for 29 years, finally submitting his resignation in 1958.

I remember Mr. Miller as a small, dapper man with bright blue eyes, assisted by pince-nez glasses. Mr. Miller was the brother of Mrs. Roy A. Hunt, whose husband was responsible for the Aluminum Company of America. There were three Hunt boys: Alfred, Torrence, and Richard. As a MFA, Torrence Miller (Uncle Tod) instilled a true love of foxhunting and horses in his nephew, Alfred. Abbie would become a Master of the Rolling Rock Hunt and a very prominent figure in the hunting and steeplechasing scene.

It has been a privilege for me to read the informative old hunt files preserved by Bobby Martin Watson (Odell) a former Joint Master of Westmoreland Hunt. Mr. Torrence Miller kept a meticulous record of the 1925–1927 meets of the Westmoreland Hunt. Although written in pencil on yellow legal paper, it is still very legible. They hunted from October into January, primarily drag but with some live fox hunting in 1926. Jack Potter was the huntsman and Alfred Fletcher was the whipper-in. They hunted 12 and a half couple of American hounds and 5 couple of English hounds. The hounds were kenneled at Cabin Hill, with beautiful farmland open to them.

Many of the riders in the field are familiar names to me, since they were the parents of my generation and they remained interested in horses. The most often mentioned names of those in the field were Jim and Betty Bovard, Henry Coulter, Margaret Coulter, Arthur Martin, George McNary, Chuck Lynch, Ralph Lynch (when home from school), J. Kelly and F. and Betty Schiller. Other names recorded were Armstrong, F. Arensberg, Barnhart, Harry Bughman, Walter Dowling, Julian Kraft, John Lawrence, J. O. Miller, George McCook, George Paull, Bud Richardson and J. Stewart.

The Westmoreland Hunt preceded the forming of the Rolling Rock Hunt, and R. K. Mellon had enjoyed a season of hunting with them in 1920. Dick Mellon was so enthusiastic about the sport that he started hunting his own hounds at Rolling Rock in 1921. With just 18 miles separating the two hunts, they had a close relationship and enjoyed participating in each other's activities. On Thanksgiving 1925, Richard King Mellon, MFH of the Rolling Rock Hunt, and twenty members of the hunt came to Westmoreland for a joint meet. The weather was about 30 degrees but warmed up during the day. The hounds ran well and they had a terrific hunt. The weekend was celebrated with a Hunt Ball given by the Rolling Rock Hunt on Friday at the Pittsburgh Club in the city of Pittsburgh, with 700 people attending.

Torrence Miller carefully recorded the following in his diary. The Joint Meet at Westmoreland with Rolling Rock on Thanksgiving 1926 was a clear day with a temperature of 30 degrees. The field of 37 had an invigorating hunt. Mr. Miller recorded the following riders—R. K. Mellon MFH, Rex and Dolly Flynn, Edith Patterson, M. McGriffon, D. Donnelly, James and Betty McKinney, J. Hess, J. Hamilton, Miss Preest, Mr. Gilder, Alan Scaife, George McCook, Edward McCague, Lucie Love, B. Walters, Mr. Thomas, Bob Waters, Elizabeth Laughlin, John Ricketson, Herbert May, Elizabeth and Jim Bovard, H. Coulter, Margaret Coulter, John Lawrence, A. C. Martin, George McNary, J. Stewart, Chuck Lynch, Walter Dowling, F. Schiller, B. Schiller and J. Kelly.

The mention of these 1926 foxhunters brings memories back to me, and it is fun to see their names listed. They obviously had a great time hunting together. This list also demonstrates how connected the members were within the various Western Pennsylvania hunts.

Another description from Mr. Miller's diary contains this observation: "The weather was not as cooperative when Westmoreland went to Rolling Rock for a joint meet on Armistice Day. It was only 20 degrees with a cold wind blowing. Although the hounds worked hard for five hours, the scenting was poor." I would think that the field of 50 must have experienced a disappointing day, but the fun they had the previous night at the Rolling Rock Club would have compensated for it. Plans for good hunting can easily be decimated by inclement weather.

The first year the Westmoreland Hunt Race Meet was held in 1926 on George McNary's Huntland Farm. The event was well covered by the newspapers. Besides the local people, members of the hunts from Pittsburgh, Indiana, Sewickley and Rolling Rock were invited to participate. There were two races over a regulation brush course—one for half-bred horses and the other for thoroughbreds. The other two races were for Farmers and one for Farmer's Sons. As an added attraction there was a Mule Race, which was pictured with a farmer persuading his white mule to cross the finish line at a fast walk.

In 1934 Westmoreland and Rolling Rock each shared a consecutive two days of racing, and the following year the entire race meet was held at Rolling Rock with the Westmoreland Cup, a two mile brush race, becoming an annual part of the program. When the two race meets combined, it was the beginning of the annual Rolling Rock Races, which developed into a truly notable race meet.

In 1932 Miss Margaret Coulter had become Master of the Hunt, and she provided good sport for the next 10 years. A small, soft-spoken lady, she knew how to do things properly. In 1942 with the advent of World War II, she did not wish to continue hunting. Torrence Miller again became Master and the hunt was put on a subscription basis. The field discarded their formal hunting attire for more somber colors, and the members pitched in as panel builders and whips.

The marvelous Lynch Field in Greensburg has always been a center of activity and is now a great sports center, well used by the community. It has a colorful history, starting with being the home of the Greensburg Driving Club from 1902–1909. The horse activity later evolved into polo, and it became the location of the Westmoreland Hunt stables and their annual horse show. Thomas Lynch, the owner of the field, had first come to Greensburg in 1889, excelled in the coal business and was a substantial member of the community. The Lynch family had 14 children, many of whom have remained in Greensburg to become pillars of the community.

Riding in the Westmoreland Hunt Horse Show in the 1930s created an indelible picture in my mind. It was held in September at the lovely Lynch Field in Greensburg and it was very festive. So many of my family's friends attended this picturesque event. There was a modest wooden grandstand, a nice tent for luncheon and refreshments, an outside course, and parking places around the ring which was made of sheep fencing. The passing trains on the elevated track of the Pennsylvania Railroad adjacent to the field added an unusual element to the scene but the horses quickly accepted its presence. Fred Emery, employed by the Coulter family, was perfectly turned out and acted as ringmaster in a kind but efficient manner. He was a fine man and an excellent horseman.

I can still picture Libby McNary (Weidlein) and her cousin, Libby Eireman (Slaughter), riding their large matching palomino ponies. I was green with envy. Bobby Martin (Watson, later O'Dell) rode lovely horses with beautiful soft efficiency. In my petulant way, I concluded that she beat me because she did not train her horses herself. How wrong I was. Bobby was a very good, subtle rider and she performed very well. I met with more success at the Westmoreland Horse Show when I started showing Miss Walker's *Lawn Fete*. This lovely small chestnut mare seldom made a mistake and deserved the admiration of the judges. My sister, Molly, rode the Mellon's show string in the hunter classes, and with her prowess and those quality horses, they were a hard combination to beat.

It is not surprising that the Westmoreland Hunt experienced wonderful years between 1923 and 1974. They had excellent leaders and a tight-knit group of loyal supporters. Sherwood C. Martin, the son of Arthur and Florabelle Martin and brother of Bobby, became a Joint Master with Mr. Miller for the season of 1949, but after he married Evie Thompson, he joined Evie as Joint Master of the Chestnut Ridge Hunt.

Dr. Ralph Lynch became Joint Master with Mr. Miller in 1951. Dr. Lynch was the youngest son of Thomas Lynch and never lost his loyalty to Greensburg. He and his charming wife Tommy lived in Fox Chapel to be closer to his practice at Mercy Hospital. They had been active in the Fox Chapel and Harts Run Hunts, but he responded when he was needed at Westmoreland. It was quite a commitment due to the 45 minute commute. When the Huntsman, G. Albright, retired in 1954, Dr. Lynch hunted the hounds. In 1956 Dr. Lynch broke his leg while skiing, and Eli Scurry, a local horseman, was persuaded to hunt the hounds.

The kennels for the hounds had changed several times. After Cabin Hill, they were moved to Lynch Field. The next move was to Union Cemetery Road and the final place for the Westmoreland Hunt stables and kennels was at Ralph and Sally Taylor's farm, which was located between the farms of the Martins and E. C. Bothwell.

Mr. Bothwell had worked for Gulf Oil Corporation and on his retirement he moved to Greensburg. He had always been interested in horses and had participated in the shows and hunts around Pittsburgh. When he moved to his new farm, Westmoreland Farm, he decided to raise Anglo-Cleveland horses to produce a large sensible hunter, and was helped in this endeavor by his capable trainer, Jack MacDonald. Mr. Bothwell was a nice, competent, large man who was supportive to the hunt in many ways. He ran the well-attended Westmoreland Horse Show on his farm, after the show was moved from Lynch Field, and his farm was also used for many Pony Club events. The setting was lovely and all of the events were beautifully run. The people of Greensburg knew how to pitch in to get things accomplished. His granddaughters, Merrily, Nikki and Susie Bachman (daughters of Vinnie Bothwell Bachman) were very active members of the Pony Club and the hunt.

Although Dr. Ralph Lynch kept up his practice, his real loves were sports and people. He was small in stature, and his intense blue twinkling eyes were shaded by bushy eyebrows. He was a superb raconteur and vitally interested in conversation. He was quick, intelligent, efficient and great fun. He was also a very talented writer.

My friend Becca Humphrey was so kind to let me copy a delightful letter that Dr. Lynch wrote to her mother. He had a marvelous sense of humor and expressed it in his eloquent writing. Dr. Ralph Lynch captured the fun of being in the Westmoreland Hunt Club in a letter he wrote, as membership Chairman, to a prospective non-hunting member, Mrs. John Barclay, Jr., on April 29, 1941:

> My Dear Mrs. Barclay:
>
> Miss Margaret Coulter, with whom, I believe, you are acquainted, has commissioned me to write you on the subject of a non-hunting membership in the Westmoreland Hunt.
>
> Doubtless you are already aware of the high character, and sterling worth of the members of this club, but I deem it my duty to point out one or two advantages that derive from membership in this organization.
>
> Membership in the Club will enable you to do your drinking in the presence of people who smell of horses, talk of horses, eat like horses and look like horses. And where else, Mrs. Barclay, could you indulge olfactory, auditory, gustatory, and visual sensation all at once and at the same time?
>
> Another advantage of membership is that it will give you contacts with widely divergent types of people. We have for example, within our membership, extremely tall persons (Mr. Dowling), extremely short persons (Mr. Miller), extremely fat persons (Mr. Hoffstot), extremely thin persons (Dr. Lynch), and one of the delightful features of the club is that at any of the formal meetings, you may see all of these widely divergent types, singing or fighting together—depending on the mood of the evening.
>
> Mood is stressed at the Club; in fact some of the members get so moody now and then, that they just go to sleep in the pantry.

As you majored in mood at Smith College, I should think that the club would be just the place for you, though, of course, you would not necessarily have to spend all your time in the pantry.

At the moment, I find myself a bit vague about the financial details involved in a non-hunting membership. I do know that a bona-fide check must be deposited in the lap of Miss Coulter before one is officially elected. But I cannot recall the exact amount of the check required.

I am sure, however, that Miss Coulter will know the correct amount, and as you are just the type of member we are looking for, I can promise you that Miss Coulter will pare costs to the bone, and put you in for strictly the lowest figure consistent with union scale. Proposed members are usually required to submit to an examination, and they must be passed as serviceably sound by Murray E. Patrick, V.M.D. However, Miss Coulter has decided to waive this in your case, so if you are a little over at the knees, it need not concern you in the least.

With pious and profound regards and with all good wishes including Happy Motoring.

Ralph Lynch
Chairman, The Membership Committee

Mrs. Henry K. Watson (Bobby Martin) became a Joint Master with Dr. Lynch in 1957. She is an exceptional lady. Bobby is beautiful, soft-spoken, indomitable, efficient, and charming, with a quick laugh. She sets high goals for herself and achieves them. When Dr. Lynch retired, Bobby hunted the hounds with Alice Mansmann as Joint Master and whipper-in. The children of these two ladies provided great support as whips. Libby McNary Weidlein was the hard working Honorary Secretary.

I had known Alice Walton Mansmann for years and she was an outstanding horsewoman, very capable and industrious. She and Bobby started the Westmoreland Hunt Pony Club in 1967 and did a fabulous job with the children. They encouraged the pony clubbers to become an efficient, hard working group, and they had a lot of success and still had great fun. These children enjoyed a marvelous experience and many became dedicated hunt members. It was a model of a good Pony Club.

Pony Club

There is no better description of the Westmoreland Pony Club than the information that George Weidlein, the son of Bob and Libby Weidlein, sent to me. It captures the essence of what an excellent pony club should be able to attain. George describes it well and these are his words:

> The Westmoreland Hunt Pony Club was my primary activity from the age of six until I went to college. My mother, Bobby Watson and Alice Mansmann started the group in the late 1950s. (The United States Pony Club was started in 1954.) From that time until we merged with Rolling Rock, there were mounted meetings twice a week during the summer and monthly meetings during the other months. The club had a very successful run, fielding winning teams at regional and national level competitions for years.

Random Thoughts

> Mounted meetings for riding instruction were complemented by special clinics where the club hosted some of the finest instructors in the country, many of them members of the United States Equestrian Team (USET).
>
> The club proudly produced 5 "A" level riders and about twice that number of "B" riders during its run.
>
> We were extremely fortunate to have the excellent organizational and horsemanship skills of the Mansmann family. Dick and Pat, two of our "A" riders gave tirelessly of their time and patience to coach and instruct, making the drive daily from Bakerstown during the summer months. They were often accompanied by their mother, Mrs. James Mansmann, or their sister Barbara. (Dick Mansmann is presently a successful practicing veterinarian in California.)
>
> When I was small, my mother would tack up three or four horses early in the morning and supervise a mule train of young riders from our farm to the Pony Club ring at the Taylor farm. Bobby Watson would do likewise. Then the lessons would begin. There were never enough horses, so one group would work on stable management while

the other took lessons, and after an hour they switched. I remember clouds and clouds of dust as we all practiced our walk, trot, canter and took some fences at the end.

A typical Pony Club summer started off with a two-day clinic with the visiting expert, then twice weekly mounted meetings for the general club, plus daily preparation for the Regional Rally in July. We worked on dressage and cross country fitness, had rigorous drilling from the Pony Club manual for the written exams and spent many an afternoon covering anything that didn't move with Purple Paint for our unforgettable tack-rooms. Following the Regional Rally, the teams spent time preparing young riders for the local "D" rallies held in August. The end of the summer featured a Pony Club Horse Show, organized by the club members. Some years we went on to add a one-day event, early in September. Club members and their parents cleared trails, designed courses, built fences, manned refreshment stands, set up speaker systems and worked non-stop to ensure a successful day.

The families who gave so much deserve to be mentioned. Aside from the Mansmanns, Watsons, and Weidleins, we would have perished without the Reeds, Shrivers, Humphreys, Jamisons, Carsons, Skelleys, Kelseys, Foxes, Paxtons, Shopes and Troys. They hauled horses, kids, and equipment spending countless hours and dollars to benefit the group.

I am not sure that it would be easy to recreate the club we had. For one thing, children now participate in so many activities. Most of the pony clubbers in my time had only one interest, horses. And the budget for additional activities was severely restricted. Plus it would be hard to find a rural setting of a small interlocking group where horses were the main interest.

During the fall and winter, most of the Pony Club turned to hunting. At Christmas time, there was a tea, usually at the Martins, where hunt members and pony clubbers gathered and awards were presented. "A"s and "B"s were recognized and colors were presented to the juniors who had earned them.

There were groups of pony clubbers before us in Greensburg and also groups that came after. Some blended in and out, but over some twenty active years in Greensburg, I would imagine no less than 200 youngsters had a taste of the Westmoreland Hunt Pony Club.

—George Weidlein

Pony Clubbers in George Weidlein's time:

Basset, Alison
Basset, Ruth
Boge, Marisa
Carson, Patty
Exton, Barbara
Exton, Marilynn
Fox, Janet
Gunter, Barbara
Harris, Patty
Herrington, Heidi
Humphrey, Peggy
Jamison, Connie
Kelsey, Craig
Kelsey, Mark
McLaughlin, Joseph
Poerio, Christine
Paxton, Linda
Paxton, Lisa
Quinn, Mary
Reed, Paul
Saddock, Jamie
Shope, Tim Kimmel
Shope, James
Steel, Sally
Shriver, Polly
Shriver, Maggie
Skelley, Candy
Troy, Alice
Watson, Kathy
Weidlein, George
Woodward, Susan

I want to emphasize George's great report on the Pony Club. The riders could progress through the classifications of D, C, B, and A. By the time a few of them become B's or A's, they were extremely knowledgeable and proficient horsemen. Westmoreland did such a superb job with its Pony Club members that quite a few attained B and A ratings.

It is the custom of most of the hunts in our area to have a "Spillwine" dinner at the end of the hunting season that officially closes at the end of March. Closing the season then enables the vixen to raise her family undisturbed. At the dinner anyone who had "parted company with their steed" during the season is required to bring a bottle of wine for the spill and sometimes a rider has to bring more than one bottle. It makes for a lively party and everyone has a really good time. I have included at the end of this chapter two delightful verses and a list of people attending the special Spillwine dinners of the Westmoreland Hunt.

The Westmoreland Hunt in Greensburg had enjoyed 58 years of good hunting. Unfortunately, with the development of their country and their shrinking membership, the hunt was faced with difficult choices about its future. It was sad, but necessary, when Abbie and Bobby resolved to continue the Westmoreland Hunt by merging it with Rolling Rock. In January of 1974 Alfred M. Hunt, Joint Master of Rolling Rock Hunt, officially welcomed the members of the Westmoreland Hunt to the new Rolling Rock–Westmoreland Hunt. Facilities were made available to keep the Westmoreland Hunt horses in the Colonial Stable of Rolling Rock Farms, or nearby stables. Alfred M. Hunt made the transition easy by observing, "We want you to feel the Rolling Rock–Westmoreland Hunt is as much your Hunt as was the Westmoreland Hunt."

Spillwine Dinners of the Westmoreland Hunt

The toasts at the Spillwine Dinners of the Westmoreland Hunt were memorable events, highlighted by homemade verse delivered by the Masters. Here is the opening of the 1968 toast, composed by Bobby Watson and typed by her Joint Master, Alice Mansmann:

> 'Tis the night of the spill wine & tux here at the club
> We are all assembled in optional tux
> Our Popsei has DONE it—we all knew she would
> Reservations & flowers, the food—extra good
> For the wine we thank you who sat in the mud
> By next year some others will land with a thud . . .
>
> Dr. Lynch was our master for many a season
> How we did love him not without reason
> But Alice and I resting up for next year
> Thank all of you riders who went without fear
> Over fences, wet fields, *new* lawns & even after deer
> Silvia Fink, the two Freds are always good friends
> With farmers and landowners they help make amends. . . .

Here is the Master's Toast at the 1970 Spillwine Dinner:

> What do we simple folk do
> To help us escape when we're blue?
> The Doctors who are ailing
> The housewives who are glum
> The students who are waiting—just thinking they're dumb.
> We find relief in a clever way
> Hunting at Westmoreland brightens up our day.
>
> Thru rain and sun gray skies and blue
> We'll rather ride than work, it's true
> That's what simple folks do
> To perk up their hearts and get thru

When all the doldrums begin
What keeps each of us in our skin
This ancient native custom
Provides the needed glow
So that's what we simple folks do or did you know.

Names from Spillwine Dinner 1969—Mrs. Henry K. Watson and Mrs. James A. Mansmann: Joint Masters, Ed Mullan (Hunt Secretary and Field Master), Barb Mansmann, Butch Goodman (2 whips), Robert B. Weidlein (President), Emma R. Exton, Carole McDaniels, Mrs. Martin (Popsie) Saddock, Dr. Roland K. Stickler and Dr. William B. Shope helped in maintaining the hunting country, Helen Johnson, George Weidlein, Tim Kimmel Shope, Heidi Herrington, Janet Fox, Maggie and Polly Shriver, Paul A. Reed, Patricia Mansmann, Margaret B. (Peggy) Humphrey, Connie Jamison, Suzanne Bachman, Elizabeth Rial, Robert Davis, Judith Ware and Katherine M. Watson. Social Members: Fred Emery, Edgar C. Bothwell, Mrs. A. C. Martin, Mrs. George R. McNary and S. Silvis Fink.

1970 additions—Erika and Roland Strickland, William B. Shope, Candice Skelley and Frank Shabella.

Spillwine 1971—Mrs. Henry K. Watson, Mrs. James A. Mansmann (Joint Masters); Mrs. Henry, Helen Johnson, Mrs. Burk Kelsy, Martha Deemer, Lisa A. Paxton, Rebecca Lula; Dr. Roland Stickler (President); Ed Mullan (Horse Show advertising chairman and Field Master); Robert B. Weidlein (Horse Show announcer); Polly and Maggie Shriver, Janet Fox, Nancy and Peter King, James P. Shope, Patty Carson, Linda Paxton, Susan Woodward, Courtney Sellers, Robert Carson, Paul A. Reed, George M. Weidlein, Margaret B. Humphrey, Connie Jamison, Heidi Herrington and Barbara Gunter.

Social members—Dr. and Mrs. Alan W. Shriver, Mr. and Mrs. Martin Saddock, Martha Warren, Mr. and Mrs. Edgar L. Paxton, Mr. and Mrs. Robert Gunter, Mrs. A. C. Martin, Mrs. George R. McNary and Mr. and Mrs. Robert B. Weidlein.

1973 Westmoreland Hunt Roster

Dr. Ralph Lynch
Mrs. H. K. Watson
Edward Mullan
Helen I. Johnson
Mrs. G. Wm. Exton
Frank Shabella
Mrs. John K. Tabor
Robert Troy
Mrs. Gary Rosenthal
Mrs. Barbara Silk
S. Silvis Fink

Junior Roster

Kathy Watson
George Weidlein
Peggy Humphrey
Polly Shriver
Maggie Shriver
Patricia Carson
Paul Reed
Kerry Warren
Joseph McLaughlin
Alice Troy

Family membership: Dr. and Mrs. James A. Mansmann, Barbara, Patty and Dr. Richard Mansmann.

Social: Mrs. A. C. Martin, Mrs. G. R. McNary, Mrs. R. B. Weidlein, Dr. and Mrs. Alan Shriver, Mr. and Mrs. Arthur Warren, Mr. Edward Sapone, Mr. and Mrs. E. L. Paxton and Mr. and Mrs. E. C. Gunther.

Westmoreland Hunt
MFHA Data

1916 Master: Julian B. Huff.

1920 Master: Torrence Miller.

1924 Hon. Sec.: Margaret Coulter. Huntsman: (prof) Jack Potter. Whippers-in: (prof) P. Albright.

1925 Whippers-in: (prof) P. Albright and (prof) A. Fletcher.

1926 Whippers-in: (prof) P. Albright and (prof) F. Emery.

1932 Master: Miss Margaret Coulter. Hon. Sec: Joseph P. Wentling. Huntsman: (prof) G. Albright. Whippers-in: (prof) F. Emery.

1936 Whippers-in: (prof) F. Emery and (prof) Archie Leone.

1942 Master: Torrence Miller. Hon. Sec: A. C. Martin. Huntsman: (prof) Geary Albright. Whippers-in: (prof) Joe Dascoglis.

1946 Whippers-in: (prof) Charles Topes.

1949 Jt. Masters: Torrence Miller (1942) and Sherwood C. Martin, Jr.

1951 Masters: Torrence Miller and Dr. Ralph Lynch. Hon. Sec: Torrence Miller. President: E. C. Bothwell.

1953 Hon. Sec: Mrs. Robert Weidlein. Huntsman: (prof) Geary Albright. Whippers-in: Hon. Mrs. James Mansmann and S. Silvis Fink.

1954 Whippers-in: S. Silvis Fink.

1955 Whippers-in: S. Silvis Fink, Mrs. James A. Mansmann and Anna Mary Koppitz.

1956 Masters: Torrence Miller and Dr. Ralph Lynch. Huntsman: (prof) Eli Scuri.

1957 Masters: Dr. Ralph Lynch and Mrs. Henry K. Watson. Huntsman: Dr. Lynch. Whippers-in: S. Silvis Fink and Mrs. James A. Mansmann.

1957 After 29 years of Mastership, Torrence Miller resigns.

1961 Dr. Ralph Lynch retires.

1962 Mrs. Henry K. Watson: Master and Huntsman. Hon. Sec: Mrs. Robert Weidlein. Whippers-in: Mrs. James A. Mansmann, Miss Barbara Mansmann and Junior Whip Knox Watson and (prof) Gerry Boyle. Kennelman: (prof) Gerry Boyle.

1962 Whippers-in: Mrs. James A. Mansmann and Eli Scuri.

1964 Whippers-in: Mrs. James A. Mansmann, Richard Mansmann and Junior Whip Knox Watson.

1965 Whippers-in: Mrs. James A. Mansmann, Barbara Mansmann, Junior Whip Knox Watson and (prof) Gerry Boyle.

1966 Masters: Mrs. Henry Watson and Mrs. James A. Mansmann. Hon. Sec: Mrs. B. W. Kelsey. Whippers-in: Mrs. James A. Mansmann and Barbara Mansmann.

1967 Whippers-in: Barbara Mansmann.
1969 Hon. Sec: Helen Johnson. Whippers-in: Barbara Mansmann and (prof) Byron Goodman.
1970 Whippers-in: Barbara Mansmann and (prof) Byron Goodman.
1974 Westmoreland merges with Rolling Rock.

Jolly Bassett

Chestnut Ridge Hunt

Est. 1932

1942–1974

Uniform: Scarlet with white collar. Evening: Scarlet with white facings. Button: Gold "C.R.H."
Foxhounds: 6 couples American (Baily's Hunting Directory, *1933*).
Foxhounds: 15 couples American (Baily's Hunting Directory, *1950*).
*Country hunted is approximately 22 by 28 miles. Rolling pasture lands, woodlands and waste lands; chicken coops, post and rail, worm fences and stone walls (*The Chronicle of the Horse, *September 25, 1953).*

The Thompson family was synonymous with the Chestnut Ridge Hunt in Fayette County. The hunt was originated by Andrew Thompson, but as his son Mark Thompson aptly said, "The heart and soul of the Chestnut Ridge Hunt from 1939 until her death in 1974 was Evelyn Thompson."

Uniontown, the county seat, is approximately 50 miles southeast of Pittsburgh. The area did play an interesting role in the early history of western Pennsylvania. The nearby Fort Necessity is the site of George Washington's defeat by French and Indian forces, but he and his remaining men were permitted to retreat under the terms of surrender. The Cumberland Road was the well-traveled road to Pittsburgh, the gateway to the West. The Washington Inn (now a museum on Route 40) was a famous coach stop for weary travelers. Later, Uniontown became a thriving center of the coke and coal industry, largely developed by Josiah Van Kirk Thompson, Evelyn Thompson's grandfather.

The Chestnut Ridge Hunt was established in 1932 by J. V. Thompson's son Andrew. It began at the Lazy Hour Ranch in Dunbar, 10 miles north of Uniontown. Bert Cence, an affable, industrious man, who owned and farmed this large property, was the Huntsman. He had previously been the Huntsman for the Pittsburgh Hunt. It was a drag hunt and the surrounding farmland was open to the hunt. After 22 years there, Evie Thompson, the MFH, moved the hunt to Friendship Hill in New Geneva, Pa. where they hunted live fox.

My friend Mark Thompson remembers, "My father was interested in hunting, fishing and shooting. He rode horses all of his life and was interested in foxhunting as a boy. He hunted at Rolling Rock a lot and was a close friend of Dick Mellon. He hunted with the Pittsburgh Hunt too."

I remember the Lazy Hour Ranch because I went to several excellent horse shows there. At the end of this chapter I have included a list of the two-day horse show in 1939. It is an impressive list of people participating from other hunts, and includes the names of Chestnut Ridge members on the committee. I was surprised to see my sister Molly listed as secretary. Molly was a good friend of the Thompsons, but being a secretary was not a typical role for her.

Andrew Thompson's children became involved with the hunt, and they took their turn as Masters. It was his daughter Evie who became the key figure in the success of the hunt. The hunt gained in stature and uniqueness when Evie moved it to Friendship Hill in 1954.

In 1941 Evie moved from Fox Hill in Uniontown to the estate of Friendship Hill that her grandfather J. V. Thompson had purchased in 1910. Evie started a dairy operation there, and her friend Helen Shaw (Roberts) helped her run the farm for a couple of years. Evie truly loved living in this old house but it presented interesting problems because of its age, and its historical significance as the home of Albert Gallatin.

Albert Gallatin, a Swiss immigrant, bought the land in 1788 and built the original brick house in 1789 to receive his bride Sophia Allegre, who sadly died five months later. Gallatin married Hannah Nicholson and he added a frame addition to make room for his growing family. He loved Friendship Hill and the New Geneva area, but sold the house in 1832. Gallatin made significant contributions to his adopted country in the fields of finance, politics, diplomacy and scholarship. He is best known as serving as Secretary of the Treasury under Presidents Thomas Jefferson and James Madison.

Josiah V. Thompson had acquired Friendship Hill after it passed through several owners. J. V. was very successful as a banker and was in the coal business. At his peak, he was reported to be worth 70 million dollars. He married Mary Anderson and they had two sons, Andrew and John. In 1889 he became President of the First National Bank, gaining tremendous respect and confidence in the community for his brilliance and control of coal properties. Fayette County was the zenith of the Coke Region, producing a superior commodity that was in great demand in the surrounding industrial areas. Josiah's civic and business accomplishments are duly recorded in *Cloud By Day*, written by Muriel Earley Sheppard, who knew and loved the Uniontown area.

Unfortunately his wife, Mary, died in 1896 and J. V. became a workaholic, building his empire. According to his family, his demise commenced with his marriage to Hunnie Hawes, who loved spending his money. In 1903 they took a fifteen-month honeymoon trip to Europe and Hunnie had a field day acquiring anything that took her fancy to furnish their new mansion on the outskirts of Uniontown. In time, Oak Hill became an opulent showplace, but Hunnie was never completely accepted. In 1913 they were divorced. The "walls came tumbling down" on J. V. after his million dollar settlement to Hunnie, and his creditors, waiting like vultures, foreclosed on his extended properties. Bankruptcy was declared in 1919, but despite this J. V. never lost his optimistic point of view.

I feel privileged to have known his granddaughter Evie Thompson (Mrs. Sherwood Martin) from the numerous horse events in which we both participated—shows, hunting, and point-to-points. Evie was a wonderful person, loved and respected for her capabilities and true sportsmanship. She was small in stature with a brown, weathered face, twinkling eyes and a spontaneous smile. She was a very special person and deserved her accolades.

Her brother Mark was closer to my age and we had lots of fun together. It was a special treat when Mark would invite me for a hunting weekend at Friendship Hill. This was truly an amazing place, not only because of its historical background, but also for the remarkable manner in which Evie coped with the innumerable tasks involved. She managed the working farm, ran the Chestnut Ridge Hunt, and after the hunts threw great parties with drinks and food for the multitudes.

Evie was ably assisted by Fred Newton (Newt), who had been with the family for years. Newt was a small sprightly Englishman who seemed completely undisturbed by the overwhelming functions. The parties lasted well into the night, and there was little concern about the treatment of the valuable antiques spread throughout the house. I remember that there was electricity in the kitchen, but the remainder of the house was illuminated by candles or kerosene lamps. It was amusing that on certain days the house was open to the public, with ropes cordoning off the rooms and "please do not touch" signs placed all about. Everyone who had spent the night had to make the bed properly, hide their belongings, and put in place the rope that protected the room. The tourists enjoyed their tour through the interesting house, oblivious to all the previous activities. It was incredible—only Evie and Newt could have coped with such a double standard.

In 1950 Evie married Sherwood Martin, the son of Mr. and Mrs. A. C. Martin, who had been an MFH of the Westmoreland Hunt in Greensburg. They were blessed with three children, Flora Belle, Fredericka, and Sherwood III. The indispensable Newt helped raise the children along with his other duties. Although the house opened to tourists in 1946 under the auspices of the Friendship Hill Association, it did not become a Historic Site until 1954.

Evelyn Thompson Martin described her life at Friendship Hill in a newspaper interview ("Life in a Landmark" by George Swetnam, *The Pittsburgh Press*, Sunday, Sept. 12, 1965):

> Life in the historic mansion, she said, had its drawbacks. When asked how she enjoyed it, she would say to people, "You mean what a gas it

is to having the whole world trying to get in or look over the transom?" After the building was accorded the status as a National Landmark in 1965, Evie Thompson dealt with the problems as well as the pleasure of owning a famous man's home. She laughed about the time she was wheedled by a chapter of the Daughters of the American Revolution into letting them have a tea at the home. They planned for 30 guests, but 600 showed up, leading to a call from the state police to ask what was going on.

When the house was first opened to the public in 1955, many of the small artifacts fell prey to tourists who wanted to collect antiques. Many of their dinner parties were interrupted by enthusiastic tourists, who thought the party was part of the tour and would help themselves to the buffet. Evie learned how to regulate visiting hours.

A large part of the mansion was not used by the family, and was kept under wraps. She and her sons had major cleaning to do when the house opened to the public. Like many old houses, she recalled, "In the winter it's drafty, and in the summer there is a shortage of water—not that it is plentiful at other times. What running water there is in the house is by no means potable. Jugs must be filled at a spring below the hill and carried to the kitchen."

But the pleasures were also great for Sherwood Martin and his wife Evie and their three children. They lived very close to nature, and she felt that at Friendship Hill her children had a beneficial exposure to life. By the nature of their existence on the farm the children became knowledgeable about many things, and proficient at many tasks. She saw it as a life unlimited in opportunities for learning, for self-development and self-realization.

Apart from foxhunting, daily life was according to Evie, "Pretty much what anyone would expect on any 800-acre farm. Our Guernsey herd, containing over 200 cows, calves, and bulls, was one of the oldest such herds in the state, requiring constant maintenance. Our 20 horses and ponies must be fed and worked. Our 40 foxhounds must be cared for and exercised. Our house pets—two Irish wolfhounds, a miniature poodle, and a Siamese cat—also require our attention."

But foxhunting was special to Evie. "Perhaps dearest to my own heart is the opportunity we have to continue the time-honored tradition of

> foxhunting. For the last ten years [this was 1965] the hounds of the Chestnut Ridge Hunt have made their home with us. And every year, from the first of October to the first of May, we have pursued this ancient sport of sports. The cry of the hounds, the strident sound of the horn, the rhythm of the horses' hooves, and the colorful sight of the scarlet coats and black caps have become a part of life at Friendship Hill."
>
> "In the evening we have enjoyed the pleasant company of many of our hunting friends gathered together around the long table under the candlelit chandelier in the dining room, or around the piano in the music room, or before the warm fire in the sitting room. This has meant so much to me and my family that in my mind Friendship Hill and foxhunting are forever intertwined."

In 1953 Evie and Sherwood had moved the hounds and their horses to Friendship Hill. Bob Neff was their kennelman and whippers-in, and the hunt stables were at Old Frame, the farm owned by Bill and Jody Balling. The Ballings were a great help to the hunt in many ways—as secretary and whippers-in. Jody also took on the responsibility of the Chestnut Ridge Pony Club and did a great job.

Mark Thompson remembers, "The Hunt was very fortunate to have three fine gentlemen who served as secretary in a very dedicated way—Issay Horwitz, of Connellsville (1932–1946), William S. Jenkins, of Frostburg, Maryland (1946–1958) and C. William Balling, from Old Frame Farm (1958–1947). In addition to the enthusiastic membership, many people had the pleasure of hunting as guests at Chestnut Ridge and they were assured of having a good time."

Mark recalls, "We always hunted live fox at Friendship Hill. Our country could be classified as 'rough.' People knew they needed a good horse to handle Chestnut Ridge because it was 'trappy' country—with fences in odd places so a horse had to be able to jump off his hocks. The horse also had to be clever on his feet to go up and down the steep slopes." It was challenging hunting country.

The Chestnut Ridge Hunt attracted many visitors. Abbie Hunt would hunt with Rolling Rock on Saturday and hunt with Evie on Sunday; Posie

Boyd would hunt at Sewickley and the next day she came up to Chestnut Ridge; they often had Bill Hanley, Johnny Slaughter and Helen and Joe Roberts, among others.

Joe Roberts described one amazing trail near the Friendship Hill mansion, perched on the heights above the Monongahela River. "You had 10 to 15 people in the field and when you followed them to the end of this log, suddenly the horse in front of you would disappear. It was scary to see a horse turn left and vanish from sight. You then realized there was a hairpin turn on the trail as you started to drop sharply down towards the river. You had to zigzag back and forth until you reached it. Every time you took that trail your heart would start pounding."

Another delightful description was written by Robert Gigliotti, a member of the Chestnut Ridge Hunt (and later a member of the Rolling Rock Hunt). He published his recollections in *The Chronicle of the Horse* (December 22, 1972), of a hunt in December, 1967, that he never forgot. At that time he was part of a joint hunt at Chestnut Ridge with the Rolling Rock Hunt, and he recalls the charm of Friendship Hill, and the features of the country:

> It was in late December, after success in finding one fox, that Rolling Rock Huntsman Lovell Stickley cast his hounds again and soon got up another fox, which in contrast to the first fox led them on a strenuous four-mile chase. The "Hounds went screaming through covert and open fields, down dirt lanes and along paved roads, ending in a complex of coal stripping cuts on the Smithfield-New Geneva road, where the hounds marked their fox to ground in one of the many earths of this most difficult part of our country.
>
> At the end of the day the hunters returned "under a full moon that illuminated the frosty landscape" to Friendship Hill. "There, in the glow of wax candle candelabra, friends toasted good hounds, good horses, good friends, good foxes of today and other days." The toasting over, the members adjourned to the dining room. "The candles burned brightly in their crystal chandeliers, there was a glitter of silver and glassware on the table, and ruddy faces still glowed from the excitement of the hunt and from the day's cold. Hunters threaded their

way around the table in their pink coats, and hunt buttons gleamed in the candlelight. There was a clatter of glasses and plates and knives, and the sounds of eager talk from several conversations. It was a time to be long remembered.

On Thursday, December 21st, the same fox was suddenly started again. Now the hunters called him affectionately "the Four O'clock Fox" because of the time the hounds regularly got him up. He eluded them again that day. But then, on the day before Christmas, the hounds picked up his line once more. It was a clear, cold 26-degree day, and the fox led them on an exhausting chase. "We went through field after field, and covert after covert," and over post and rail, and back and forth across the same highway until the hounds were lost. The maddening pattern was finally ended "as a view holloa was raised by hilltoppers, in cars parked on the side of a road about a quarter of a mile away." Galloping to the view they glimpsed the very tired fox climbing up the almost sheer side of a coal strip called the "high wall." The hounds lost him again, and during the confusion "the music was almost deafening after it echoed off the surrounding hilltops." Finally, "a cry went up as someone pointed halfway up the sixty-foot face about fifty feet ahead of us. There, our auburn-coated pilot, the Four O'clock Fox in all his glory, rested condescendingly on a slim rocky ledge, a safe thirty feet below the hounds and an equally safe thirty feet above the hunt. . . . A few brave hounds tried to get down the sheer face to him, but rolled harmlessly past him, head over tail, landing at our horse's feet."

Agreeing that it was a most successful and unusual hunt, and the strangest "Gone to Ground" that Chestnut Ridge had ever seen, the hounds were called off, with the special hope that they could run the Four O'clock Fox another day.

—Robert Gigliotti

After the death of Evelyn Thompson Martin, the Chestnut Ridge Hunt disbanded in 1974, but I am happy to say that Will and Pam Thompson Burkland, the daughter of Mark and Patty, have moved their family to Ligonier. They have three boys, Stewart, Elliot, and Ian, who are good riders and the family hunts with Rolling Rock. Also Mark Thompson, Jr. and his wife, Shelley with their boys, Bert and Peter, are staunch hunting members and trailer to the meets from Uniontown. It is wonderful to have so many Thompsons still devoted to the sport.

Of all the hunts in Western Pennsylvania, Chestnut Ridge was the most unique. I am indebted to G. Markle Thompson, who contributed so much to the description of the hunt. Evie was a magnetic person whose love and dedication to foxhunting attracted many people. Her hospitality, and the aura of the Friendship Hill setting, provided her guests with indelible memories.

Chestnut Ridge Hunt MFHA Data

1932 Master: Andrew A. Thompson.

1934 Hon. Sec.: Mary R. Thompson. Huntsman: Robert Herron. Whippers-in: J. V. Kirk Thompson, Thos. M. Whyle, Evelyn L. Thompson and James Hustead Semans.

1933 Hon. Sec.: J. L. Hankins. Huntsman: B. C. Cence. Whippers-in: J. V. Kirk Thompson, Thos. M. Whyle, Evelyn L. Thompson and James Hustead Semans.

1935 Hon. Sec.: Mrs. Wendell Stone. Huntsman: (prof) B. C. Cence; Whippers-in: J. V. Kirk Thompson, Thos. M. Whyle, Evelyn L. Thompson and G. F. Rieman.

1936 Joint Masters: Mrs. Mary R. Thompson and Thomas H. Whyle. Hon. Sec.: Miss Fredi Thompson. Huntsman: (prof) B. C. Cence. Whippers-in: Hon. J. V. Kirk Thompson, Evelyn L. Thompson, G. F. Rieman and Wendell Stone.

1937 Joint Masters: Miss Mary R. Thompson and G. Fred Rieman. Whippers-in: J. V. Kirk Thompson, Evelyn L. Thompson and Wendell Stone.

1939 Master and Huntsman: Miss Evelyn Thompson. Hon. Sec.: I. L. Horewitz. Whippers-in: Fred Baer and Mark Thompson.

1940 Joint Masters: G. Fred Rieman and Evelyn L. Thompson. Whippers-in: Miss Posey Boyd, Miss Helen B. Shaw and Mark Thompson. Huntsman: (prof) Ralph Taylor. Whippers-in: Miss Posey Boyd, Mark Thompson and Fred Baer.

1947 Master and Huntsman: Evelyn L. Thompson. Whippers-in: Miss Elizabeth McNary, G. Markle Thompson and Fred Baer.

1949 Master and Huntsman: Evelyn L. Thompson. Joint Master: Mark Thompson. Whippers-in: Fred Baer and Susan Walker.

1950 Masters and Huntsman: Mrs. S. C. Martin and G. Markle Thompson. Whippers-in: Mrs. Susan Walker and Fred Baer.

1951 Masters and Huntsman: Mrs. S. C. Martin. Joint Master: Mr. S. C. Martin. Hon. Sec.: William S. Jenkins. Whippers-in: Mrs. Susan P. Walker, Fred Baer and G. Markle Thompson.

1952 Whippers-in: Mrs. Susan P. Walker, Fred Baer and James Fuller.

1954 Whippers-in: Mrs. Susan P. Walker, Fred Baer, Miss Joanne Bygate and William Balling.

1956 Whippers-in: Fred Baer and Mr. and Mrs. William Balling.

1957 Whippers-in: Mr. and Mrs. William Balling and Donald Andrade.

1958 Masters and Huntsman: Mrs. S. C. Martin. Joint Master: G. Markle Thompson. Whippers-in: Mr. and Mrs. William Balling and Donald Andrade.

1960 Whippers-in: William Balling, Donald Andrade and Ernest Beglin.

1962 Whippers-in: William Balling, Ernest Beglin and (prof) Robert Neff.

1965 Joint Masters: Mrs. Sherwood C. Martin and Mr. William S. Jenkins. Hon. Sec.: C. William Balling. Huntsman: Mr. and Mrs. Sherwood C. Martin. Whippers-in: William Balling, Ernest Beglin, Dr. N. W. Brian Craythorn and (prof) Robert Neff.

1966 Whippers-in: C. William Balling, Dr. N. W. Brian Craythorn and (prof) Robert Neff.

1967 Joint Masters: Mrs. Sherwood C. Martin and G. Markle Thompson. Hon. Sec.: C. William Balling. Huntsman: Mr. and Mrs. Sherwood C.

Martin. Whippers-in: Miss Carolyn Martin, Dr. N. W. Brian Craythorn and (prof) Robert Neff.

1968 Whippers-in: Miss Carolyn Martin and Susie Steidling.

1969 Whippers-in: Miss Carolyn Martin, Miss Flora Belle Martin and Miss Susie Steiding.

1970 Whippers-in: Miss Carolyn Martin, Miss Flora Belle Martin and Robert Gigliotti.

1971 Huntsman: Mrs. Sherwood C. Martin.

1972 Huntsman: Mrs. Sherwood C. Martin and G. Markle Thompson. Whippers-in: Flora Belle Martin and Robert Gigliotti.

1974 Master: G. Markle Thompson. The Chestnut Ridge Hunt becomes inactive as of August, 1974 and does not plan to hunt its country in the 1974–1975 season.

Chestnut Ridge Horse Show

From *Chronicle of the Horse* Aug. 25, 1939; 2 days; 106 horses

Hunter Division Judges

O'Mally Knott of New York

Murray P. Fleming of Canada

Draft Horse Division Judges

R. K. Mellon, MFH of Rolling Rock

George P. McNary of Greensburg

Officials of Horse Show

Evelyn L. Thompson—Chairman
G. Fred Rieman—Vice Chairman
Molly Hays—Secretary
Bertram C. Cence—Manager

Dutch White—Ringmaster
R. L. Dolan—Veterinarian, Uniontown
F. N. Sherrick—Veterinarian, Connellsville

Chestnut Ridge Hunt Committee

Mrs. W. B. Parshall—President
R. B. Wood—Vice President
J. L. Horewitz—Secretary Treasurer
Mrs. Wyley Byers, Jr.
J. L. Hankins
Lida B. Lanahan
James McGee
George Paul
W. B. Parshall
Mary R. Thompson
Mrs. H. G. Thorndike
Thomas M. Whyel

Stronger

Dutch Fork Hunt

Est. 1968

1970–1979

Hunt livery and colors: Black melton, scarlet; colors: Burgundy.
Foxhounds: 30 couples American, 1 couple English, 1 couple Cross-bred.
Hunt country consists of a part of Washington County, Pa., and Brook and Ohio Counties, West Virginia, comprising an area approximately 10 miles by 10 miles consisting of hilly farmlands and woodlands. Paneling is in process at present. Fences consist of coops and posts and rails (Baily's Hunting Directory).
Hunting colors: burgundy.
Hounds: American, 7 couples.
Kennels: West Alexander, Pa.
Season: October 1–March 31, Tuesdays and Sundays.
Hunt Country: Hunt country consists of all Washington County, and part of Green County, Pennsylvania, and all of Brook and Ohio Counties, comprising an area approximately 50 by 30 miles, consisting of extremely hilly farmland and woodlands. Paneling is in process at the present time (1969). Fences consist of coops and post and rails.

Unfortunately I have no personal knowledge of this hunt, but I feel that they have the right to be included in this history of western

Pennsylvania hunts. As we all know, it takes a great deal of effort to establish a hunt and it is impressive that they gained recognition. I gather from friends that they held horse shows and were invited to participate in Joint Meets with other hunts. They must have had a good time and I apologize for my lack of knowledge.

Dutch Fork Hunt
MFHA Data

Joint Masters: James D. Ashton and Phillip Falconi
Honorary Secretary: Mrs. James D. Herron
Whippers-in: Caroline T. Ashton, Michael Burke and (prof) Steve Neff
Kennelman: Porter King

1970 Masters: Caroline T. Ashton and Michael Burke. Hon. Sec.: Mrs. James D. Herron. Huntsman: (prof) Robert Neff. Whippers-in: Susan Craig and (prof) Debbie Pforsich.

1971 Masters: James A. Ashton and Caroline T. Ashton. Whippers-in: Jimmy Ashton, (prof) Janet Smith and (prof) Janet Smith.

1972 Masters: James A. Ashton, Caroline T. Ashton and Jack Kalkreuth. Hon. Sec.: Dr. Lynn Herron. Whippers-in: Jimmy Ashton and Hon. Randy Mullens.

1973 Masters: James A. Ashton and Caroline T. Ashton. Hon. Sec.: Lee C. Paull, III. Whippers-in: Dort Dickinson and Ellen McFarland.

1975 Masters: James A. Ashton and Eric Halverson. Huntsman: Mr. Ashton. Whippers-in: Jack Adamson and Jennifer Ruffolo.

1976 Master: Mrs. Ellen Holdsworth.

1977 Master: James A. Ashton. Hon. Sec.: Luana Beinhauer. Whippers-in: Jack Adamson, Luana Beinhauer and Megan Sandercox.

1979 The hunt was inactive during the 1979–1980 season.

Saxonburg Hunt

Est. 1976

1987–1997

Uniform: Scarlet, Kelly green collar with navy piping. Evening: scarlet with Kelly green.
Foxhounds: 22 couples American.
The country is farmland, pasture and woodland. Paneled with board panels, coops, gates and telephone pole jumps.

The Saxonburg Hunt was established by E. P. Moriarty in 1976 on his farm in Saxonburg, Pennsylvania, located 25 miles northwest from the former Hart's Run Hunt area. The Saxonburg Hunt country was approximately eight-miles square in the townships of Clinton, Jefferson and Middlesex in Butler County. It was mostly open farmland, with grain and grass farms, and small 10-acre wood lots on two of the farms. Paneling consisted of mostly coops and panels, and there were natural divisions provided by the terrain and creeks.

Recently I had the pleasure of listening to Barbara and Buss Moriarty and hearing his description of the Saxonburg Hunt. When he established his hunt I was living in Ligonier, and did not know this dynamic man other than by his reputation. Buss had been in the lumber business, and acquired a beautiful farm in Saxonburg. He was a leader in the Pennsylvania Horseman's Association, offered his farm for Pony Club Rallies, and held many other excellent horse events at Moriarty Farm. After he had two knee replacements, it was difficult but necessary for him to give up his farm and his great interest in horses.

We talked about the problems that hunt committees often create, and with a soft smile, Buss said, "It was advantageous for me to have the power of a dictator, listening to suggestions but doing things my own way." There is no doubt that it simplifies running a hunt if one can afford to own a private pack.

He also lent me some snapshots of the hunt. I was pleased to see a photograph of Peggy Skinner, who was a staunch supporter of the Harts Run Hunt. Peggy supplied me with many details of that hunt, and Buss was very complimentary of this efficient lady.

I am grateful to Buss for writing the following description of how he started his own hunt—which was a very big undertaking.

The Saxonburg Hunt, by E. P. Moriarty

> I was raised with the love of foxhunting. My father, E. P. Moriarty, Sr., rode with the Pittsburgh Hunt. I was also a member of the Harts Run Hunt for several years and our children Mike and Adele also rode with that hunt.
>
> The Bancroft family were unable to continue running the Harts Run Hunt and in 1976 the hunt was disbanded. I then decided to start the Saxonburg Hunt, and drafted four couples from the Harts Run Hunt and three couples from Rolling Rock. Our hunt started as an unrecognized farmer's pack. My dear wife Barbara was not a rider but she gladly accepted the role of hunt secretary for several years. As the hunt grew, Barbara provided a delicious soup and her homemade bread for our guests on Sunday afternoons. It was not until 1985 that I began the paperwork for registering the hunt, and in 1987 it was registered.
>
> When we started our project, we accepted the excellent advice of Tod Addis, V.M.D., from Philadelphia, to have our kennels and runs attached to the stable. This enabled the hounds to be a part of the daily stable schedule, and it proved to be a healthy arrangement for all concerned.

I never regretted this decision, but I must admit that taking care of a pack of hounds took a total commitment. The exacting hours required for feeding, cleaning the kennels, breeding, exercising and training the hounds took a dedication that was fully repaid by their response. I am indebted to the support of my family and the help of other hunting members as we maintained our pack and improved our facilities. I loved working with the hounds and will never forget the unique experience.

Drag hunting was standard for the Saxonburg Hunt from 1976 to 1980. Our son Mike and I originally laid the drag until Mike left for college. Mike was also whipper-in during this time, cleaned the kennels and exercised the hounds with me. After Mike left, I planned and laid the drag for the day. The lively way of drag hunting lost its appeal and in 1980 we started live foxhunting. Four couples of hounds were drafted from Rombout Hunt in upper New York, and three couples from Tryon, North Carolina. It was fascinating to learn this sport and to watch the diligent hounds work. Every outing was a challenge.

The Saxonburg Hunt went out three days a week: Tuesdays, Thursdays, and Sundays. We learned that Saturdays should be reserved for the farmers to hunt game. The presence of our hounds was apt to stir up the game, and Sunday suited us just as well.

Our fields were small during the week, but on Sunday we would have an average of 12 riders. As a small private pack, we invited guests from Erie, and Sewickley, Pennsylvania, and Bath and Chagrin in Ohio. Some of the names that come to my mind: Buzz Anderson, Charlie and Jimmy Arensberg, Mary Armstrong, Karen Chabal, Ray Firestone, Al Gordon, Joan Goswell, Dr. Hansen, Kim Hay, Colleen Hofstetter, Nancy King, Lloyd McKlintock, Michael Moriarty, Linda Moyes, Dr. Guy Pietz, V.M.V., Lois Sarver, Peggy Skinner, Dr. John Stremple, and Katie Wilson. Ray Firestone often brought a group with him from his Bath Hunt, in Ohio.

I regularly visited the farmers and township landowners regarding permission to travel over their fields and along their property. Barbara and the whippers-in delivered goodies to many of the landowners during the holiday season as a small thank-you for the use of the land during the foxhunting season.

The guests of the hunt offered many compliments about how well the hounds worked, and how enjoyable the open and natural terrain was to hunt. The 70 or so landowners not only granted us the right, but also enjoyed watching and following the hunt, which offered great sport and was a terrific sight.

The clubhouse began originally in the tack room of our barn, and was always filled after the Sunday hunt. Eventually, as more people participated, the clubhouse moved to the Moriarty's kitchen, where there was always plenty of Barbara's hot soup and delicious homemade bread for the members as they relived the excitement of the chase.

(Buss admitted that it was quite an experience to start his hunt from scratch):

First of all, I had to meet with the homeowners, landowners and farmers to gain their trust and use of their land. Then I had to learn about foxhunting from the roles of the Master, Kennelman and Huntsman. I spent may hours with the hounds gaining their love and trust. We handled them daily and trained them by walking and teaching them to respond to my horn while hunting. In time we developed a biddable pack that was a pleasure to hunt, and one to be proud of.

E. P. Moriarty

The Saxonburg Hunt
MFHA Data

1987 Masters: E. P. Moriarty, Jr. and Mary Armstrong. Hon. Sec.: Barbara Moriarty. Huntsman: E. P. Moriarty, Jr. Whippers-in: Kim Hay and Nancy King.

1988 Whippers-in: Kim Hay, Karen Chabal and Nancy King.

1989 Master and Huntsman: E. P. Moriarty, Jr. Whippers-in: Kim Hay, Karen Chabal and Joan Goswell.

1990 Whippers-in: Kim Hay, Karen Chabal, Joan Goswell and Linda Moyes.

1991 Hon. Sec.: Lois Sarver. Whippers-in: Dr. W. Guy Pietz and (prof) Sam Osche.

1992 Whippers-in: Dr. W. Guy Pietz and (prof) Joan Livitski.

1993 Whippers-in: Dr. W. Guy Pietz and (prof) Joan Livitski Broussard.

1994 Whippers-in: Dr. W. Guy Pietz and (prof) Kim Hay

1995 Whippers-in: (prof) Kim Hay. Hon. Sec.: Barbara Moriarty (1995–1997)

1996 Whippers-in: (prof) Kim Hay.

1997 Disbanded

Odiferous

What Now

Rolling Rock Hunt

Est. 1920

1922–present

Uniform: Scarlet coats with blue collar and R.R.H. buttons. Evening: Scarlet, with blue facings (Baily's Hunting Directory, *1931*).
Foxhounds: 12 couples of imported English (Baily's Hunting Directory, *1924*).
Country: approximately 8 miles by 15 miles, but is really unlimited. It is a rolling country, good with post and rail fences. It has more flat country than any in Western Pennsylvania, and is filled with native foxes (Baily's Hunting Directory, *1926*).

The Rolling Rock Hunt is located in Ligonier, Westmoreland County, Pennsylvania. Greensburg, the county seat, is 18 miles west and Pittsburgh is 50 miles west. The beautiful undulating valley lies between Laurel Mountain and Chestnut Ridge and provides breathtaking views of the rolling land and the forested mountains. In the early days it was a farming community with large tracts of cleared land. Presently the land is still open to the hunt but with the lack of farming, nature is reclaiming many open fields.

Much of the information about the earliest years of the hunt I have gathered from J. Blan van Urk's excellent book, *The History Of Rolling Rock*, published in 1950. This well-written book was accomplished under the auspices of Richard King Mellon, and it is filled with pertinent facts. J. Blan and his attractive wife Ginny spent a great deal of time at Rolling Rock and became an integral part of the community. They were fun to be with—Jack in the hunting field and vivacious Ginny at the bridge table or on the golf course.

There are several horse-related activities that play an integral part in the story of the Rolling Rock Hunt. These are Polo, the Rolling Rock Races, Point-To-Points, Beagling, Horse Shows, and Pony Club. They span various time frames, and, rather than interrupt the flow of my story, I have placed their descriptions at the end of this chapter. This arrangement does not imply that these events were not important. All of them have been a source of great enjoyment for the sportsmen and spectators of the Valley over the years.

Background

I found it interesting that the Mellon family had a close affinity to Ligonier since Judge Thomas Mellon had married Sarah Negley, the daughter of Jacob and the granddaughter of Alexander Negley. Alexander Negley, a Swiss immigrant, had been a veteran of the General Forbes campaign in 1758 and was stationed at Fort Ligonier. He settled on a farm between Ligonier and New Florence (this farm was later owned by his grandson James Ross Mellon, the older brother of R. B., and he named it "Rachelwood"). After a close encounter with a band of raiding Indians, Alexander Negley decided to move his family to Pittsburgh. His son Jacob was born in Ligonier but spent most of his life in Pittsburgh. He married and was responsible for developing the area near the present East Liberty, calling it Negleystown. Jacob's daughter Sarah fell in love with Thomas Mellon and they were happily married. Thomas and Sarah Negley Mellon had eight children; Thomas Alexander, James Ross, Samuel Selwyn, Andrew W., Richard Beatty, George Negley, and two girls, Sarah Emma and Annie Rebecca.

In 1877 Judge Mellon decided to purchase the Ligonier Railroad, which was incomplete after the financial panic of 1873. He put his sons, Thomas and Richard Beatty in charge of the venture. R. B. worked on the railroad in many capacities for the next three years. The family loved Ligonier and in 1882 Judge Mellon purchased Burnett Springs, the property near the St. Clair Show Grounds. It is presently the home of Mason and Gil Walsh.

Richard Beatty Mellon married Jennie Taylor King and they had two children, Sarah Cordelia (married Alan Scaife in 1927) and Richard King. The R. B. Mellons contributed immensely to Pittsburgh. They were interested in people, the East Liberty Presbyterian Church, the financial world, and scientific research. R. B.'s favorite motto was "It can be done." This busy couple also mutually enjoyed nature.

With R. B.'s love of the Ligonier valley, and his penchant for hunting and fishing, he bought the Burnett Springs property from his brothers. By enlarging his property with the purchase of the Saltzmann place, and the Stitley and Anderson farms, he had a good start in establishing his shooting preserve. The name of the area was inspired by the beautiful mountain stream that poured its waters down over the rocks, hence the name of Rolling Rock Farms. This stream was eventually developed into the famous well-stocked fishing stream of the Rolling Rock Club.

The Rolling Rock Club House was open in 1921 to accommodate Richard Beatty Mellon's sporting friends and guests. The old cabin and the Stitley farmhouse located near the present gate of the inner driveway to the club proved inadequate for the number of people who wanted to come to the valley. Forming a club afforded more freedom for R.B.'s friends to enjoy the area, and they would feel more comfortable paying their own way. In 1917, the Club had been incorporated for the purpose of "maintaining a club for social enjoyments and to provide and maintain facilities for shooting, hunting, fishing, riding, golf, tennis, and other athletic sports." The founding members and first Board of Governors of the Club were: Richard B. Mellon, A. Marshall Bell, Wilson S. Arbuthnot, Frederick C. Perkins, J. Denniston Lyon, William C. Robinson, Walter S. Mitchell, William B. Scaife, George M. Laughlin, Jr., William B. Schiller, Herman Griffin. Francis S. Guthrie (my uncle, married to my father's sister) and William S. Moorhead.

1920–1933

The Rolling Rock Hunt was formed in 1920 by Richard King Mellon (1899–1970), the son of Richard Beatty Mellon and the grandson of Thomas Mellon. In this chapter he will be referred to as Dick, R. K. or the General depending on the time in his life. To this day I still think of the hunt as his hunt.

Dick Mellon had developed a love for the sport after he hunted for one season with the Westmoreland Hunt in Greensburg. While visiting Rolling Rock with his father, he realized that the beautiful rolling country would be a perfect place for foxhunting. Richard Beatty Mellon was primarily interested in shooting and fishing, but he encouraged his son Dick to follow his dream.

The conception of the Rolling Rock Hunt started on a very small scale. In 1920, one year before the Rolling Rock Club was built, Dick, with the blessings of his father, purchased two and one-half couples of American foxhounds. As Master, he employed Alfred Fletcher as Huntsman and Jerry Lawson as whipper-in.

After Torrence Miller, the MFH of the Westmoreland Hunt, brought their pack to Rolling Rock for a day of drag hunting, Dick and his friends were truly convinced that foxhunting in Ligonier would be successful. Richard King Mellon had been raised to do things well, and he made plans for the future. Accompanied by his supportive father, R. B. Mellon, and his good friend W. L. G. (Bill) Gibson, Dick went to England in his quest for foxhunting knowledge. During their trip, they decided on the handsome scarlet and blue colors for Rolling Rock, reminiscent of the Conestoga wagons. With the aide of George Evans, eight and one-half couple of fine English foxhounds were purchased and returned with them to America by ocean liner. In 1921 the Rolling Rock Hounds were officially established as a private pack. Under the detailed guidance of Richard King Mellon, the Rolling Rock Hunt would become one of the finest hunts in America

In 1924 Dick imported more English hounds and employed the colorful Frank Smith as his huntsman. One of the most important parts of establishing a good hunt is to develop the hunting country, and it took a great deal of diplomacy and time to get permission from the landowners to traverse and panel their land. Ligonier Valley was a farming community, and the land was cleared with great galloping fields. There was a lot of barbed wire so it was essential to install jumping panels. Richard K. Mellon was a born leader, a good organizer, attentive to details, a man of vision who set high goals and accomplished them.

By 1925 there were enough people interested in his private pack that Dick decided to make it into a membership-subscription hunt. He felt the involvement of the membership would be very beneficial to the hunt. The officers were: Richard K. Mellon, Master; Malcolm McGiffin, President; L. G. Gibson, Secretary; Matthew T. Mellon, Treasurer.

Dick Mellon was the energetic catalyst in developing the interest in riding and hunting at Rolling Rock. In 1928 there were 65 horses entered in the first annual Hunter Trials held in the center of the racecourse. In this period the various hunts of the area interacted and participated in each other's hunt events. The annual hunter trials continued in the same location until 1983 when the Rolling Rock Races were terminated. The land was then transformed into an excellent shooting area.

The architecturally perfect Rolling Rock Stable was built in 1928, designed by the firm of Janssen & Cocken of Pittsburgh, and the lovely stone Rolling Rock Kennel was built in 1929. (By the early 1980s the stable had been adapted into attractive apartments and the kennel became a museum for the extensive collection of horse and hunting memorabilia. The newly renovated Colonial Stables have become the center of the hunt with excellent kennels and an attractive home for the huntsman.)

Dick's well-chosen pack of Rolling Rock hounds not only hunted brilliantly, but they were also winners at notable Hound Shows. The handsome pack of English hounds had been carefully selected for both looks and ability. Every aspect of Rolling Rock was handled with a standard that was no less than perfection. It was also affordable, since in those days it only cost $50 a month to keep a hunter at the Colonial stable.

The 1920s and 1930s were superb for the Rolling Rock Hunt under the mastership of Richard King Mellon, who surrounded himself with a group of enthusiastic members. The good sport attracted riders from many surrounding areas. I think the height of grandness was the planned lunch break on a Saturday hunt. Luncheon would be served at an appointed place, some riders had a second horse brought out, and grooms were present to hold the all of the horses during the pleasant luncheon.

Memories of the Hunt

It was a special occasion when the foxhunters of 1998 had the pleasure of hearing a first-hand account of the early days of Dick Mellon's hunt. At the Hunt Ball I felt very honored to be seated next to the guest speaker, The Honorable Adolph W. Schmidt, accompanied by his charming wife Patsy. The customary ball held during Race Week had ceased when the Races were terminated in 1983. The new masters, Sophie Mellon, Phipps Hoffstot, and Tom Slater decided to reinstate the lovely affair and appropriately asked Adolph to be their guest speaker. Adolph was recognized as "The Honorable" when he was appointed Ambassador to Canada. A small handsome man, he looked elegant in his old, perfectly fitting evening scarlet, as he spoke of his hunting days with the Rolling Rock in the 1930s.

Adolf Schmidt was a graduate of Princeton University and Harvard Business School, and in 1929 he started with the Mellon Bank. There he experienced the stock market crash and then the mandatory Bank Closing of 1933. He recalled that Richard Beatty Mellon, President of the Mellon Bank, stood on the top of a ladder and advised a multitude of nervous customers that they could withdraw their money if they desired. But Pittsburgh fared relatively well, while all of the Cleveland banks remained closed.

During the spring of 1930, Adolph joined Chauncey Hubbard and George Wycoff, classmates at Yale University with Paul Mellon, at Mrs. McManus's Boarding House in the East End of Pittsburgh. Chauncey encouraged Adolph to hunt at Rolling Rock in 1932. In the orientation sheet it was noted that, "Membership in the Hunt does not include membership in the Rolling Rock Club, which is by invitation only." He received his invitation in 1934.

He mentioned the notable members that he had met while hunting–the same as the people I have listed as the early members. It was in the 1932 season that he met his future bride, Pat Mellon, the daughter of Thomas A. Mellon, while she was hunting with her good friend Nancy Byers of Sewickley. They were home on holiday from the Fermatta School in Aiken, South Carolina, where they hunted frequently with the Aiken Hunt.

He remembered Bing Byers and Malcolm McGiffin, who both suffered fatal falls in the hunting field in 1932. They were both dear friends of Dick Mellon and it is a tribute to them that their handsome hunting portraits, painted by Frank B. Voss, still adorn the walls in the Pipe Room at the Rolling Rock Club.

Adolph concluded with an amusing story about Chauncey Hubbard at the Hunt Ball in 1935. "At an intermission most of the men had retired to the Log Room. Chauncey Hubbard had ordered a drink at the bar when he noted Richard Mellon was seated at the first long table facing the bar. Whatever possessed him no one will ever know, but he began an address that went as follows: "Dick, I need a raise. Just look how shiny my Huntsman tails have become." Then lifting them up–"Look at the seat of my pants—they're getting threadbare: my elbows are beginning to stick out." (At this point he had the attention of the whole room and everyone was howling.) Then taking off his Maxwell of London dress pumps, "Dick, in heavens name, I sure need a raise. Look at the holes in the bottom of my shoes. What will people think of this Mellon banker?" By this time people were laughing so hard it became contagious. Ordinarily sober Clarence Stanley, who had just been elected President of the Union Trust Company, was doubled up."

In closing, Adolph said that foxhunting produced for him a sense of exhilaration and sheer pleasure not found in other sports. In the fall of 2000, Adolph W. Schmidt passed away—a fine man who had made his mark in the world.

1933–1946

After R. B. Mellon's death in 1933, the ownership of Rolling Rock Farms was handed down to his son and daughter, Richard K. Mellon and Mrs. Alan Scaife (Sarah). Alan was a close friend of Dick Mellon and they worked very well together.

Since it fits chronologically I must mention that I remember the thrill I had in the late 1930s when my friend Betty Blackburn and I brought our horses from Fox Chapel to hunt for a day at Rolling Rock. We were young and inexperienced foxhunters, but fortunately we could ride. The country was beautifully groomed and we were safely chaperoned by the unforgettable Tommy Spinks. He was so kind and encouraging that we had a truly marvelous time. Tommy, employed by the Rolling Rock Hunt, was a gifted horseman, and although he was not loquacious, he was as inspiring to people as he was to horses. He was capable of schooling horses, of showing them, and was a good whipper-in. When I became Joint Master in 1977, I instigated a second flight similar to Tommy's role in the field, and it was rewarding to see the glowing faces of the young riders in the field—many of them the great grandchildren of early members of the Rolling Rock Hunt.

In 1936 Richard King Mellon married Constance Prosser Mellon. She was a lovely person in so many ways. Connie was beautiful, competent, and caring. She was a good rider, liked foxhunting, and enjoyed accompanying her husband on their numerous shooting trips. She was instrumental in starting the St. Michael's of the Valley Church in Rector and later the Valley School of Ligonier. Connie, like her husband, knew how to accomplish her goals with dedication. The Mellon children were Richard Prosser, Cassandra King, Constance Barber, and Seward Prosser. All of the children were exposed to riding but only Connie and later Sandy's daughter Christina showed any real interest in foxhunting. In the later years I enjoyed being with them in the hunting field. They were both good riders and pleasant company.

The General received his commission in the army during his dedicated service in World War II. Although I never felt close to the General, I certainly admired his accomplishments. My sister Molly became very good friends with R. K. and Connie when she showed their great string of show horses. I was impressed by his interest in every detail of the club and the farm. With his manager he would drive around the property inspecting everything. I recall meeting him while he checked on the construction of a new beautifully built stonewall. On the other hand, I felt very comfortable with Connie, who was so open and friendly. She had a remarkable ability in getting important projects done and still had time to personally select gifts for people when the occasion arose.

During the war, General Mellon appointed Harry C. Bughman as Master. It was a difficult time, and the hunt became inactive and the hounds were dispersed. The Bughmans had been active in the Sewickley Hunt before they moved to the Ligonier Valley in 1939. The Bughmans were the parents of Betty (Burton) and Lenny.

Lenny Bughman was a talented young man who would play an important role in many sporting events at Rolling Rock. He announced for the Rolling Rock Races, and the Polo, keeping the spectators well informed in a delightful way. In 1942 he had married Catherine Taylor, known as Kit, who was a very dear friend of my sister Molly (Off). Their friendship went back to the days when they hunted with the Fox Chapel Hunt. The Offs and Bughmans became very close friends when both couples lived in Ligonier.

Molly and Kit were both attractive girls and loved having a good time. They had a ball during race week and their husbands were not pleased with the attention they received from the jockeys and trainers. Molly also loved telling a rare story about a return trip from Virginia, when the ladies were pestered by a car following them closely. They tried to escape with speed, and were finally pulled over by a siren. It evolved that the followers were FBI agents who gave them a serious warning about their dangerous driving but had to accept the ladies' explanation.

The Bughmans had three girls Pam (Dovey), Jill (Clement), and Cathy. Although I knew all of these girls well, I became close to Pam when she worked at our shop The Daisy and rode a great deal with me at Foxley Farm.

Molly and Sam Off's children, Susan and Sammy, maintained a close relationship with the Bughman family. My friendship with these younger people grew stronger with time, demonstrating the integrity of the close-knit community that we have in Ligonier Valley.

1946–1977

When General Mellon returned from the service after WW II, he realized that he did not have the time to devote to the hunt, and in 1946 he engaged Sidney Watters as Master. Although Sid was young, he had hunting experience and certainly won the support of the field with his humor and charm. The hunt thrived under his delightful leadership. When he first came, it was impossible to import English hounds and it was even difficult to find enough suitable American hounds, but a pack was formed and trained into an excellent drag pack.

In the beginning, the hounds ran like smoke on the straight laid drag, resulting in a pace similar to that of a steeplechase. Dicky Wallach, who was in charge of the Rolling Rock Club, suggested sending Bill Wallace to the Moore County Hounds to learn the finesse of laying a good drag. Bill learned his lessons well and trained his men to lay a very realistic line. A well-laid drag simulates the trail of a fox with the tricks that it might use to elude the hounds. The drag should be imaginative and challenging to a good pack of hounds. The members found the hunting exciting and invigorating. Bill's grandchildren Shirley and Pat later became enthusiastic riders and Pat is now happily hunting with Rolling Rock.

Anyone who hunted with Rolling Rock in the 30s and 40s will certainly remember the colorful Roy E. Sibel, an undertaker, who was amongst the first group of men from Ligonier to accept Dick Mellon's invitation to hunt with Rolling Rock in 1934. Roy was a great addition to the hunt and by 1946 he and his buddies from the Hardly Able Stable were avid foxhunters. Some of these men were Abby Graham, Harry Mears, Don Paxton and Ronald G. Boyce. Due to Roy's enthusiasm and charming attitude he became a member of the Hunt Committee in 1948. It was about this time that three other men came to love the sport offered at Rolling Rock—George J. Bronder, Dr. V. E. Beldham and Guy Hunter.

In 1950 George C. Clement became a Joint Master with Sid Watters. When Sid left to devote his full time to training racehorses, George continued as MFH until 1965. The 1950s and 1960s were congenial hunting years with the field filled with Rolling Rock residents and their children as they took up the sport. Among the foxhunters was Cordie May, the daughter of Alan and Sarah Scaife. She married Herbie May, Jr. After Cordie gave up hunting, she remained a member and is a staunch supporter of the hunt to this day. Like the young Mellon boys, her brother Dick Scaife rode but was not interested in hunting.

The Clement family was a delightful addition to the growing group of young people in the valley. Anne and George had come from the Boston area with their four children Alice, Elise, Eddie, and Kim. By 1953, George became Master and Huntsman with Lovell Stickley and Billy Fletcher as professional whippers-in. George was a delightful man who made friends easily and people really enjoyed hunting with him. His wife Anne acted as whip on her good gray horse *December*. She also was a great help to Kit Bughman in organizing the Pony Club. Her children were enthusiastic riders in the Pony Club and members of the hunt. As you will see, George Clement was also responsible for starting the popular sport of beagling in the valley.

Another lady who contributed immensely to the hunt was Mary Louise Flinn Stringer (later married Larry Knapp, then Jim Davidson). Her parents, Rex and Dolly Flinn from Fox Chapel, were dear friends and early members with Dick Mellon. Mary Louise, known as Weasel, was an exceptionally attractive lady who loved horses and hunting. Before the Stringers moved to Ligonier, I had the pleasure of driving from Fox Chapel with Weasel and Diana Osborn to enjoy foxhunting. Later Weasel often acted as Field Master but she did not want to be a Master. She also played a vital role during race week organizing the activities and being a charming hostess. The Steve Stringers offered a magnificent Stirrup Cup at their Braemar Farm for the

Opening Meet of the hunt held on Friday during Race Week. The field was always large and festive because many of the racehorse owners brought their favorite hunter to enjoy a day with the Rolling Rock Hunt.

For those who might be interested in recalling the list of people who were members of the Rolling Rock Club, and had residences in the area, please see the 1954 Loyalhanna Register list at the very end of this chapter. With only a few exceptions, I remember with pleasure most of these people. Just seeing their names brought back such warm memories of the individuals that I experienced a strange desire to call them on the phone.

The community was pleased to welcome Bill and Jean Stirling when they moved to the Valley in the 1960s. They were an attractive couple, truly involved with horses, and were very helpful with the horse shows. I had known the Stirlings when they lived in Bakerstown and hunted with the Harts Run Hunt. Jean Hansen (Stirling) and her friend Mary Lou Armstrong (Mele) were two beautiful girls who started their riding career with Milt Selznick in the 30s when he had his stable on Beechwood Boulevard. Although we were very good friends, I have to admit that I was jealous of Jean and Mary Lou because, with their long shapely legs, they created such an elegant picture astride a horse. Bill, President of the Busy Beaver Lumber Company, became involved with horses when he married Jean. They were primarily interested in showing and did very well with their two exceptional horses *Extravagance* and *Café Tan*. The Todds were delighted when this attractive couple moved to Ligonier. Mary Lou Mele also moved to Ligonier, and she and Jean helped with the teaching of the Pony Club. All three of them were members of the hunt and Bill became a Joint Master with Abbie in 1965. Unfortunately, the Stirlings extended their interest into racing and moved with their children Kent and Jill to Florida to be closer to the racing scene. Burt and I had a marvelous time visiting them in Stuart and then West Palm Beach, which is a fabulous horse area.

Alfred M. Hunt (MFH 1965–1977) deserves special mention for his indefatigable effort for the Rolling Rock Hunt. In 1949 he was President of the hunt and never stopped working for it in many capacities. Abbie was a small man in stature with the heart of a lion. Eve Fout from Middleburg, Virginia supplied him with beautifully schooled hunters. Eve said "It was not a problem to find horses for Abbie because he never bothered a horse." Abbie was a true sportsman who gained the admiration of horsemen in the fields of hunting and steeplechasing. With the aide of multifarious friends he helped in putting on an impressive three-day, A-rated horse show, worked on making the Rolling Rock Races into a bigger spectacular event, and invited many different guests to enjoy hunting with the Rolling Rock Hunt. Abbie depended on his capable secretary, Dolores Sinopoli in his many endeavors. Abbie approached all of these tasks with such contagious enthusiasm that people willingly gave their support.

In 1975 Abbie Hunt MFH asked his good friend Bobby (Mrs. Henry K. Watson, MFH of Westmoreland) to merge with Rolling Rock. Westmoreland was experiencing the loss of country and a shrinking membership. There was a strong feeling of loyalty between the two hunts from the very beginning of their existence. Abbie was the nephew of Todd Miller, a former Master of Westmoreland and he had often hunted with them. The merger seemed like a perfect solution to retain the name of the fine hunt and still offer good hunting for its members. Abbie and Bobby made an excellent team and the Rolling Rock-Westmoreland Hunt flourished with the support of the Mellons.

Bobbie Watson and Alfred Hunt were wonderful Joint Masters (1975–1977) and the field enjoyed the marvelous sport they provided. One outstanding member of the hunt who deserves special mention was Mrs. Howard K. Walter (Alison). Mr. and Mrs. Howard K. Walter had been members of the Hunt since 1925—the year that I was born! Mrs.Walter continued to hunt even after her husband retired from the field. She rode an outstanding horse called *Laurel Beau*, and although she was not a strong rider, nothing seemed to intimidate this combination. Sallie Sullivan and I distinctly remember galloping along on our tired horses after a really long run and having Mrs. Walter pass us with a big smile on her face. Sallie was a good friend of mine and she kept her horses with us at Foxley Farm. We had lots of fun together, hunting and keeping our horses fit.

It was not until 1988 that the members voted to drop the name of Westmoreland. There were very few members remaining from Westmoreland, and it was appropriate to return the name to its original title as the Rolling Rock Hunt.

1977–1997

In 1977 it was announced that the Rolling Rock Hunt was to be disbanded. Abbie and Bobby did not wish to continue as Masters. This shocking news made the members rally together. At a well-attended meeting of some sixty people, Perk Oliver, Susie Todd and Stite Vipond were asked to become Joint Masters with Jack Tierney, Jr. as Hon. Secretary. Mrs. Peter Burrell, the former Mrs. R. K. Mellon gave her consent with the contingency that the hunt would be maintained in the proper tradition. Without the strong support of the Mellon family the hunt was financially pressed. I had a large list of people who annually came to our party before the Rolling Rock Races on Saturday. They loved the races, which were synonymous with the hunt, so I started an annual newsletter with an appeal to subscribers. The response was superb and it was so gratifying to realize that people did believe that R. K. Mellon's hunt played an integral part in the Rolling Rock tradition.

Persifor S. Oliver is another man who deserves an "honorable mention." Before I pursue his accolades, I must say that he had an outstanding wife, Eleanor (Didi) Maxwell Oliver. Didi was a competent attractive lady who had been successful in many careers and excelled in the position of Resident Secretary of the Rolling Rock Club from 1971 to 1982. She replaced Isabel Bayard who was loved and respected for the marvelous job that she did. Isabel's tenure was from 1955–1972. The Louis Bayards were good friends of my parents and I was very close to these fine people. Isabel was a hard act to follow but Didi rose to the mark, following her predecessor's reputation with ease and grace.

The Oliver's had three nice children: Brad, Ping and Gail (Mrs. Richard Barrett). Gail inherited her love of riding from her father, and is a member of the hunt. Life in Ligonier appealed to all of them and they plan to spend their later years in the Valley.

Perk loved foxhunting and in his competent quiet way he gained the respect of everyone in the hunt. He had served as Honorary Secretary and then became Joint Master with Stite Vipond and me in 1977. Besides coping with the finances, he kept in close contact with the huntsman and staff. In his later years, despite his sparse figure, he would brave any weather and happily finish the hunt. Due to a broken hip, he retired in 1994. H. Phipps Hoffstot was elected as Joint Master in his stead, but no one could completely replace the remarkable Perk Oliver.

Over the years my fellow masters have done most of the work in supervising the hunt but occasionally a woman's opinion proved beneficial. I enjoyed conducting the second flight, writing the newsletter, and keeping in touch with the wonderful landowners. During my tenure (1977–1997) the hunt had been successful and provided good sport, but it has not always been easy. Finances are always the major problem for any hunt. As most Masters know, there is also the volatile human factor to contend with—immediate attention must be paid to unhappy landowners, temperamental huntsmen, and errant, complaining members. I often wonder why so many people aspire to becoming a Master. It is a labor of love and the title hardly compensates for the dedication that the position demands.

During my twenty years as Joint Master I have had the pleasure of hunting with many wonderful people, far too many to include by name. I will say that Sheila Selznick, Milt's wife, was a special help to me with the second flight. Sheila often rode a green horse that she wisely started in the back of the field. She understood horses and hounds, and I often asked her advice about which way we should go, especially when my hearing started to deteriorate. I enjoyed taking the second flight because it took a great deal of thought and anticipation. It was challenging to keep my group up with the hounds when they were running a fox. Since the second flight went at a slower pace, I had to guess where the fox might run and often our group was in the right place to view the fox. Occasionally, I would get in the way of the huntsman, but they were always very nice about my unintentional mistake.

As Mark Thompson, Sr. said (see the Chestnut Ridge chapter), "The Honorary Secretary deserves high recognition and sincere thanks from the hunt." It is a time-consuming and important role needed for the running of a successful hunt. Sheila Selznick replaced George Weidlein in 1986 and competently fulfilled the position until 1995. Mrs. Richard (Betty) S. Smith took over after Sheila. Betty was devoted to the hunt and despite several falls during her hunting days, she never lost her enthusiasm. In 1998 Mrs. Richard (Georgia) K. Smith, an ardent foxhunter, willingly accepted the task and is still fulfilling her complex duties in the year 2001. To avoid any confusion I want to point out that the two Smith ladies are unrelated. All of our Honorary Secretaries have done a great job.

During the years of our joint mastership we had quite a few different huntsmen. Mark Stickley, the son of Lovell Stickley, started us off in 1977 and was a wonderful young man, who did not get ruffled by our naïve ways. I must say that I particularly enjoyed hunting with Joseph Hardiman. He was a delightful Irishman. I would come away from a conversation with Joseph feeling that I had experienced a bit of Irish Spring. Joseph gave the hunt a very good time because he was conscious of the field, and if the scenting was poor he simply provided everyone with an active ride. Joseph is now the huntsman for Chagrin Valley and they are very lucky, and happy, to have him.

In 1984 Tom Slater replaced Stite Vipond as Joint Master. Stite continued to hunt, often against the wishes of his doctor, until he was 80 years old. Stitler A. Vipond grew up in Hollidaysburg, where his father Paul Vipond was Master of the Frankstown Hunt. Stite said, "I did not hunt much there because I was away at school," but he loved to ride and especially enjoyed racing over fences. I nervously watched as Stite headed his horse into the highest panel of a line fence, but his horse coped nicely. Stite is a most endearing man and in his 80s will play golf with his buddies Perk Oliver and Burt Todd and then go fishing on the trout stream. What energy!

Tom C. Slater with his quick wit and sharp business mind was a great help to Perk. The hunt had taken over the responsibility of running the Matthew barn where the members kept their horses. Tom oversaw the thankless task of trying to keep all the boarders and employees happy. Due to the need for insurance coverage the owners of horses at the Matthew Barn have to be members of the hunt. Tom Slater is a large man and has two big Irish hunters who successfully keep him up with hounds. Tom has become quite knowledgeable about hounds and thoroughly enjoys them. Tom had a serious fall in the spring of 2000, but with sheer determination he was hunting again in the fall—an admirable feat.

Although I was Joint Master until 1997, during the last few years my hunting was curtailed by arthritis. I should have retired but the prospective replacements did not completely fill the requirements that we thought were necessary. It was with great pleasure that I relinquished my position to Sophie (Mrs. Armour N.) Mellon. Although she had small children and did not have much hunting experience, I knew that she was the right person because she was competent and wanted the hunt to grow in the right way. Armour is very supportive of Sophie's endeavor but he does not wish to hunt. To the delight of the community he has acquired a pack of Basset hounds. With the support and interest of the Mellon heirs, the Rolling Rock Hunt is rightfully in the hands of the family.

1997–2000

Although many of the members in 1997 felt that they were losing control of the hunt that they had worked so hard to maintain, it was exciting to look forward to a new era of revitalization. There was much to be accomplished and the credit rightly goes to Sophie Mellon who rallied together the young members of the Mellon family.

I am sure that General Mellon would be so proud to know that his children's children wish to restore his hunt to its former excellence. To have a fresh start, in April of 1998 the hunt was returned to the status of a private pack with subscribers.

The Rolling Rock Hunt Committee consisted of:

Mr. and Mrs. Armour N. Mellon
Board of Directors: (Mrs. Mellon: Joint Master)
Mr. and Mrs. W. R. G. Byers III
Mrs. Scott McBroom
Mr. and Mrs. W. R. G. Byers
Mr. H. P. Hoffstot: Joint Master
Mrs. Scott McBroom
Mr. Thomas C. Slater: Joint Master
Mr. Hugh Robards: Joint Master

To help you identify the above grandchildren of R. K. Mellon—Armour Mellon is the son of R. K. Mellon's son Richard. Russell Byers is the son of his daughter Constance. Russell's wife Anne is an enthusiastic foxhunter. Christina McBroom is the daughter of R. K.'s daughter Cassandra (Henderson now Milbury). Just as R. K. would have done, the Mellon heirs have improved the Colonial Stables to accommodate proper housing for a Huntsman and an excellent kennel for the hounds.

I cannot close this writing without mentioning R. K.'s sons, Richard Prosser (Dick) and Seward Prosser (Pross), who have been supportive of the hunt despite the fact that they do not hunt. Dick has spent a good deal of time on the east coast enjoying boating, but also has a lovely house overlooking the old racecourse at Rolling Rock. Pross and his wife Sandy (Springer) excel in their sports of golf and shooting. They still have time to keep a close eye on the functions of the Rolling Rock Farms and the Club. Sandy Springer's grandparents owned the land known as Springer's Bottom and their family home is the present refurbished stone house on Route 381.

To bring the Rolling Rock Hunt back to its original excellence, the family searched for a special huntsman. They interviewed Hugh Robards from the Limerick Hunt in Ireland, who had a superb reputation as one of the finest huntsmen of the time. Hugh took the position as Joint Master and Huntsman, bringing with him his charming wife Caroline and young daughter Emily. It was a challenge for them to work with a new pack in a hilly country so unlike the Irish countryside. The family, including Emily, work diligently with the hounds, and many new hounds have been acquired to improve the pack and start a good breeding program. Hugh's reputation has been fulfilled and the field is in awe of his excellent control of the hounds.

Despite her youth, Emily Robards is the capable Kennelman and Huntsman for the McGinnis Run Basset Hounds. She is doing a marvelous job with the support of her parents. Armour Mellon is the MBH and he is assisted by Gary Houston, Tom Stickle and Pat Wallace acting as whippers-in.

The future of the Rolling Rock Hunt looks bright and I am pleased that I was able to play a part in the interim period. The Rolling Rock Hunt is a tradition worth saving for future generations.

Rolling Rock Hunt
MFHA Data

1924 Master: Richard K. Mellon, Esq. Huntsman: (prof) Frank Smith. Whippers-in: (prof) John Cully and (prof) William Bale.

1926 Hon. Sec.: Matthew T. Mellon.

1927–1948 Hon. Sec.: H. A. May.

1927 Whippers-in: (prof) O. Newell and E. Newell.

1932 Kennel Huntsman: (prof) J. Woodyatt. 35 couples of English foxhounds.

1933 Huntsman: (prof) Fred Hedges.

1940 Whippers-in: (prof) Nat Brown and Edmund Ladue.

1942 Master: H. C. Bughman, Jr.

1943 Hunt inactive. Master: H. C. Bughman. Jr. Hon. Sec.: H. A. May. Huntsman: (prof) Fred Hedges. Whippers-in: (prof) Nat Brown and Jim Regan, Jr.

1946 Hunt activated. Master: (prof) Sidney Watters. Jr. Huntsman: (prof) James J. Regan. Whippers-in: (prof) Lovell Stickley and (prof) Alfred Fletcher.

1947 Whippers-in: (prof) Lovell Stickley and (prof) Alfred Fletcher.

1950 Joint Masters: Sidney Watters, Jr. and George C. Clement.

1953 Master and Huntsman: George C. Clement. (1955) Hon. Sec.: George T. Oliver. Whippers-in: (prof) Lovell Stickley and (prof) William Fletcher.

1958 Master: George C. Clement. Whippers-in: Mrs. George C. Clement and Mrs. Henry J. Stringer. Huntsman: (prof) Lovell Stickley.

1960 Hon. Sec.: Persifor S. Oliver. Whippers-in: Mrs. George C. Clement and (prof) R. McClean.

1965 Joint Masters: Alfred M. Hunt and William Stirling, Jr. Huntsman: (prof) Lovell Stickley. Whipper-in: (prof) R. McLean.

1968 Master: Alfred M. Hunt. Whippers-in: (prof) R. McLean and (prof) Barbara Kraeling.

1971 Hon. Sec.: DeCourcy E. McIntosh.

1975 Merged with Westmoreland, name changed to Rolling Rock-Westmoreland Hunt. Joint Masters: Alfred M. Hunt and Mrs. Henry K. Watson. Hon. Sec.: John T. Tierney, Jr. Whippers-in: (prof) Barbara Kraeling and (prof) Mark Stickley.

1977 Masters: Persifor S. Oliver, Mrs. Burt K. Todd and Stitler A. Vipond. Hon. Sec.: John T. Tierney. Treasurer: John T. Tierney, III. Huntsman: (prof) Mark Stickley. Whipper-in: (prof) Lovell Stickley.

1979 Hon. Sec.: George Weidlein. Huntsman: (prof) John Roche. Whipper-in: (prof) Dennis Stickley.

1980 Whipper-in: (prof) Maggy Roche.

1982 Huntsman: (prof) Maggy Roche. Whippers-in: Dr. Bill Smith, (prof) Tim Northrop and (prof) Tyrell Lecocq.

1983 Huntsman: (prof) Tim Northrop. Whippers-in: Dr. Bill Smith and (prof) Alice Northrop.

1984 Whippers-in: Nancy Cairns, (prof) Alice (Bayo) Northrop and (prof) Joseph Hardiman.

1985 Huntsman: (prof) Joseph Hardiman. Whippers-in: (prof) Michael Hardiman and Kim Hardiman.

1986 Hon. Sec.: Dr. Sheila Selznick. Whippers-in: James Wolf, (prof) James Gibson and Kim Hardiman.

1989 Whippers-in: James Weaver and Kim Hardiman.

1991 Whippers-in: (prof) John Hardiman and Kim Hardiman.

1992 Whippers-in: James Weaver, (prof) John Hardiman and Kim Hardiman.

1994 Persifor S. Oliver retires (1977).

1995 Joint Masters: Henry Phipps Hoffstot, Thomas C. Slater and Mrs. Burt K. Todd. Hon. Sec.: Mrs. Richard S. Smith.

1997 Mrs. Burt K. Todd retires (1977).

1997 Joint Masters: Henry Phipps Hoffstot, Mrs. Armour N. Mellon and Thomas C. Slater. Huntsman: (prof) John Macey. Whippers-in: Mark Thompson and (prof) Heather Colt.

1998 Hon. Sec.: Mrs. Richard K. Smith. Huntsman: (prof) Hugh Robards. Whippers-in: Caroline Robards and Kris Weaver.

2000 Joint Masters: Henry Phipps Hoffstot, Mrs. Armour N. Mellon, Hugh Robards and Thomas C. Slater. Hon. Sec.: Mrs. Richard K. Smith. Huntsman: Hugh Robards. Whippers-in: Caroline Robards and Kris Weaver.

Early Foxhunters in the 1920s and 1930s

Alderdice, Jane
Alderdice, Nancy
Arensberg, Charles
Bell, "Pinkie"
Benny, George
Bissell, Jack
Brett, Dick
Bughman, H. C., Jr.
Bughman, Leonard
Byers, "Bing"
Byers, Nancy
Chalfant, Martha
Cook, "Sis"
Cook, Janet
Denton, M/M Frank
Donnelly, M/M Dorwin
Eagan, Dick
Evans, "Lollie"
Everett, Jim
Fagan. Charles
Flinn, Rex and Dolly
Hamilton, J. C.
Harris, Betty Jane
Hays, Charlie
Hilliard, Raymond
Hodge, Frances
Hubbard, Chauncey
Jones, T. M., III
Laughlin, M/M George
Lawrence, John
Love, Russell and Lucie
MacDonald, R. H.
Masten, Dean C.
Matthews, Charlie
May, Herb
McCague, Dr. Edward J.

McCreery, T. K.
McEldowney, Jane
McGiffin, Malcom
McKay, Betty
McKinney, Jim
McKinney, Robert
Mellon, M. T.
Mellon, Paul
Mellon, Richard Beatty
Mudge, Leonard
Nohl, Louis
Oliver, George T., II
Page, Ben
Park, Mrs. Lewis A.
Patterson, Edith
Patterson, Nancy
Paxton, Don
Reed, McCook
Reed, "Weezie"
Ricketson, John
Robinson, Lew
Rogers, Mrs. D.
Scaife, M/M Alan
Scaife, Verner
Schmidt, Adolph
Scribner, Joe
Sibel, Roy
Smith, M/M Theodore
Thomas, W. R., Jr.
Thompson, Arthur W.
Thompson, Mary
Todd, Charles S.
Walter, M/M Howard K.
Walters, J. P.
Walters, Phil
Waters, Bob

Rolling Rock Hunt

Members 1949

Alfred M. Hunt, President
A. Perry Osborn, Jr., Vice-President
Herbert A. May, Jr., Secretary and Treasurer
Sidney Waters, Jr., Master of Foxhounds

Hunt Committee

Richard K. Mellon, Chairman
Alan Scaife
Leonard W. Bughman
Herbert A. May
Blaine Fairless
Roy E. Sibel

Active Members

Dr. V. E. Beldham
E. C. Bothwell
George J. Bronder
M/M H. C. Bughman, Jr.

M/M L. W. Bughman
Mrs. J. M. Dovey
Charles M. du Puy
Blaine F. Fairless
M/M Alfred Hamilton
Miss Susie Hays
Alfred M. Hunt
Guy Hunter
A.W. Kennedy
David I. McCahill, Jr.
M/M Allan MacDougall, Jr.
Mrs. William M. McEldowney
Herbert A. May
M/M Herbert A. May, Jr.
Paul Mellon
M/M Richard King Mellon
Mrs. Samuel W. Off
M/M George T. Oliver, II
M/M A. P. Osborn, Jr.
Mrs. Simon T. Patterson
H. Donald Paxton
Mrs. H. H. Phillips
Mrs. Joseph P. Replogle
Mrs. John Richardson
M/M Alan M. Scaife
Roy E. Sibel
Mrs. H. J. Stringer, Jr.
George E. Thackray, Jr.
Miss Mary Ellen Thackray
M/M Gordon Thompson
Paul S. Vipond
M/M Howard K. Walter
Robert S. Waters

Junior Members

Louis Balken
John Barclay, III
Edith Anne Binney
Billie Hodge
Polly Kinnear
Fronk E. Lainbeer, III
Emil Lang, II
Margaret Love
Heath McBain
Hale Matthews
Henry M Matthews
Margey Murray
Marcia Scott
Grover Stephens
George E. Thackray, III
Geoffrey Walter

Rolling Rock Hunt

Members 1973

F. C. Anderson
Bob R. Dorsey
F. H. Guthrie
Peter A. Hanko
Alfred M.Hunt
Dr. J. Jedruch

Mrs. Betty J. Kelsey
Mrs. Paul Klim
Mrs. Lawrence W. Knapp
DeCourcy McIntosh
Mrs. Cordelia S. May
Persifor S. Oliver
Henry Poerio
Mrs. Joseph P. Replogle
Mrs. Henry K. Sherman
M/M Walter Suppes
John T. Tierney, Jr.
Mrs. Burt K. Todd
Stitler A. Vipond
Mrs. Howard K. Walter

Limited Members

Mrs. Leonard W. Bughman
Mrs. Arthur R. Fawcett, Jr.
Dick Fitzsimmons
Robert B. Gigliotti
Sue Kraeling
Martin O'Rourke
Edwin McConnaughey
Mrs. H. Houghton Phillips
Dr. Laura Schrock
Mrs. Milton Selznick
William Stirling
Mrs. William Stirling
John R. Steitz
John T. Tierney, III

Junior Members

Susan Anderson
Deborah Davidson
Ellen Dorsey
Lauren Fawcett
Mary Goodwin
Christine Graver
Amy Greenwood
Mrs. Christine Gegory
Larry Martin
Debbie Mays
Jeff Mays
Lee Ann McClatchey
Marcia Murray
William Purvis
Thomas Stewart
Ann Stringer
Kate Sullivan
Phillip Thackray
Lulu Tito
Franny Todd
Laurie Todd
M. M. Vipond
Susan Woodward
Priscilla Zimmerman

Rolling Rock—Westmoreland Hunt

Members 1977

F. C. Anderson
Mickey Burke
Robert Cummins
Ray Dortenzo
Phillip Falconi
Dr. John E. Frazier, II
Vivian Harbison
Mrs. Phillip Holland
Robert L. Hunker
Alfred Hunt
Mrs. Betty Kelsey
Mrs. Phillip Davidson
Mrs. Cordelia May
M/M Thomas Miller
Mr. Robert Allerton Miller
Persifor S. Oliver
Henry C. Poerio
Donna J. Reefer
Mrs. Richard Ridilla
Mrs. Joseph P. Replogle
Sheila Selznick, V.M.D.
Frank Shabella
Thomas C. Slater
M/M Peter Sikora
Dr. Bill Smith
Mrs. Barry R. Sullivan
M/M Walter Suppes
John L. Tierney, Jr.
Mrs. Burt K. Todd
Stitler A. Vipond
Mrs. Howard K. Walters
Mrs. H. K. Watson
Mrs. Robert T. Woodings
Daniel O. Burger

Limited Members

Mrs. Richard Beinhauer
Barbara Burke
Mrs. Nicholas Claudy
Robert B. Gigliotti
Jerry Goldberg
Dr. Jacek Jedruch
Gigi Sedor
Mrs. Max Lammers
Mrs. David Lindell
Edwin McConnaughey
Page Oberlin
Martin O'Rourke
Jack Spink
Mrs. Edward C. Schmidt
Mark Thompson
Holly Tucker
Bob Troy
Linda Peters
Dick Fitzsimmons

Junior Members

Lisa Bailey
Nancy Cairns
Deborah Davidson
Mary Goodwin
Elizabeth Goodwin
Keli Krumenacker
Robert N. Lake
James Y. Lake
Sue Latterman
Sandra Stringer
Lisa Miller
Patricia Nenoff
Amy Rawlings
Megan Sherman
Maggie Shriver
Polly Shriver
Kerry Slate
Michele Slater
Mary Beth Spakowski
Kate Sullivan
Courtney Suppes
Laurie Todd
Franny Todd
Lulu Tito
Judy Wise
George Weidlein
Rena Weisz
Suzanne Woodings

Rolling Rock—Westmoreland Hunt

Members 1981

Daniel O. Burger
Michael D. Connolly
Mrs. Philip J. Davidson
Mrs. Katherine Suppes Dean
Mrs. Emma Lou Fetter
Dr. John Frazer, II
Vivian Harbison
Mrs. Philip Holland
Alfred M. Hunt
Mrs. Betty Kelsey
Mrs. Cordelia S. May
Persifor S. Oliver
Henry Poerio
Mrs. Richard Ridilla
Richard M. Scaife
Sheila Selznick, V.M.D.
Frank Shabella
Mrs. Peter Sikora
Thomas C. Slater
Dr. Bill Smith
Mrs. Richard S. Smith
Mrs. Barry Sullivan
M/M Walter Suppes
John T. Tierney, Jr.
Mrs. Burt K. Todd
Stitler A. Vipond
Mrs. Howard K. Walter
Mrs. R. T. Woodings

Limited Members

Mrs. Richard Beinhauer
Robert B. Gigliotti
Mrs. W. R. Harris
Mrs. Cornelia Mueller-Heubach
Martin O'Rourke
Ms. Donna J. Reefer
Mrs. Joseph Replogle
Mrs. Paul F. Rizza
Jack Spink
Miss Margaret Skinner
Miss Franny Todd
Miss Laurie Todd
Robert Troy
Melody Valmont
George Weidlein
Mark Lucas

Junior Members

Missy Davison
Miss Lauren Fawcett
Elizabeth B. Goodwin
Mary Goodwin
Lauren Jamison Hawkins
Christina Henderson
Mary Hudson
Sara Hudson
Marguerite S. Kahrl
James Y. Lake
Robert N. Lake
Douglas Larson
Marion Love
Vickie Love
Kit Nimick
Gregg Sikora
Kathleen Slate
Michele Slater
Dana Smith
Laura Smith
Lauren Smith
Sandra Stringer
Kate Sullivan
Greg Suppes
Lulu Tito
Terri Tokay
Alice Troy
Robert Woodings
Suzanne E. Woodings

Rolling Rock Hunt

Members 1998

Barensfeld, David E.
Bohenko, Dr. Lori L.
Brentzel, Ms. Cathy M.
Burkland, M/M William S.
Byers, Mrs. W. R. G. Jr.
Carrera, Mrs. Geraldine
DeMayo, Mrs. William M.
Douglas, Barry

Eichleay, Miss Anne Haven
Fisher, Mrs. Chester G.
Frazier, Dr./Mrs. John E. II
Gano, M/M James
Gardill, Ms. Julia
Gladstone, Master Chase
Gladstone, Mrs. Richard C.
Gladstone, Miss Shepard
Gnazzo, Joseph
Gruber, Mrs. E. John
Hardiman, Mrs. John
Hanley, William H.
Held, Miss Julie
Hencher, M/M Dennis
Hill, Mrs. Ronald C.
Hill, Miss Autumn
Hoechstetter, Harvey
Hoffstot, H. Phipps
Jewell, Miss Jessica
Johnston, Ms. Margaret
Jones, Mrs. Michael Mc.M
Lazzaro, Dr. Theodore A.
May, Mrs. Cordelia
McGraw, Dr. Donald J.
McGraw, Miss Constance E.
McGraw, Miss Jayne
Mellon, M/M Armour N.
Milbury, M/M E. Van R.
Mullan, Edward
Murfey, Miss Libby
Nahorniak, Mrs. Nicholas
Nahorniak, Miss Victoria
Oliver, Persifor S.
Orwig, Mrs. Dennis
Palmer, Miss Amanda
Raizman, Dr./Mrs. Richard E.
Reefer, Ms. Donna
Rizza, M/M Paul
Samloff, Ms. Kristine
Selznick, Dr. Sheila V.M.D.
Sharp, Ms. Tyrell C.
Slater, Ms. Michelle
Slater, Thomas C.
Smith, Mrs. Richard K.
Smith, Mrs. Richard S.
Smith, Mrs. Vance M. III
Speicher, M/M Raymond
Stickle, Miss Gretchen
Teroerde, M/M Friedrich
Thompson, M/M G. Markle Jr.
Todd, Mrs. Burt K.
Turjan, Miss Marcie
Turnquist, Mrs. Paul
Vipond, Stitler A.
Vittone, Mrs. Paul R.
Wallace, Patrick R.
Weaver, M/M James
Widing, M/M Eric P.
Wine, M/M Floyd
Wood, Mrs. Daniel

Rolling Rock Hunt

Members 2000

Barensfield, David E.
Barrett, Mrs. Richard J.
Brentzel, Ms. Cathy M.
Brentzel, Miss Stacey

Burkland, M/M William
Byers, M/M Russell
Cairns, Miss Sarah
Carrera, Mrs. David
Crookston, Mrs. Albert
DeMayo, Mrs. William
Douglas, Barry
Everson, Ms. Nancy
Fisher, Mrs. Chester G.
Frazier, Dr./Mrs. John E. II
Gano, M/M James
Gardill, Mrs. Robert
Gladstone, Mrs. Richard
Gnazzo, Joseph
Gruber, Mrs. E. John
Hardiman, Mrs. John
Hill, Miss Autumn
Hoffstot, H. Phipps
Hoffstot, Henry
Hoffstot, Miss Maeve
Houston, R. Gary
Iscrupe, Mrs. Richard
Jewell, Miss Jessica
Jones, Mrs. Wm. McMichael
Lazzaro, Dr. Theodore
Lyons, James E.
Lynch, Dr. James
May, Mrs. Cordelia
McBroom, Mrs. Scott R.
McGraw, Dr. Donald J.
Mellon, M/M Armour N.
Milbury, M/M E. Van R.
Mullan, Edward
Nahorniak, Mrs. Nicholas
Oliver, Persifor S.
Palmer, Miss Amanda
Penticost, Mrs.Alex
Raizman, Dr./Mrs. Richard E.
Reilly, M/M Christopher J.
Rizza, M/M Paul
Robards, M/M Hugh
Samloff, Mrs. Andrew
Schreck, M/M Albert
Selznick, Dr. Sheila
Sharp, Ms. Tyrrell C.
Slater, Thomas C.
Smith Mrs. Jamie
Smith, Mrs. Richard K.
Smith, Mrs. Richard S.
Speicher, M/M Raymond E.
Teroerder, M/M Friedrich
Thompson, M/M G. Markle, Jr.
Todd, Mrs. Burt K.
Turjan, Miss Marcie
Turnquist, Mrs. Paul
Vipond, Stitler A.
Wallace, Patrick R.
Weaver, M/M James
Widing, M/M Eric P.
Wine, M/M Floyd

Polo

Polo was another horse related activity that came to the Ligonier Valley in the 1930s. Gordon and Rolland Thompson had played the game while attending the Arizona Desert School, and they persuaded their mother, Mrs. Arthur W.

Thompson to seed their field in Rector. It was a lovely location, privately set back from the road, surrounded by trees and sided by two bubbling creeks. In 1935 and 1936, Lew Brown, former Captain of the University of Arizona Polo Team, helped the Thompson boys assemble a team. The fourth player was Joe Thompson from Uniontown, and since he did not have any polo ponies, he practiced on his Chestnut Ridge foxhunters.

In 1940 Gordon Thompson and Lenny Bughman conceived the plan of having an International Polo Tournament. In whirlwind Rolling Rock fashion, they incorporated their Polo Association with an enthusiastic committee of Gordon Thompson, A. M. Byers, Blaine F. Fairless, John (Rip) R. Bigelow, R. K. Mellon, George R. McNary, Dr. Ralph Lynch, James O. Flower, William C. Robinson and Leonard W. Bughman.

Lenny Bughman, with his usual enthusiasm and interest, volunteered to help organize the polo and take charge of the publicity, a field in which he excelled. He was an excellent announcer, accurately catching the action and reporting it with captivating feeling. He had many fine talents and he knew how to use them.

The first 3-day tournament was held in August of 1940, and the proceeds went to the Allied War Relief Fund. It was a huge success, attracting an audience of 12,000. The Polo Association vanned in the teams from Meadow Brook (N.Y.), Fairfield (Kansas), Huntington Valley (Ohio), and Fauquier-Loudoun (Va.). One of the greatest polo players of all times, Thomas Hitchcock, Jr. was the referee and Thomas Brady was the umpire. Mrs. A. W. Thompson awarded the Challenge Trophy to the Fairfield team.

After this accomplishment, the second Annual was held the next year with an improved field and additional grandstands. Teams came from Blind Brook (N.Y.), Houston (Texas), Meadow Brook (N.Y.), and Fauquier-Loudoun (Va.). The trophy was won by Meadow Brook, ably assisted by their 10 goal player, Mike Phipps. Although they had an audience of 16,000, the next tournament had to be postponed due to the war.

With memories of the pre-war polo successes, the Rolling Rock Polo Association organized its own team in 1947. They engaged the delightful Cyril

R. Harrison, a seven goal player, to coach them. The Association purchased six ponies and rented more from Fred Terjan. It was great fun when they even allowed the ladies to try a practice stick and ball. The Rolling Rock team that year consisted of Mark Thompson, Gordon Thompson, Jack Kenny and Roy Bates. The following group of men also enjoyed practicing the game.

F. Carl Anderson, Jr.
Reynolds Bell
Leonard W. Bughman
Charles M. Du Puy, Jr.
Alfred Hunt
Herbert A. May, Jr.
David I. McCahill, Jr.
George McNary
George Oliver, II
P. Osborn, Jr.
Roger Phillips
A. R. Reed, III
J. C. Reed
Arthur Scully
Gordon Thompson
G. Markle Thompson
John Troutman

The Polo Association tried to have regular Sunday games, but could not arouse the necessary interest of spectators. In 1949 they had a Fourth Annual Invitation Tournament. The players for Rolling Rock were Mark Thompson, Bill Hanley, Cyril Harrison, and Dave McCahill. They were victors over the competing teams of Meadow Brook, New York Athletic Club and Harbor Hill (Ohio). This was the last of a beautiful era, since it was so financially draining.

Polo reappeared in Ligonier Valley when Jess Gift arrived some 40 years later, and made a field on his property on Forbes Road. It was a lovely setting and with the hard work of Dan Connally and Vick Smith, Jr. there were two successful years in 1983 and 1984. But the effort finally did not work out satisfactorily for all concerned.

In 1989 Dr. and Mrs. Richard E. Raizman brought polo back to the valley by creating a polo field on their farm at Stom Hollow Road. Richard had enjoyed playing for teams in Sewickley and Darlington, Pa, and he began having games on his own field with players from the Mid-States circuit of the USPA. This created an interest for new players and the Ligonier Polo Club was formed. They now host several tournaments and the Club is active on the circuit.

The highlight of their season is the annual benefit game (since 1989) held in September, pitting players from the Ligonier Club against a team from Germany. The German team is sponsored by Mr. Friederich Teroerde, President of ELG Metals, whose son, Patrick is the captain of the German team. In addition to the polo game, the teams and friends are magnificently entertained by the Teroerdes on Thursday night, and the Raizmans the following night. Both the Raizmans and the Teroerdes are members of the Rolling Rock Hunt, and the hounds are paraded during intermission, plus other displays of horsemanship. It is a very festive weekend and the proceeds are donated to the Leukemia Society of America. The event generally raises over $100,000.00 yearly for this deserving charity.

In the year 2000 the players for Ligonier were: Richard Raizman (captain), Mark Powers, Glenn Watterson, Glenn Watterson, Jr., Kent Watterson, Ken Fawcett, Dennis Collingwood and Jim Watson. The players for Germany: Patrick Teroerde (captain), Thomas Winter, Mattieu Von Delden, Mickey Kuyper, Thomas Geisler, Ezekial Kraft, Cesar Guina-Azu and Tim Zekany.

Rolling Rock Races
1935–1983

The Rolling Rock Races are a thing of the past but will long be remembered for their magnificence. In 1935 the first two-day meet of the Rolling Rock Hunt Racing Association was held on the lovely racecourse designed by William Almy, Jr. of Boston. One of the most prodigious races was for the "King of Spain" perpetual trophy (renamed the Rolling Rock International Gold Cup). R. K. Mellon had been the most recent winner of this cup, and with the closing of Grassland, the race was moved from Tennessee to Rolling Rock. The Race Meeting was an instant success.

I could not remember the precise program of the Rolling Rock Races. Perk Oliver's estimate of six or seven races was more accurate than mine. The affable, efficient George E. Carr III, the former manager of the Rolling Rock Farms, fortunately had kept the Wednesday and Saturday 1983 programs. There were six races on Wednesday and seven races on Saturday.

The race meets were originally held by the Westmoreland Hunt in Greensburg. In fact, George McNary retired the Western Pennsylvania Hunt Cup in 1931 by winning it for three consecutive years. In October 1934 Rolling Rock held its first Wednesday Meet with Westmoreland retaining the Saturday Meet. In 1939 it was the first year that the Rolling Rock Races were held for the benefit of The Home for Crippled Children in Pittsburgh, (later the name was changed to The Rehabilitation Institute of Pittsburgh). The event was such a tremendous social and financial success that it donated over one million dollars to the well-deserving institute during the ensuing years.

It may interest the reader to see the names of the memorable Pittsburgh horsemen who had donated trophies for a selected race. For each race day there were two races over national fences, which were hurdle fences. These were appropriate fences to introduce a horse to jumping races. The term National Fences referred to the more challenging brush jumps. Timber fences were stout impressive solid timber fences. A flat race, of course, was run on the turf.

Wednesday, Sept. 14, 1983

First Race—The Torrence Miller Cup—about two miles over National Fences

Second Race—The A. M. Byers, III Cup—about two miles over Timber

Third Race—The Edith Flinn Patterson Cup—about two miles over National Fences

Fourth Race—The William Christopher Robinson, Jr. Cup–about two miles over National Fences

Fifth Race—The Rolling Rock Hunt Cup

Sixth Race—The Ligonier—about seven furlongs on the Turf

Saturday, Sept. 17, 1983
First Race—Malcolm McGiffin Cup—about two miles National Fences
Second Race—Second Divisioin of McGiffin Cup
Third Race—Western Pennsylvania Hunt Cup—about three miles over Timber
Fourth Race—The Herbert A. May Cup—about two miles over National Fences
Fifth Race—King of Spain International Gold Cup—about two and half miles over International Championship Course
Sixth Race—Thurston Wright Cup—about one and a quarter mile on the Turf
Seventh Race—The Laurel Ridge Amateur Cup—about two miles on the Turf

The course, the stabling, and the fabulous entertainment lasting from Tuesday through Sunday could not be surpassed. There was a pool dinner on Tuesday night; Wednesday—an informal dinner dance; Thursday—private party for the Race Committee, owners and trainers; Friday—pool dinner. The fabulous Hunt Ball was held on Saturday evening, and on Sunday a brunch was held by Barry and Sallie Sullivan for the racing group.

The meet on Wednesday attracted people who were more interested in racing, but it still provided all the colorful attractions. Saturday was the highlight of the Race Meet and a multitude attended. It was exciting, and a beautifully done event. The course was laid out in the valley and could be viewed from the parking places on the hill, the grandstands (one for contributors and one for general admission) or the coveted raised boxes.

Lenny Bughman, the talented announcer, and the racing officials were in the three tiered decorated tower, keeping close tabs on all the activity. R. K. Mellon and friends climbed up on a gorgeous coach stationed near the tower to observe the races. Everyone was well turned out for the impressive event. It proved to be an energetic day if you wanted to inspect the horses in the paddock before each race, say hello to friends, and rush back to a good viewing spot in the grandstands. In addition to this, the Rolling Rock Hounds were paraded on the course in front of the stands, attended by the huntsman and two whips. There was usually another crowd-pleasing exhibition, such as the trained Lippizan horses. The Rolling Rock Race Meet attracted the best horses, owners, and jockeys, and everyone loved Race Week.

In the 1970s, at the request of Abbie Hunt, we entertained the visitors at Foxley Farm on Thursday evening. It gave everyone a change of scene for an evening of dinner and dancing. Our big room was perfect for such entertainment, and with the staff from the Club and the Race Week orchestra, it was a most enjoyable evening.

It was decided in 1939 to hold the Race Meet for the benefit of the Industrial Home for Crippled Children. People worked very hard to make it a fantastic event—it was socially accepted and appealing to the general public. But bigger is not always better and the tremendous success of the Race Meet finally brought it to a close. The crowds grew out of proportion, and the emphasis changed from that of a Race Meet into a fancy drinking party. It was incredible to see the exotic parking areas adorning the hillside, each one trying to surpass the next in accoutrements. Even the State Police had difficulty clearing the area at the end of the day.

For quite a few years, we had held a pre-race party at Foxley Farm on Saturday. Burt Todd called it the Tressop-Trolls Hunt Party (named after a defunct Irish hunt of which he considered himself Master). The party mushroomed into hundreds of people, many of whom we did not even know. It was fun in the beginning when we entertained friends and their guests, but it too got out of hand. It was sad but necessary to close the important fall event of the Rolling Rock Races in 1983.

Rolling Rock Hunt Racing Association, Inc.
October 7, 1978

Race Committee

Honorary Chairman: Peter F. Burrell
Co-Chairman: Alfred M. Hunt and Richard P. Mellon

Vice Chairmen: L. L. Biddle III, Leonard W. Bughman and Mrs. Philip J. Davidson
Racing Secretary: Charles T. Colgan

General Committee

Co-Chairman: Mrs. Richard M. Scaife and Mrs. William H. Woodwell
Vice-Chairmen: Mrs. L. L. Biddle, III and Mrs. Robert W. Off

Mrs.George S. Amory
Mrs. Henry H. Armstrong
Mrs. Louis P. Bayard
Mrs. James S. Beckwith, III
Mrs. Leonard W. Bughman
Mrs. Peter Burrell
Mrs. Davis C. Burroughs, Jr.
William J. Connelly, Jr.
Bob R. Dorsey
Mrs. John C. Dovey, III
Miss Jane Flaccus
Mrs. Clayton Flagg
F. Warrington Gillet, Jr.
Spencer R. Hackett
Mrs. George M. Henderson
Mrs. James H. Knowles, Jr.
Charles Lockhart, Jr.
Dr. Ralph Lynch
Mrs. John A. Mayer
Mrs. Donald R. McLennan, Jr.
Mrs. Constance Mellon
Mrs. Richard P. Mellon
Mrs. Seward P. Mellon
Mrs. Albert C. Muse
Mrs. Thomas H. Nimick, Jr.
Mrs. Samuel W. Off
Mrs. Persifor S. Oliver
Mrs. Joseph P. Replogle
Mrs. Frank E. Richardson, Jr.
Mrs. William C. Robinson, Jr.
Arthur M. Scully, Jr.
Mrs. William P. Snyder, IV
Mrs. William Stirling, Jr.
Henry J. Stringer, III
Gordon Thompson
John T. Tierney, Jr.
Mrs. Burt K. Todd
Stitler A. Vipond
Mrs. Howard K. Walter
Mrs. James Mellon Walton
Mrs. Henry K. Watson, II
Mrs. John D. Weidlein
Richard Wright

Point-to-Points

The first annual point-to-point was held in 1941. The three and one-half mile course over natural type fences was laid out in the landscape of the Rolling

Rock Farms with the end on the finish line of the racecourse. This type of race is limited to members of the various hunts, and there are three races—the ladies race, a men's race, and a man's heavyweight race. The latter race gave the larger weight-carrying horses a chance to compete in their own class. People rode their hunters and loved the competition.

In 1947 I had the pleasure of riding Mrs. John O. Burgwin's nice horsc *Vodka* in the three point-to-point series at Rolling Rock, Chestnut Ridge and Frankstown. He was the best horse running in the ladies races and should have won them all, but in my first race at Rolling Rock I cut a flag just before I turned for the finish.

Point-to-Points seemed to have lost its appeal in western Pennsylvania but in the 1990s Mark Thompson, Jr. and his wife Shelley decided to hold a hunter pace, which is not a race, during the fall season at Log Cabin Farm. The beautiful Rolling Rock Race Course is now utilized for bird shooting. Log Cabin Farm, previously owned by Edwin C. Hodge, is now owned by Rolling Rock Club and is used as a shooting preserve. The Club is generous in availing this lovely property to the hunt and riders when it is free during the busy shooting season. The winners of a class are determined by timing and points as the riders perform individually over a flagged course.

I think there is an advantage to entering your favorite hunter in a hunter pace rather than a point-to-point. It takes time to make your hunter quiet in the hunting field and it may be wise to avoid the competition of point-to-points. The hunter pace provides a good time for the foxhunters to gather and compete. Donna Reefer, a responsible hunt member, has recently taken over the organization of the popular event.

Beagling
1954–1981

George C. Clement, MFH of the Rolling Rock Hunt, brought the beagle pack from New England in 1954. It had belonged to his father, Kimbal Clement, and the beagles were descended from the Waldingfield Beagles of

Virginia, the oldest pack in the United States. George hunted the beagles from 1954 to 1965. Lovell Stickley was Kennel Huntsman, and the whippers-in were David Burton (later a Joint Master) and Ann C. Clement, Mrs. Leonard W. Bughman and John Rathbun.

Beagling has been very popular in the valley. Following on foot a pack of beagles or basset hounds as they hunt rabbits can be an active sport. The rabbit circles more than it runs in a straight line, but our rolling country gives people plenty of exercise while hunting. Since I would foxhunt every Saturday, I never felt the need to cover the countryside on foot, but other people loved it. It also provides a congenial sport for the whole family. Of course, there were often enjoyable hunt teas as well.

In 1965 William C. O'Neil and William R. Oliver were elected Joint Masters. Bill O'Neil and his charming wife, Polly, remained devoted to the pack and were very sad when they gave the pack to the West County Beagles in Bath, Ohio in 1981. The O'Neils had been totally involved and would take the Ligonier Valley Beagles to the National Beagle Club Institute Farms in Aldie, Virginia where they successfully competed with the other recognized beagle packs.

Bill O'Neil was a successful lawyer at Thorp, Reed, & Armstrong and had more time to devote to the beagles when he retired. The O'Neils built a house in the Rector Hill Road. They were a very special couple and adored by the community. Polly and Bill also had two delightful daughters, Barby and Joannie. I have previously mentioned Joannie and her prowess with her marvelous mare, *Tammy*, in the chapter on Foxley Farm.

Unfortunately, I cannot list the many people who were members over the years. I do know that Frank Doak was a Joint Master with Bill from 1968 to 1978. Charlie Fagan was also a very devoted member. When he attends the Rolling Rock Hunt Ball, he looks so handsome in his beautifully fitted green coat that he still holds the right to wear while others don their evening scarlet.

The beagles hunted rabbits every Sunday during the season, which ran from mid-October to the end of March. With the permission of the landowners, the Ligonier Valley Beagles used the same country as the Rolling Rock

Hunt. It was a very popular sport and attracted many members who enjoyed traversing the beautiful countryside while watching the beagles work. There usually was a hunt tea provided at the end of the invigorating day.

I was pleased to find an article in *The Chronicle of the Horse* (December 11, 1970) about the Ligonier Valley Beagles written by William C. O'Neil. He tells of starting a new program to keep beagles well exercised during the summer months, so they would be fit for the season. The Joint Masters were William C. O'Neil and William R. Oliver, and their pack of nine couples provided very good sport for 1969–1970. On October 25th at 2:30 PM the meet was held at Log Cabin Farm, owned by Mr. and Mrs. Edwin Hodge. Participating were William C. O'Neil—Joint M.B./Huntsman; Whippers-in; Lovell Stickley, Dennis Stickley, Gordon Thompson and Frank Doak; Field-master—William V. Brock and a field of 24. The scenting was good and they ran six rabbits with a kill of one.

In March of 1971 the Rolling Rock Hunt and the Ligonier Valley Beagles held a successful ball attended by 200 members of Western Pennsylvania hunts and beagle packs. It was through the kindness of the Hunt that the beagles and the foxhounds were kept at the Rolling Rock Kennels in the 1970s; both of these packs were capably cared for by the Huntsman, Lovell P. Stickley.

I am very grateful to John (Pete) K. Goodwin who gave me an article about the Ligonier Beagles, which was published in the *Tribune-Review* in 1981. The bold type stated that this was the last hunt for this pack and the end of a 27-year era. There was a nice picture of Bill Kennicott, William O'Neil and Ed Button surrounded by their adoring beagles. Nancy and Pete Goodwin were enthusiastic beaglers, with their daughters Frances and Mary. Mary was a devoted whipper-in for several years and became a Joint Master just before the hunt ceased.

I am glad to report that Armour Mellon has acquired a pack of bassets and with the help of Hugh Robards, Joint Master and Huntsman for the Rolling Rock Hunt, Armour is learning the fine art of hunting his pack. The pack is called McGinnis Run, and the capable young Emily Robards is its Huntsman and Kennelman. Gary Houston, Tom Stickle and Pat Wallace are enthusiastic whippers-in and the field is growing in numbers.

Horse Shows

Horse Shows are usually an annual event for most hunts because they give their members an opportunity to compete locally and the show is a good means of raising funds. In the 1950s the two day Rolling Rock Shows attracted many out-of-towners, and were lovely affairs held at the attractive grounds of the St. Clair Stables. The grounds with two rings are in a valley surrounded by trees and the main ring opened up to a challenging but inviting outside course. The accommodations and ambience of the weekend were appealing to the out-of-towners. The exhibitors from Virginia and Ohio raised the standard of competition, but the shows still maintained a pleasant atmosphere.

In the 1970s, under the guidance of Abbie Hunt and the William Stirlings, it was decided to hold a prestigious three-day A-Show. Danny Lenehan was put in charge of the 1976 event and they employed a team of notable people. Chris Black was the Secretary, Ted Mannison—the ring Steward and the judges were George Morris, Katie Monehan, Betty and Ernie Oare and Dave Kelly. Extra tent stabling was erected and with everything well planned—disaster struck; it did not rain, it poured buckets! Literally, the only creatures that enjoyed the event were the ducks floating around in the virtual pond in front of the ring. With the great financial loss incurred, it was never tried again.

Later it was decided to hold schooling shows. These were successful but did take a great deal of effort. Tom Slater took his turn at running them for several years. The next chairman was Sheila Selznick who did an excellent job. Marcia Brown had gotten some experience from Sheila and she did a great job for the next few years. It was a time-consuming job and the hunt was very grateful for the funds raised by all of these hard workers.

Presently the Pony Club has a very nice one-day show in July for its members and other riders of the area.

Rolling Rock Hunt Pony Club
1955–present

The young riders of today are fortunate to have so many good teachers available. There is also The United States Pony Club, an inspirational source of developing knowledgeable young horsemen. This is an excellent organization offering strict but intelligent guidelines for local District Commissioners to follow. The USPC was founded in 1954 by a group of foxhunting enthusiasts and much of the leadership is still drawn from the foxhunting community. In the year 2000 there were 625 Pony Clubs (including Alaska and Hawaii) and more than 13,000 members. The children have fun and are guided in the safest way possible to learn about horse care, competition at all levels, and foxhunting.

Prior to the Pony Club at Rolling Rock, Connie Mellon wanted to encourage riding for the children of the community. With the assistance of the staff from the Colonial Stables, she organized picnic rides where they rode up the Fishing Stream and stopped for a nice luncheon. The staff would hold the multiple horses during luncheon and then everyone would ride home. They were popular rides that occurred before my time in the valley, but both Pam Bughman and Jim Walton told me about them. Jim remembers the time when, "I was riding my naughty pony and it took off on the ride home. A firm hand reached down and stopped her. I looked up and saw Mrs. Mellon's wonderful face and I was so grateful." The picnic rides were usually lots of fun and the children adored them.

In 1945 Kit Bughman organized the Loyalhanna Junior Horse Show held at her mother's (Mrs. Stephen Taylor, later Mrs. Armstrong) lovely place in Ligonier. Under Kit's supervision the juniors did all the necessary chores of putting on the show. They loved it and learned a great deal from their hard effort. It was so successful that it became an annual event and it was the predecessor of the Pony Club.

Kit Bughman and Anne Clement started the Rolling Rock Pony Club in 1955. They became District Commissioners (DCs) and later on I joined them. It was a worthwhile but time-consuming job and we had a lot to learn. Many of the riders did not have their own horses so I arranged to rent some for the summer from a helpful dealer in Virginia. Although the scheme generally worked out well, I recall one scary event. We were holding a meeting outside of the ring at the Nimick's field near the Rolling Rock Bass Pond. For some unknown reason, the small bay horse that Lizzie Magee was riding took off in a wild bucking spree and dumped its rider hard. Lizzie was a good rider and regained her composure a lot faster than the unnerved instructors.

When our children were little in the 1960s, I was a DC for the Rolling Rock Hunt Pony Club. I remember Billy Bale, the excellent manager of General Mellon's successful stables, asking me "Why do you work so hard with those children when most of them will move away?" My sincere response was that the interested riders would continue and take their knowledge with them to a new community. If the children did not continue riding, their Pony Club experience would certainly enhance their lives. Working with an animal, understanding sportsmanship, and contributing to a team effort are invaluable lessons.

Although I well remember most of the Rolling Rock Pony Clubbers, I do not have complete lists and therefore will not use their names. One person that I must mention however, is Susie Macdonald (Grill), a wonderful person and an excellent rider. As a child she rode a marvelous gray pony *Desert Owl* that she bought from Sandra Stringer, Weasel's daughter. Susie is the daughter of my good friends, Ann and Dick Macdonald, and we have always been close to the family. I was crushed when she moved away, because she was so helpful, especially with our ponies. I love having Susie ride with me when she comes home, because she really understands horses.

The Pony Club was fortunate when the Westmoreland Hunt merged with Rolling Rock, and we had the benefit of the exceptionally well-trained group of Westmoreland Pony Clubbers. They were a great group of young people and were so helpful to our riders. See the list at the end of this section for the years of 1975 and 1976, submitted to me by George Weidlein, who has been wonderful in supplying all kinds of information. George was an active hunting member at Westmoreland and became the secretary for the Rolling Rock–Westmoreland Hunt from 1978–85.

In the 1980s I was truly impressed with the training of young Pony Clubbers when we had invited all the Tri-State clubs to join us for a day with the Rolling Rock Hunt. The children and horses kept arriving until we had over 100 riders in the field. My first reaction was "Alert 911 for ambulance service," and the Joint Masters hastily agreed to divide the field into three groups, according to their ability and desire. We requested that each Pony Club have adequate adults to supervise their own group, and our own members were very helpful. I did have to ask one young rider to take her horse home because the horse became frantic and potentially dangerous. A friend escorted them back to our stable and all was well. The rider was capable, but I know she was relieved to make a dignified exit. The rest of the day went very well, and the enthusiasm shown at the following luncheon was a testimony of the memorable experience we all shared.

The Rolling Rock Pony Club is still going strong with its headquarters at the St. Clair Stables on the Rolling Rock show grounds. There have been many wonderful District Commissioners who have devoted valuable time to the club. I think it is fair to say that the DCs play their role while they have their children involved, and after that, it is time for the next group to take responsibility. They all do a very good job, and I hope that the Pony Club will always continue its excellent instruction.

Generally speaking, it is safe to say that the pony club is more popular with girls than boys, but there have been many young male riders who benefited from the experience. Some of our U.S. Olympic riders are graduates of the Pony Club system. Unfortunately, boys in general are apt to crave other sports, such as baseball or football.

Riding fulfills many avenues for girls who love horses. They want to take care of their equine friends and they have a great learning experience with many of their buddies. It is a perfect interest for a young lady as she matures. Marcie Turjan's mother glowingly thanked me for playing a small part in Marcie's riding experience. Mrs. Turjan was sincere when she said that riding had played such an important role in the raising of her daughter, and she was so appreciative. I totally agreed that horses and pony clubs teach a young person many valuable lessons in coping with life.

Rolling Rock–Westmoreland Hunt Combined Pony Club Roster 1975–1976

*Names Submitted by George Weidlein for the 1975 Roster

Ansick, Georgeanna *
Bonarrigo, Gerrie
Bonarrigo, Kathy
Cairns, Nancy *
Carson, Robbie
Davison, Ann
Davison, Deborah
Donahue, Lorraine
Fink, Paulann
Getty, Amy
Goodwin, Betsy
Goodwin, Caroline *
Goodwin, Mary
Graver, Christine
Hanes, Kitty *
Hudson, Mary
Krumenacker, Kelli *
Luscombe, Mark
Luscomb, Thomas
Mays, Debbie
Mays, Mindy
McClatchey, Lee Ann *
McLaughlin, Joe *
McConnell, Patricia
McConnell, Jill
Meierkord, Susan
Mellon, Richard A.
Miller, Lisa
Miller, Kathy
Murray, Cary
Murphy, Martha
Neff, April
Reed, Paul *
Remington, Brenda
Ridilla, John
Ridilla, Lynn
Scaife, Jennie K.
Schultz, Carole
Sheedy, Clare *
Shriver, Maggie
Sherman, Tanya
Sherman, Megan
Slate, Kathy
Slate, Kelly *
Slate, Kerry *
Smith, Dana
Smith, Lauren
Stout, Stacy
Strickland, Laura *
Strickland, Olita *
Sullivan, Kate
Suppes, Courtney
Sweeney, Kirsten
Sweeney, Nina

Tito, Lulu *
Troy, Alice
Walsh, Connie
Warren, Kerry
Watson, Kathy
Weidlein, George

Rolling Rock Hunt Pony Club 2000 Roster

Officers

D.C. Jennifor Sacksen
Co-D.C. Pam Burkland
Co-D.C. Alison Romano
Sec. Jancee Wilson
Treas. Monica Puskar

Members

Boyd, Anita
Burkland, Elliott & Ian
Clifford, Leila
Eichleay, Haven
Enos, Molly and Ellie
Gary, Scott
Hughes, Salina & Ashley
Jamison, Eliza
Kassel, Jessica
Lammert, Sarah
McConnell, Justin, K. C. & Elaine
McConnell, Madi
Matchett, Lauren
McGraw, Stancey
Nelson, Elizabeth, Scotty & Ginger
Pentecost, A. J.
Puskar, Alyse
Romano, Emily
Sacksen, Ben, Sam, Rachael & Sophia
Sheperd, A. J.
Simkovich, Paul
Speicher, Dan, Ellie & Krista,
Trabbold, Jessica
Turjan, Marcie
Walton, Rita
Wilson, Heather
Wilson, Taylee
Wood, Sarah & Julia

Loyalhanna Register 1954 Residents of Rolling Rock

With the help of Sam Off and Perk Oliver, we compiled an extensive list of people living in the valley in the 1950s, but we would have missed many names. I am very grateful to Peggy Caves, the nifty lady presently in charge of the Rolling Rock reservation office, who found three rare Loyalhanna Registers. I have chosen to use the 1954 list. I do realize that some of these people were not full time residents but they had houses. At that time the register was named after the Loyalhanna Creek, which runs through the Rolling Rock Farms. I am sure that the readers will enjoy remembering their friends and next of kin in this complete list.

In the case of my family, I would like to note that Sam and Molly Off were not on this list because Sam's job with U.S. Steel had them temporarily living in Virginia. Burt and I were "write-ins" because we did not move into the Parson's farmhouse until late November.

Arensberg, M/M F. L.
Austin, M/M J. Shirley
Bell, M/M Davitt S.
Bell, M/M James A.
Berdan, M/M John
Biddle, M/M L. L. III
Blair, M/M George M.
Blair, M/M Oliver
Blair, M/M William W., Jr.
Boardman, M/M Wm D.
Borntraeger, M/M Henry
Bright, M/M John
Bughman, M/M H. C., Jr.
Bughman M/M L. W.
Burchfield, M/M A. H., Jr.
Burton, M/M David C.
Byers, M/M J.F., Jr.
Cheever, Dr./M F. Sargent
Childress, M/M Wade T.
Childs, M/M Harvey, Jr.
Clement, M/M George C.
Corse, Mrs. Irving P.
Crandall, M/M Francis
Dauler, M/M Lee V.
Denton, M/M Frank R.
Dodds, M/M Robert J., Jr.
Ebbert, M/M, George S., Jr.
Eierman, M/M H. D.
Elliott, M/M Wm A.
Ernst, Dr./M Paul B.
Evans, Mrs. Howard S.
Evans, M/M John D., Jr.
Evans, M/M Thos. M.
Fairless, M/M Benjamin F.
Fairless, M/M Blaine F.
Fleming, M/M Murray P.
Foster, Dr./M George V.
Fownes, Mrs. Henry C., II
Frazer, Mr. John G., Jr.
Frazer, Mrs. John G.
Freeland, M/M E. B.
Gaub, Mrs. Otto C.
Gordon, Dr./M Harold E.
Greene, M/M Orland

Gwinner, M/M Frederick
Hackett, M/M Samuel E.
Hackett, M/M Spencer R.
Hamilton, M/M A. R., Jr.
Haxall, M/M John D.
Hazard, M/M Leland
Heinz, M/M H. J. II
Hodge, M/M Edwin, Jr.
Hoffstot, M/M H. P., Jr.
Howard, M/M William E.
Howell, M/M Max Don
Hughes, M/M Joseph D.
Kelly, M/M L. H.
Knapp, M/M L. W., Jr.
Knowles, M/M James H.
Langdon, M/M Courtney
Lazear, M/M John M.
Lockhart, M/M Charles
Lockhart, M/M George H.
Love, M/M George H.
MacBain, M/M Hugh D.
Macdonald, M/M C. K.
MacDougall, Mrs. E. Laughlin
Magee, M/M Edward J.
Mann, M/M Kenneth D.
Marshall, M/M John N.
Marshall, M/M William G.
Matthews, Mrs. Chas. H., Jr.
May, Mrs. Cordelia S.
Mayer, M/M John A.
McCargo, M/M David
McCargo, Mrs. Grant
McClintic, M/M Robert H.
McCluskey, Dr./M E. R.
McCutcheon, M/M T. G.
McKay, M/M Lawrence
Mellon, M/M Richard K.
Messer, M/M Peter C.
Moorhead, M/M H. R., Jr.
Mudge, M/M Leonard S.
Murray, M/M Lawrence N.
Muse, M/M A. B.
Nimick, Mr. T. H., Jr.
Oliver, M/M George T. II
Oliver, M/M William R.
O'Neill, M/M William C.
Parsons, M/M Lewis M.
Patton, Mrs. R. L.
Price, M/M Gwilym A.
Price, The Rev. and Mrs. Charles
Purnell, M/M J. Stanley
Rains, M/M L. F.
Rathbun, M/M W. T., Jr.
Raymond, M/M J. S.
Rea, M/M Cleveland D.
Rea, M/M James C.
Rea, M/M Wm. H.
Rhodes, M/M G. P.
Roberts, M/M Albert S.
Robinson, M/M Lucius W.
Robinson, M/M W. C., Jr.
Ross, M/M Walter L., III
Ryan, M/M John T., Jr.
Sarosdy, M/M Aurel F.
Scaife, M/M Alan
Schaefer, M/M F. M.
Schmertz, Mr. Louis R.
Schmidt, M/M Adolph
Scully, Mrs. Arthur M.
Smith, M/M Theodore F.
Stringer, M/M H. J., Jr.
Swensrud, M/M Sidney A.

Taylor, Mrs. Stephen C.
Thompson, M/M Gordon
Thompson, M/M Gordon
Thompson, Mrs. Arthur W.
Todd, M/M Burt K.
VanBuskirk, M/M A. B.
Veatch, M/M Raymond R.
Wallach, Mrs. Richard
Walter, M/M Howard K.
Walton, M/M John F., Jr.
Ward, M/M T. C., Jr.
Weidlein, Dr./M E. R.
Weidlein, M/M E. R., Jr.
Woods, M/M L. C., Jr.
Wurts, M/M Thomas C.
Wyckoff, M/M George W.

Loose horse

Index